Catering
Like a Pro

FROM PLANNING TO PROFIT
Catering
Like a Pro

REVISED EDITION

FRANCINE HALVORSEN

John Wiley & Sons, Inc.

Copyright © 2004 by Francine Halvorsen.

Published by John Wiley & Sons, Inc., Hoboken, New Jersey.
Published simultaneously in Canada.

Library of Congress Cataloging-in-Publication Data:

Halvorsen, Francine.
   Catering like a pro : from planning to profit / Francine Halvorsen.—
2nd ed.
        p. cm.
   ISBN 0-471-21422-1 (Cloth)
   1. Caterers and catering—Handbooks, manuals, etc. I. Title.
   TX921.H3 2004
   642'.4--dc21

                                          2003009972

10 9 8 7 6 5 4 3 2 1

To the memory of
those whose
last day was at
Ground Zero
in New York City
September 11, 2001

ACKNOWLEDGMENTS

I want to thank "the pros" for spending time with me and generously sharing their knowledge and experience. They give truth to the saying that if you want something done, ask a busy person. Simon Andrews, Annemarie Colbin, Linwood Dame, Ronnie Davis, Peter Dent, François Dionot, Monika Henry, William Henry, Bob Kinkead, Eric Lilavois, Joe McDonnell, Jim McMullen, Liz Neumark, Jacques Pépin, Stanley Poll, Steve Rowan, Jason Scholz, Allen Smith, Sylvia Weinstock, Virginia Wyman—thank you all.

Each of them works, as Joe McDonnell said, ". . . every day but St. Swithun's," and all hours except 2 to 5 in the morning and sometimes even then.

Thanks to Ellen Gallo of Starwood Hotels and Resorts and Laura Bright of Maverick Southern Kitchens for their insights and gracious introductions. Jan Anderson at FrancisFrancis! and Myra Fiori of Illy Caffè were very giving of their coffee expertise. My gratitude to Irena Chalmers for her generous vote of confidence and encouragement when I needed it.

At John Wiley I would like to thank Katherine Schowalter for acquiring this book and offer my appreciation to Claire Thompson Zuckerman for nurturing the first edition. For this revised edition, Susan Wyler, my editor, handled a cumbersome job with enthusiasm and decisiveness and Pamela Adler contributed invaluable final touches. My appreciation to David Sassian for his thoughtful attention to detail, and to Jeff Faust, who understands that sometimes a book is judged by its cover.

A special thank you to Jesse Halvorsen, Linda Lee, Lionel Halvorsen, and Peggy Hoban as well as Sarah, Benjamin, Isaiah, and Emilia, who have contributed a lot of cooking, eating, and laughing to this project. And for Robert Feldman, who makes me feel very catered to, X O ♥.

CONTENTS

FOREWORD

I have always been fascinated with small bits of information, like knowing mathematicians are often music lovers because they respond to the strong mathematical discipline of music that goes way beyond the superficial beat of one, two, three. Lawyers and doctors have a lot in common because both require extensive deductive reasoning skills. It does not, therefore, come as a surprise to discover the new breed of food professionals are expert in both the arts and the sciences.

Francine Halvorsen is a painter and poet. She also uses the language of food as her palette and food as her canvas. It has made her an exceptional cook. Francine is the caterer and friend we could all wish we had in our neighborhood. She is generous in contributing her own unique style of cooking and presentation to raise funds for dozens of causes and her generosity is reflected in her dedication to make every party an event and every event a party. Always she errs on the side of bringing a little more of everything for everyone.

Francine has the experience and qualifications to write this book. She has staged literally hundreds of parties under all manner of abundant and circumscribed conditions. She has thrived in the rich beauty and resources of Florence, Italy, and has come up with brilliant on-site solutions when faced with a scarcity of food and equipment in remote locations.

In *Catering Like a Pro,* Francine describes in detail all the behind-the-scene techniques necessary to be a professional. Reading it is an apprenticeship in catering from start to finish. It is a book that should be kept nearby and called upon as a dependable consultant to confer with again and again.

Catering is among the most demanding areas of the food business. A caterer must be charming and inspire confidence or no client will be willing to entrust what may be the most important event of his or her life. A caterer must be knowledgeable and flexible while simultaneously being an astute businessperson who remembers to carefully add up all the hidden costs so that there are no surprises either for caterer or for client. A caterer must combine the skills of a psychiatrist, plumber, electrician, and flat-tire changer and be able to cope with everything that can go wrong—from finding the furnace is on fire to calming a host or hostess in full heat. In addition, a caterer must have the skills to organize the event, plan the meal, cook the food, serve it, wash the dishes, and get the pots back to home base after a fourteen-hour day. That anyone would take this on is amazing. That anyone would be prepared to reveal how it can be done is inspiring. That Francine Halvorsen has written this book is her gift to us.

—Irena Chalmers

PREFACE

It was difficult thinking about the relevance of this edition of *Catering Like a Pro* after September 11, 2001. Not only were the events absolutely staggering, but I was displaced from where I lived and worked, a block and a half from the south tower. In time, I became aware that perhaps food service was not an inconsequential subject. Volunteers in the food industry—caterers, suppliers, distributors, restaurateurs, chefs, and servers—all did their part. Catering outposts were set up where they were needed. Many donated their services, even as emergency services funded the food for literally millions of meals.

Among the people interviewed in this book are Liz Neumark and Ronnie Davis. Great Performances and Ronnie Davis Productions coordinated the serving of over two million meals on behalf of the American Red Cross and the City of New York Emergency Services beginning on the September 12, 2001. Many others contributed their services directly and through fund-raisers, privately and publicly. In addition to providing food, City Hall Restaurant in Tribeca made available a constant supply of much-needed fresh water for people to help themselves to as they needed.

I hope that this book's attention to detail will free readers to be confident and creative as they pursue their careers. People often omit professional requirements because they seem obscure and overwhelming. The chapters will take you all the way from first thoughts and how to clarify them to organizing a large off-premise party. I have been gratified to see that the first edition of *Catering Like a Pro* has been a useful tool for many burgeoning professionals. Many institutions use it and recommend it. On the other side of the fence, it has also helped individuals hire caterers or create their own events. Pretty much anyone can follow these recipes.

The phrase "easier said than done" was invented for the applied arts. This book has been devised to enable someone using it to follow step by step all the stages that, when completed, make for successful client-centered events. All practical considerations are covered: Some are technical, and some are common sense. They range from business-office management and finance to computer catering programs to Internet links and telephone hot lines.

Simon Andrews, Annemarie Colbin, Linwood Dame, Ronnie Davis, Peter Dent, François Dionot, Monika Henry, William Henry, Bob Kinkead, Eric Lilavois, Joe McDonnell, Jim McMullen, Liz Neumark, Jacques Pépin, Stanley Poll, Jason Scholz, Sylvia Weinstock, and Virgina Wyman all contributed their clarity of thought and vision, to say nothing of their great recipes. Their combined expertise is an embarrassment of riches and they have unselfishly shared their experience.

A catered occasion is a social event first and an eating event second. That being said, the food should be excellent. The menus in the book can be used as they are or as inspirations for your own menus. All the recipes in the main section of the book are for 20 or more, and most of them can be halved or doubled. The recipes provided by the "pros" are as they submitted them. Most regional markets have all the ingredients you will need, but the detailed directories will provide endless food resources and a lifeline to large-scale recipes that suit any tastes.

Given the varieties of conditions and circumstances in which a caterer has to operate, knowing the basics is everything. If you are uninformed about food storage and sanitation, your clients' goodwill and good humor will be short lived. And your delicious food is useless if there are too few place settings or the service staff is late and grumpy. The checklists and charts in this book will help you to keep track of everything you need.

The names, addresses, websites, and phone numbers in the resources directories will give you access to your own independent network and enable you to build up personal data files. This book is not meant to be read and discarded, but to be kept on hand as a reference. Amateurs and professionals alike will find particular ways to bring order and organization to their ideas and to execute them. As you learn each element, you are encouraged to build on what you know.

Catering is a profession that evolves with perseverance, and though it requires substantial skill, in the long run it is the personal and necessary intangibles that you bring to catering—your signature touches and the relationships you develop with colleagues and clients—that will build your reputation.

—Francine Halvorsen

Catering
Like a Pro

1

The Client-Centered Approach to Catering

Catering is a perfect business for goal-oriented people who find problem-solving challenging and pleasurable. It's sometimes like being the ringmaster of a traveling circus, guiding performers and guests through a series of events that appear to be wonderfully spontaneous but are, in fact, the result of dozens of practical decisions.

If you are like most people who think about catering as a profession, you love food, parties, and people. When your family and friends ask you to take charge of events at holidays and personal celebrations, you say yes almost every time. You enjoy making special occasions memorable and prefer the hard work and rewards of these endeavors to whatever else you are already doing. Developing an equal enthusiasm for learning, planning, organizing, and earning more money than you spend on any event will transform you from an amateur to a professional caterer. Add the stamina to deliver the event, and you are a thriving entrepreneur.

Off-premise catering, which usually means having a professional kitchen and office but no fixed banquet hall or dining area requires personality traits that at first seem contradictory. While catering appeals to many free spirits, it demands a great deal of organization and administration to channel bursts of inspiration and creative impulses. Everything down to the last detail must be planned; yet all must be carried out with extreme flexibility. That is the only way the caterer can respond to the wishes of clients, technical difficulties, people problems, and the vicissitudes of weather. Many people feel that stamina and a smile are more important than culinary skills, but your clients will expect both from you.

No single formula can be carved in stone. That's why experienced professionals have developed dependable client-interview techniques, good management ability, a reliable team, creative food planning, product sources, and the vitality and clear-headedness to stay on top of each job thoroughly from start to finish. Your main bankable assets are your interpersonal and negotiating skills, which will help you prosper.

By far the largest number of new entrants to this business do off-premise catering. Selling even small amounts of food from your kitchen may be a legal gray area in some communities, and you need to check your local health department codes. If you are starting out with minimum capital, look for a properly licensed kitchen you can use. Often small restaurants, specialty food shops, private schools, and religious or community centers will rent space and time in their kitchens during their off hours or lulls. This is another area where networking helps, so ask around.

Organizing procedures and estimating costs maximize results and minimize losses. By and large, catering earns a greater profit margin than the restaurant business, but there is not much room for error, as the markup on food is not very great. Even the most luxurious of foods and feasts must be analyzed economically. Schools, religious organizations, businesses, political groups, civic associations, and fund-raisers are held accountable in planning their regular and special-occasion events. People arranging private family celebrations have limited assets, whatever their bank account. Clearly, money managing will be one of your important tasks. The expensive treats and labor-intensive goodies that bring oohs and ahs from your friends and family will be few and far between; most of your clients will not give you a blank check.

Another valuable talent is flexibility. You have to be in charge of all levels of each project; every detail has to reflect your tastes and standards. Yet you cannot be overly controlling, because it is your clients'

PRODUITS

PAUL BOCUSE

COLLONGES, le 26 Août

Madame F. HALVORSEN
75. Franklin street

NEW-YORK 10003

Chère Madame,

J'ai lu avec attention votre courrier du 14 Août dernier, voici ce que je pense de la cuisine de catering :

"Il y a une réelle évolution ces dernières années, les prestations servies sur l'ensemble des compagnies sont supérieures.

Le seul conseil que je puisse donner c'est de réaliser des plats simples avec des produits de qualité.

Et. chose très importante, il faut que l'équipage ait le sourire!".

Bien amicalement.

PAUL BOCUSE

69660 Collonges-au-Mont d'Or France
Téléphone : 78.22.01.40 Télex Bocuse 375 382 Fax 72.27.85.87
S A R L AU CAPITAL DE 250 000 FRANCS R C. LYON 71 B 721

wishes that must be satisfied and your colleagues' cooperation that you must depend on. People call caterers to execute projects that are important to them, and they expect more than good food. They want the kind of memorable event that makes them feel it was something they would have done if only they could. You may be surprised at the details they feel passionately about. As your reputation increases, people will defer to you more, but your first job is to listen to the client. What makes catering different from other professional culinary fields is that each and every job is unique and must be planned from beginning to end to satisfy the demands of the individual client.

You will need to keep a pencil handy so you can make notes, organize them, and read back to your client what he or she has said. Next, your notes must be translated into an achievable plan. Your clients will vary greatly. Some will know exactly what they want, without a clue as to what it takes to achieve it; others will just want to select from the clear-cut options you have to offer. In either case, the same questions must be asked and answered repeatedly: How many? How much? Where? When? What? Why? Who? All professionals report the same two things: "You must write everything down" and "There is always something."

Caterers are often independent risk takers, but they must also be team players; they have to be excellent organizers, but not control freaks. Be prepared to deliver exactly on schedule, and be equally prepared to wait for a late guest of honor or be delayed by traffic jams, power outages, or security checks.

When you are starting out, it is ounce wise and pound foolish to scrimp on the time and money it takes to research and develop your confidence and techniques. Dry runs for family and friends or free service to charity events, at which only the materials are paid for, are an investment of your time in hands-on practice that will pay off in the future.

Professionals readily acknowledge that it takes special skills and planning to make delicious and attractive food off premises that is just right for each circumstance. They do not function impulsively, leaping from inspiration to inspiration; rather, they count on dependable tried-and-true methods and meticulously tested recipes to turn out a professional product at a profit. They know people are depending on them and that expensive experiments are rarely fun and can be embarrassments. Under a wide range of conditions, caterers must be able to provide food that looks appetizing and tastes delicious, and to make money doing it. Not one caterer calls it an easy job.

Besides requiring a personal style, this business demands that you keep current with trends in food fashions and entertaining styles. The pros all read trade journals, magazines, and the food section of major newspapers as well as many food industry newsletters. This is something you can start doing now.

The dictionary defines *caterer* as "one who supplies the viands at an entertainment . . . usually considered to be more delicate or dainty than home production; a purchaser of provisions, purveyor, provider, or preparer of eats or delicacies." As early as the fifteenth century, "catering" was a profession, but as every caterer interviewed in this book emphasizes, "cooking is the least of it."

Local markets vary in what they have to offer, and the seasons bring different foods to market; substituting ingredients in recipes or menus may be necessary. Caterers have to bear in mind the incremental cost ratios of proportions for 10, 25, and 50 people, and the accompanying proportional preparation and cooking times. Even the most experienced chefs can sometimes omit a step from their checklist if they are not mindful. Professionals have to be knowledgeable about capital and overhead costs and how to analyze and predict job expenses.

If you are going to provide provisions only—with no, or virtually no services—consider what corner of the culinary market you want to claim. Be as specific as possible. Think of the food you want to provide and evaluate your abilities and your resources. The more explicit you are about what you do and do not provide, the happier everyone will be.

Do you want to make food à la carte? Cook to order and deliver, or have the food picked up? There is potential for any single product to meet with success; people have built successful companies making only muffins, cakes, sushi, chili, pasta, soups, and so on. Is your specialty birthday parties, holiday events, portable office lunches, beach parties, elegant dinner parties, desserts? Do you feel more comfortable with buffet meals and informal settings for large groups, or do you shine when you assemble dinner from scratch for 20 people? Families are growing weary of the sameness of fast-food deliveries, and they are calling on chefs to deliver home-cooked meals to them when they return from work. Personal chefs are fast becoming in great demand.

Since many caterers start simply by making and delivering food to order, first organize your recipe files and menus. They are good merchandising tools and helpful in systematizing food and nonfood items.

Begin a personal directory of resources and potential clients that includes people you know who use caterers and people who have asked you to cook special dishes or to help them plan events and special celebrations. Start to keep a small set of file folders for your notes and the information you glean from newspapers, magazines, and other resources.

Students in the field of hotel and restaurant management are often knowledgeable about food, but they need to learn the seemingly hidden elements that make a catered event work. Whether you are starting a full-service catering establishment or specializing in a small corner of the market, you will need all the practice you can get.

The best way to begin finding clients is by word of mouth. Once you let it be known that you are willing to provide a catering service, your family and friends will be your first network. Every organization or group with which you are associated should be told you are available for catering events. Read not only the major newspapers, but the local and neighborhood papers that carry news of upcoming events, new building openings, new companies, and events coming to town. Check the library for magazines and books. The Yellow Pages are another excellent resource. Don't be reluctant to call organizations you would like as clients. Find out who is in charge of contracting caterers and either speak to them or first mail an introductory letter and then follow up by phone.

Contact people who are frequently asked if they know a good caterer, such as neighborhood merchants who specialize in gourmet food and kitchen supplies, bridal consultants and bridal clothiers, florists, and even bookstore owners. Find out who handles your local government events like Fourth of July celebrations, inaugurations, and landmark anniversaries; see if you can work with them in some capacity. Have business cards and letterhead printed so that you have a professional demeanor from the start. Treat the people you talk with as potential contacts or clients.

Catering is a versatile and fast-growing segment of the flourishing food-service industry. Do not turn your nose up at any small assignment you think you can handle; think of it as being paid to build experience and a résumé.

2

Defining and Achieving Your Goals

How do your family and friends feel about what you are doing? Are they supportive? This is an important consideration, as catering requires many long hours and an intense concentration that cannot be postponed. Deadlines have to be honored, and events are usually held on weekends and holidays.

Working for a caterer or even volunteering for a few special events will provide some experience with the kinds of on-the-job pressures that occur. It will also be an opportunity to see firsthand the unplanned glitches that must be dealt with.

What goals do you have for the next three to five years? What are your financial requirements and how are you going to fulfill them? Will you use your savings or borrow money? Will you keep the job you have and work in the food profession in the early morning or at night, or do you plan to jump in full-time from the start? Will you cater on weekends? Write down your thoughts and turn them into a strategy.

A great deal of free information is available from the Internet, public libraries, various government offices, and schools. As an example, the Small Business Administration is a remarkable online resource. It offers business plan outlines, charts and forms for you to estimate financial needs, and good advice in strategizing. You can also reach an informed counselor on their 800 number. The United States Government Printing Office, the National Association of Catering Executives, and the National Restaurant Association all have a miscellany of helpful information, as do the culinary schools in your area.

The first rush of business from family, friends, neighbors, and colleagues will probably be the cornerstone you build on. Plan carefully and deliver a little more than you promise, and the favorable impression you make on the guests at these events will increase your business exponentially. When contacted by potential clients who have been to one of your previous events, suggest food and an ambience not too different from those flavors and events that led them to choose you in the first place.

Listen to people at the events you orchestrate. This feedback will tell you the best and the worst about what you've done. Adjust and respond accordingly. Perhaps less should be spent on food and more on service; maybe the decor was too elaborate, or there wasn't a generous amount of glassware. You want each event not just to work, but to appear perfect.

Each client has a certain style of event that suits them best. Often cultural and corporate clients favor caterers who understand their goals. Thoughtful letters and menus, occasional tasting parties, and sample gift baskets remind people of your strengths.

If you are working a full-time job you are not ready to give up, you might want to make yourself available to work for a caterer or other food service on weekends to see how an event goes from beginning to end. Nothing you learn will be wasted. No matter how well staffed you plan to be, sooner or later you will have to do every aspect of catering yourself. Due to unforeseeable emergencies at one time or another, you may find yourself scraping dishes and repacking them, passing hors d'oeuvres, or scouting the premises with a flashlight for dropped flatware. But if you are doing it when the "emergency" was foreseeable, you haven't planned well. Pacing yourself and hiring the appropriate people to help you are things that must be done from the beginning.

Education is essential. Even if you are an excellent cook and manager, you do not want to reinvent the wheel. Preparing meals for large numbers of people under various conditions and serving them graciously at the appropriate temperature and time is learned in small steps. Apprenticing will prepare you for the reality of catering, and taking a few courses in a culinary school will introduce you to professional methods and systems that are invaluable.

Good culinary schools offer everything from the expected courses in food, pastry, nutrition, and sanitation to often overlooked but much-needed courses in the psychology of human relations, practical accounting, and law. Schools also present the benefits of professional networking and full- or part-time job opportunities that help build your résumé while you learn to run your own business. Many of them have first-rate restaurants where diners expect the best in food and service. Call schools and ask questions or visit them and see how you can best benefit from their programs.

Education credits and a good résumé will also help with finances later on. Purposefulness always adds to credibility. Banks or family members will need some reassurance that you take your career seriously before they invest their money.

A degree program teaches not just specific skills, but how to be professional. If you do not want to enter a long-term program, it's good to know that almost all culinary schools and college departments offer excellent individual courses. Spending from six months to two years in a school situation and apprenticing with established professionals will give you an excellent base. You may, however, decide to wing it and start to take on professional jobs that you know you can handle and learn new skills as you need them. Many professionals have started this way.

For menu planning, resources include the culinary collections at your public library and local colleges. For instance, Radcliffe has a collection of almost ten thousand volumes in their culinary collection in the Schlesinger Library (founded by the grandparents of chef and restaurateur Chris Schlesinger). The library runs a series of free seminars that are open to the public.

Chef Louis Szathmary owned the world-famous Bakery restaurant in Chicago and was an avid collector of culinary literature in many languages. His collection included 8,000 books, 3,500 pamphlets, and 100 unpublished manuscripts, and span 500 years, the earliest volume being from 1299. Szathmary willed the collection to the University of Iowa, where he knew it would be cared for, conserved, and bound. The collection can be used to research historic meals and dinners from various periods and cultures as well as culinary history and modern recipes.

As you develop your business plan, a location for your operation is important. Zoning is a legal issue that must be taken into account. The space must be adequate for work, storage, parking, and delivery facilities. It is a good idea to make sure you will not be disturbing people when you and your crew return, unload, and unpack at one or two in the morning. You also need to be sure that you are negotiating a reasonable lease for the right length of time. These days, rents can go up rapidly. If your business grows, you may need more space in the future. You might even think about buying a place outright. Clearly, much depends on your finances and cash flow. As in all other financial matters, it is wise to consult with a lawyer and accountant who can make the options very clear to you. Remember: No question is too embarrassing to ask. Asking questions now can save your business in the future.

At this point, too, you will have to decide if you want to arrange things so that clients can come to you, see your kitchen, and have a sampling, or whether you prefer to go to their home or office. If clients are going to visit your premises for tastings and meetings, your workspace must look as good as your food tastes. For the purpose of maximizing how your space looks, you are well advised to consult with a designer.

The location from which caterers function is traditionally called the commissary. The commissary is not only a kitchen, but the place where provisions and staples are received, sorted, and stored and where food is prepared and kept hot, cold, or frozen until ready to use. You will need room to pack food and equipment and a place where your staff can keep personal things, change, and eat. The space must have a completely enclosed toilet and washroom. When you are starting, your office will probably be in a corner of the commissary as well. Fire and sanitary codes must be adhered to stringently. (These are discussed fully in Chapter 9.)

Your kitchen must be well planned, and if you are going to do any on-premise catering, you will need substantial square footage. On-premise events require a reception area, a dining area, additional bathrooms, dressing rooms, etc. To calculate the square feet you need, take an educated guess as to the size your average event will be. If you think a dinner party for 100 will be the largest group to whom you might deliver a full meal, you will be able to plan accordingly. The same facilities will easily accommodate a cocktail party for 250, or three simultaneous weekend parties of 20 or 25 each.

As in all endeavors, no one single thing will guarantee your success as a caterer, but a combination of experience, formal education, independent research, and trial and error will get you where you're going.

If you pay attention to what the pros in the next chapter say, you will have insight into the business from some of the most successful people in the field. They are the people to listen to. These caterers share a love and enthusiasm for what they do. At the end of the day, after all the hard work and long hours, the pleasures and the glitches, they are happy with their profession.

3

Learning from the Pros

In this chapter, you'll hear from a select group of celebrity caterers and chefs. They offer some of their personal experiences, insider tips, and signature recipes. You will see that each has his or her own style.

Annemarie Colbin

Natural Gourmet Cookery School, New York, New York

"By going to culinary school you learn much faster what it would take a long time to learn."

When Annemarie Colbin, now a doctor of holistic nutrition with a Ph.D. from the Union Institute and University, started the Natural Gourmet Cookery School, it was considered pretty much "alternative." Yet after 25 years of business, many of the lessons taught there have become firmly mainstream. Annemarie says, "By going to culinary school, you learn much faster what it would take a long time to learn."

"Caterers don't have to specialize, but they are missing out if they don't learn about good and tasty food that is grain based, with lots of vegetables and fruit. Virtually fat-free and frequently dairy-free, these high-quality nourishing ingredients can be cooked in a wide range of dishes. As part of a larger palette, natural foods add the possibility of extending business for caterers whose clients pay attention to the nutrition of every meal they eat. Both classic and ethnic dishes can be made from fresh provisions to please any appetite. Natural foods, properly prepared and seasoned, can be as delicious and exciting as anything else on the table and to aficionados even more so. By combining textures, shapes, and colors, the various flavors are enhanced. By spending as much thought on these dishes as others it encourages people to eat a more harmonious array."

The school has a chef's professional training program and is accredited by the Accreditation Council for Continuing Education and Training (ACCET) and licensed in New York State. Most graduates go on to professional careers in the private and public sectors and incorporate their training.

Annemarie encourages students to do things that make sense to them, not just because someone tells them to do it. She has been successfully independent in her teaching and writing. Many people talk rather medicinally about food and health links, but the Whole Meal Course at the school features gourmet applications appropriate for professional chefs as well as for beginners. As researchers learn more about nutrition and the immune system, the more advantage is found in increasing the grains and vegetables in our diets. There are also fewer sanitation problems and very little waste.

Colbin says, "At a buffet you can serve two or three dishes from the natural foods menu. Seaweed salad, whole-grain pilaf, and soup are good examples. If caterers learn the basics of whole-foods cooking and perhaps take a course in desserts that use fruits poached or baked and sweetened with natural syrups, they broaden their culinary horizons. I propose that 'Wholistic Nutrition' be defined as 'the study of how different foods, both whole and refined or fragmented, affect various levels of the human being's bodymind (physical, mental, emotional, and spiritual)'."

The Natural Gourmet Cookery School specializes in mostly vegetarian cuisine featuring whole, fresh, natural, and seasonal food, including grains, beans, fruit, vegetables, high-quality oils, and natural sweeteners, as well as fish and organic chicken. They just celebrated their twenty-fifth anniversary. Many graduates go on to cater or become personal chefs for people who are interested in combining nutrition and gourmet food. Some work in spas, retreats, and wellness centers; others become personal chefs or go on to open their own restaurants. There are those who work in four-star establishments and contribute more subtly to the freshness statements in vegetables and salads that have become such an important part of culinary interests.

Annemarie Colbin's Mediterranean Fish Soup

This is a delicious and easy soup. Serve with some good crusty sourdough whole-grain bread and a salad.

SERVES 4

2 tablespoons extra-virgin olive oil

¾ cup chopped onion

3 cloves garlic, chopped

¼ teaspoon dried tarragon, or ½ teaspoon minced fresh

3 cups unsalted fish stock or water

Large pinch saffron threads, crumbled

1 teaspoon salt

4 calamari (squid), cleaned, and sliced crosswise into rings

½ pound small scallops

8 littleneck clams, scrubbed

8 mussels, scrubbed and debearded

1 pound fresh scrod or other thick white fish

2 teaspoons coarsely chopped fresh cilantro

Freshly ground pepper to taste

1. Heat the olive oil in a large pot over medium heat. Sauté the onion, garlic, and tarragon for 2 to 3 minutes, or until fragrant but not browned.

2. Add the stock, saffron, and salt. Reduce heat to low, cover, and simmer for 20 to 25 minutes. (Recipe can be made ahead of time up to this point.)

3. About 15 minutes before serving, bring the stock to a simmer if necessary. Add the calamari, cover, and simmer for 3 minutes. Add the scallops, clams, mussels, and fish. Cover and simmer for another 5 to 6 minutes, or until the clams are open. Discard any clams or mussels that do not open.

4. Serve in warm bowls and top with chopped cilantro and a few grinds of fresh pepper to taste.

Mesclun Salad with Beets and Avocado

SERVES 4

2 large beets, stems trimmed to 1 inch

4 cups mesclun or mixed baby salad greens

1 ripe California avocado

1. Cook the beets in a saucepan of salted boiling water to cover for about 1 hour, or until a sharp knife can go in easily. Let cool to the touch, peel with your hands under cold running water, and cut in half lengthwise. Slice lengthwise into thin half-moons and set aside.

2. Divide the greens among four salad plates.

3. Cut the avocado in half lengthwise, and remove the pit. (Easy way: embed your knife into the pit as if to cut it in half, then twist gently and remove the pit on the knife and discard.) Cut avocado into quarters and peel. Slice each quarter into thin lengthwise slices and fan on the greens.

4. Arrange the slices from half a beet on each plate. Drizzle with creamy lemon vinaigrette to taste.

Creamy Lemon Vinaigrette

YIELD: 1 1/2 CUPS

3 tablespoons fresh lemon juice

3 tablespoons olive oil

3 tablespoons flaxseed oil

3 tablespoons water

2 tablespoons chopped scallions (white part only)

1 teaspoon sea salt

4 ounces soft tofu (not silken)

Place all the ingredients in a blender and blend until smooth and creamy.

Bob Kinkead

Kinkead's, Washington, D.C.
Kinkead's Colvin Run Tavern, Tyson's Corner, Virginia

"It is difficult to do off-premise what can be done in my own kitchen. Catering is mainly logistics. How do I get the food there? How will it all look? Will it be up to my standards? Will it be the right amount?"

Bob Kinkead was for many years an owner and executive chef at Kinkead's, and now he has added Kinkead's Colvin Run Tavern, which opened to accolades. He does only off-premise catering for charity events and fund-raisers that the restaurant genuinely believes in. Speaking with Bob Kinkead recently, he said that even though does more private parties at Colvin Run, he does almost no off-premise catering.

"It is difficult to do off-premise what can be done in my own kitchen," says Kinkead. "Catering is mainly logistics. How do I get the food there? How will it all look? Will it be up to my standards? Will it be the right amount? Large charity events are not necessarily RSVPed too accurately. I want the food as tasty and good looking as possible."

"Does the participating place have a kitchen, even a warming kitchen so that hot food can be served hot? Do we make an assortment of food that tastes best at room temperature or cold? What do we select as an offering? Overextending the kitchen diminishes quality. Since a double standard is impossible, it has to be an event we really believe in, so we choose them carefully. It must be something that raises money for a good cause, satisfies the client, gives pleasure to the guests, and reflects well on us."

Zoofari, the large fund-raiser at the Washington, D.C, National Zoo, was an event Kinkead participated in when he was executive chef at the now-closed Twenty One Federal. The tradition will probably continue, because it is not only well run, but so much fun that the staff wants to do it. As a fan I can appreciate the fact that he never wants to compromise. And we benefit from the delicious recipes below.

Kinkead's Pear Salad with Walnuts, Roquefort, Endive, and Radicchio

SERVES 20

100 whole walnuts, toasted

1 pound Roquefort cheese, crumbled

4 ounces cream cheese at room temperature

10 pears, preferably Bosc

5 endives, cut into julienne

4 large heads radicchio, cut into julienne

Port Vinaigrette (recipe follows)

1 teaspoon salt

1 teaspoon cracked black pepper

1. Chop 40 of the walnuts and reserve the rest for garnish. Peel, halve, and core the pears. Drop into a bowl of water with the juice of the lemon half.

2. In a heavy-duty mixer fitted with a paddle attachment, add 10 ounces of the Roquefort, the cream cheese, and chopped walnuts and mix until incorporated and slightly aerated. Drain and dry the pear halves. Divide the Roquefort mixture among the pear halves, covering the core side. Place in a baking dish and, in a 400°F oven, bake until the pears are slightly tender and Roquefort is melting, about 5 minutes. Remove from the oven.

3. In a stainless-steel bowl, toss together the endive, radicchio, salt, and pepper. Divide the salad among 20 plates. Sprinkle some of the reserved walnuts and crumble the remaining Roquefort on each salad and top with a pear half. Top with 3 tablespoons dressing.

Port Vinaigrette

YIELD: 2 1/2 CUPS

2 shallots, minced

1/4 cup red wine vinegar

1/4 cup port

1/4 teaspoon salt

1/4 teaspoon freshly ground
pepper

1/4 teaspoon honey

1 cup olive oil

1/2 cup walnut oil

1/2 cup peanut oil

1 teaspoon chopped fresh chives

1. In a stainless-steel bowl, add the shallots, port, salt, pepper, red wine vinegar, and honey. Whisk to blend. Gradually whisk in each oil, one at a time, in a thin stream. Stir in the chives.

TOASTING NUTS: Spread the nuts on a baking sheet and toast in a preheated 375°F oven for 5 to 10 minutes, or until fragrant and lightly browned.

Braised Lamb Shanks with Rosemary Merlot Sauce

SERVES 20

18 large cloves garlic, peeled but left whole

¾ cup vegetable oil

6 tablespoons cold unsalted butter

2 teaspoons salt

3 tablespoons fresh-cracked black pepper

20 lamb shanks, trimmed

Salt and freshly ground pepper for sprinkling

1⅓ cups each finely diced onion, celery, and carrots

1 bunch fresh rosemary

2 teaspoons dried thyme

2 cups merlot or other dry red wine

8 quarts veal stock

Flageolets (recipe follows)

Basil Aioli (recipe follows)

1. Preheat the oven to 350°F.

2. To make the puree: Place the garlic and vegetable oil in a small ovenproof skillet and bake for about 1½ hours, or until quite soft. Strain the garlic and reserve the garlic oil. In a food processor, puree the garlic, butter, a little of the reserved garlic oil, and the salt and pepper. Cover and refrigerate the puree.

3. Salt and pepper each shank. Heat the remaining garlic oil in a large Dutch oven over medium heat and brown the lamb shanks on all sides, about 20 minutes. Remove from the pan, add the diced vegetables, half of the rosemary, and all the thyme, and sauté until starting to brown. Add the wine and stir to scrape up the browned bits from the bottom of the pan. Add the veal stock and shanks. The liquid should barely cover the shanks. Bring to a simmer and cover. Braise in the oven for 1 hour. Remove the cover and cook for about 35 minutes, or until the meat is tender but not falling off the bone.

4. Remove the shanks from the cooking liquid and let cool. Strain the cooking liquid into a nonreactive saucepan. Add the remaining rosemary and return to the stove. Cook over medium-high heat to reduce by half. Strain. Stir in the garlic puree.

Flageolet Beans

YIELD: 1 GALLON; SERVES 32

2 pounds dried flageolet beans

4 quarts water

4 quarts chicken stock

4 ounces olive oil

1 tablespoon dried thyme

1 tablespoon chopped fresh tarragon

1 teaspoon salt

1 teaspoon freshly ground pepper

3 tablespoons garlic puree

1. Rinse and pick over the beans. Soak overnight in water to cover by 2 inches. Drain.

2. In a large, heavy pot over high heat combine the beans and chicken stock to cover. Bring to a boil and reduce heat to a simmer. Cook until tender but not falling apart. Remove from heat and let cool. (Most liquid, but not all, will have evaporated.)

3. Heat the olive oil in a heavy saucepan over high heat. Add one-fifth of the beans and cook until they begin to break down. Reduce heat to a simmer. Add the thyme, tarragon, salt, pepper, and the remaining beans. Cook until heated through, about 20 minutes. Stir in the garlic puree.

Basil Aioli

YIELD: 2 CUPS

2 cups packed fresh basil leaves

3 cloves garlic, minced

1 egg yolk

1½ cups olive oil

Salt and freshly ground pepper to taste

1. Blanch the basil leaves in boiling water for 10 seconds. Drain and plunge into ice water. Drain again.

2. In a blender, combine the garlic, basil, and egg yolk. Puree. With the machine running, gradually add the olive oil to make an emulsified sauce. Stir in the salt and pepper.

Eric Lilavois, Wine Director

City Hall, New York, New York

"You can select wine initially by palate, but you have to also ask, quite simply, is it worth the money or not worth the money? I can't emphasize enough the need to balance taste and business."

Eric Lilavois is a sommelier certified with the American Sommelier Association and the Wine and Spirit Education Trust in London. Both have rigorous requirements and a complex knowledge that must be mastered. Currently, Lilavois is the wine director for City Hall restaurant in Tribeca and president of Lila Vine Consulting, a company that writes restaurant wine lists and trains staff.

City Hall is an extraordinary New York restaurant in an 1863 cast-iron building. Proximity to the center of the city's political life accounts for the restaurant's name. It is not unusual to see political luminaries chewing over their plans while enjoying lunch and dinner. Chef/owner Henry Meer and his team have until recently run two busy downtown restaurants (the acclaimed SoHo Cub Room was sold), but also have hosted parties for from five to five hundred. Neighborhood folks and out-of-town celebrities enjoy hosting parties there, and whether the event is a rehearsal dinner, a wedding party, or a movie premiere, the events are given equal attention. Henry offers the same standard of the best fresh food that governs his regular dining room. He is a purist who says, "After twenty-five years at French restaurants (La Côte Basque and Lutèce), I find nothing tastes better to me than a local tomato with sea salt, a turn of pepper, and if you want to get fancy, a little bit of olive oil." Everything chef Meer prepares tastes as good as that tomato.

Therefore, it is not surprising that he should have Eric Lilavois as his wine director. Eric keeps City Hall's cellar stocked for a wide range of tastes and wallets. There are over five hundred selections on hand, and others can be ordered. There are tiers to wine purchasing: for the glass, for the list, and for catering. Eric does the selecting for the restaurant, and for City Hall's many prestigious events in their private rooms.

I have benefited from Eric's knowledge on many occasions. I would always order Margaux, with an occasional Italian red thrown in. I enjoyed them and still do, but knowing my prejudices, Eric would cover the label and ask me to taste something. I am very glad he did. There are wonderful other reds out there from all parts of the United States as well as from Chile, Austria, Spain, and other regions of France. And I am just starting on the whites.

"You can select wine initially by palate," says Lilavois, "but you have to also ask, quite simply, is it worth the money or not worth the money? I can't emphasize enough to balance taste and business. Talk with distributors. They want to work with you and may start out with an agenda that will grow into a mutually beneficial relationship with them over time.

"If your client wants a tasting, do the best possible. You can think of it as an overhead expense. Make sure the whites are slightly chilled and the reds are room temperature and given a little time to breathe. I sometimes let the reds sit and develop in the glass and have the client taste again after we have talked for a while. Also, be certain you can deliver the selection in the amount needed.

"For catering, it is best to use larger-production wines that are not easily available retail, so that you can offer a dependable list for events. You want to price it down the middle. Most event planners will respond to selections they can make for $30 to $35 a bottle. Your clients will let you know if they want something more extravagant, and you will be able to provide something for them even if they want to spend a little less. There are no rules, but you can figure guests will drink an average of 2 glasses each (there are 4 or 5, or even 6, generous ones in a bottle)."

"I like to encourage clients to taste, but if they are not too knowledgeable and want crowd-pleasers, I will offer Chardonnay and Merlot because they have wide acceptance. In the summer, more white tends to be used and in the winter, more red, but you can't count on that. What you don't want to do is show off and talk them into a wine that is too extreme for popular taste. Which is not to say it shouldn't be the best quality they can buy. The thing is, if you give them a wine in their price range that is truly remarkable, you will earn their trust. If they want several wines and are not too specific, start with a sparkling wine—its acidity makes your mouth water. Always start light, with maybe a Sauvignon Blanc, then a Cabernet and a dessert wine.

"These days, people are more knowledgeable, and if they aren't, they want to be. Make sure that the servers know what they are pouring and encourage them to talk with guests about the wines. Sometimes, at a small catered event, the client will actually ask me to speak about the wines being served. I will sometimes bring an alternative bottle (that I have back-up for) and let the host select on the spot. Usually, things are set up by event planners who have only a general knowledge of wine but a thorough knowledge of their client's temperament and budget. This is also very helpful."

Eric advises: "If you have the skill and the self-confidence, fake it till you make it." Just as your culinary creativity and knowledge of food alone are not sufficient to make the financial element of your business thrive, your knowledge and taste in wines and spirits won't lead to success if you don't have a profitable program. Study and taste, and take any job in the industry to see how it operates. It isn't just a matter of tasting literally thousands of wines over the years, but training yourself to remember them. Apprenticing is one of the surest ways to gain knowledge.

François Dionot

L'Académie de Cuisine, Bethesda, Maryland and Gaithersburg, Maryland

"Learn to manage time. If the caterer finds himself or herself alone washing pots and pans at 2 A.M., he or she did not plan well. A young business should hire from the start. It doesn't make sense not to. Help is part of what you have to organize so that you are not burned out."

François Dionot, chef extraordinaire and director of L'Académie de Cuisine, says the hardest thing on the first job that you are responsible for is the unexpected.

"The most difficult thing at the beginning is to anticipate all the little things that are going to go wrong. We find it is never the same as the last time. It is not like when people come to you, as in a restaurant. We take food to somebody's house, and every time we serve different things to different people there are crazy unknowns. It's what makes it exciting. Here's an example: It happened to me once at a beautiful house where the reception has begun when I arrive. The band is playing, photographers are taking pictures, everyone is having a good time. I plug my coffee urn into a socket and blow everything up. The band is using electricity, the photographer is using it, but I am the last one to arrive, so I am responsible.

"The unknown is what happens even when we think we are prepared. To be extremely organized is most important. It's like a pilot before takeoff. Double-check everything each time and don't assume that things are fine. If you forget to check, it increases the chance of crashing."

Presenting and plating food comes from experience. You can study and devour books and magazines and look at pictures for ideas, but it is practice that gives direction. After learning about food and becoming confident with preparing and serving, you will build your style as your understanding grows.

"When you are starting out in catering, a strong education in all culinary arts—not necessarily just in catering—is essential," says Dionot. "A minimum would be an intensive six months to learn the professional basics. After that, make the transition to as good a cooking job as you can get, in a restaurant or catering practice. The basic food ideas are the same, but transported at the last minute.

"My experience is cooking first and then catering. It has served me best for everything. A chef must have not only a good general knowledge, but must understand timing, which you can apply to other things.

"It is possible, but very difficult, to be full-fledged when you first start out. If you don't already have a specialty or a preference, choose one. Make soups and salads, for example, then make the soups and salads available. Sell just hors d'oeuvres or desserts. Whether your clients pick these things up or you deliver them, they have to be your best.

"On your first job for a wedding of 250, become a general contractor. Hire things out. Don't think of baking the cake yourself unless that is all you are making. The client is hiring you. You don't have to tell them your resources. You take the credit and the blame. If you have built a network, you can make the client happy. There is always a way to do it or find someone to do it.

"Learn to manage time. If a caterer finds himself or herself alone washing pots and pans at 2 A.M., he or she did not plan well. A young business should hire from the start. It doesn't make sense not to. Help is part of what you have to organize so that you are not burned out.

"Start by buying only basic catering equipment, and every time you need to do something special, buy the necessary pieces. If a party requires two thousand crepes, then you buy crepe pans. You can rent practically anything, but most people feel more comfortable with dependable equipment in their possession. There are successful caterers who rent almost everything all the time. It is best to buy only the things you use frequently and have strong preferences for.

"Your main marketing device is word of mouth. Make sure whatever you do, you do it so well that everyone will want you for their next job. To attract attention, create an event, either for charity or a celebration. You might arrange with somebody who has a beautiful home to invite friends and include the press. Make it a special event or even a special day, but don't call it a demonstration.

"The newest addition to the catering field in the last five years is the emergence of an increasing number of personal chefs. A new chef who has skill and a few client contacts can go into business with no overhead expense but a business card. Private chefs can start out with no equipment, no worries about sprinkler systems and grease traps. If they are good enough to keep food costs to 20 to 25 percent, they will have a large profit. I know a fairly recent graduate (4 years out of L'Académie) who averages $15,000 a month over his basic salary. Personal chefs display their skill and creativity by cooking in someone's home several times week. Sometimes for the evening meal, sometimes preparing and putting away food for several days, and also for dinner parties and special events."

L'Académie de Cuisine recently received approval from the Maryland Higher Education Commission and the national accrediting agency, ACCET, to expand its part-time professional pastry arts program into a full-time program. François, founder and director of the school, says, "The need for professionally trained pastry cooks and chefs has grown tenfold in the past few years, and we want to assist our students in meeting the demands of this specialized field."

L'Académie de Cuisine French Onion Soup

SERVES 12

10 pounds onions

1½ cups (12 ounces) butter

Coarse salt and freshly ground black pepper to taste

4 cups white wine

3 quarts chicken stock

12 slices French bread, each ¼ inch thick, completely dried out in oven

6 cups finely grated Gruyère cheese

1. Peel the onions to remove all skin including the shiny looking one (2 or 3 layers). Cut in half and slice ⅛ inch thick.

2. In a sauté pan or skillet over medium heat, gently sauté the onions in butter for 10 to 15 minutes without coloring until translucent. Add salt and pepper and, increasing heat if necessary, allow the onions to start caramelizing turning to a golden color. Scrape the bottom of the pan if onions start to stick. Continue to caramelize until the onions are light brown.

3. Add the wine and deglaze the bottom of the pan by scraping to detach the caramelized pieces.

4. Add the stock and bring to a boil. Reduce heat and simmer, uncovered, for 20 minutes.

5. Place in onion soup crocks or heatproof soup bowls. Place a crouton on top of each bowl of soup, sprinkle with cheese, and glaze under the broiler.

Crab Cakes Dionot

SERVES 6

2 ounces scallops

¼ cup heavy cream

Salt and freshly ground pepper to taste

2 plum tomatoes, peeled, seeded, and finely diced

12 ounces fresh lump crabmeat, picked over for shell

2 tablespoons finely chopped scallions

1. Remove the muscles from the scallops. Puree the scallops in a food processor, add the cream, salt, and pepper, and blend well. Pour into a bowl and keep cold.

2. Add the tomatoes, crabmeat, and green onions to the puree. Mix gently, taking care not to break up the crabmeat.

3. Lightly butter a baking sheet. Form small patties with the crabmeat mixture and place on the prepared sheet. Cover and refrigerate for up to 3 hours until ready to cook.

4. Preheat the broiler. Broil the crab cakes for 2 minutes on each side, or until slightly golden.

Jacques Pépin, Chef, Author, and Dean of Special Studies

French Culinary Institute, New York, New York

"To develop, you have to understand a recipe. You start with an idea to make A and B and then when you have created an entity you respond to the food as it takes shape. When you become so familiar with it that you have it in depth, you adjust to the feel of it. You know it so well; you can do this and not do that and finish it with the proper result for two hundred. You will know it well enough to adjust for moisture, for dryness, for an oven too hot, or a dinner too late."

L'École is the restaurant of the French Culinary Institute (FCI) in New York's SoHo.

A calmer, more gracious host than Jacques Pépin cannot be imagined. His schedule includes not only courses at FCI and Boston University, but television and lecture appearances, writing, consulting, and creating culinary legends. His advice for beginning caterers: "Simplicity."

"A salad composé: Wash and drain the salad, marinate the chicken, prepare the mushrooms and fresh garnish. Prepare and wrap the salad, prepare the dressing, and store it separately. On the premises, sauté or grill chicken breasts and mushrooms, top with your choice of something fresh, and then prepare the plates individually and serve fifty easily. If asked to entertain fifteen hundred, I would say, yes, of course, and then buy the best bread, the best prosciutto, the best of cheese and fruit; I do not really attempt to cook for that many if I am alone. I shop and prepare and present. For five hundred, perhaps I poach several salmon and dress them cold for a buffet. If I am a beginner, perhaps for ten to twenty, every last bit is from scratch.

"The selection of materials is very important: choose selectively. Break the menu down in your head. The size of the kitchen and the equipment is critical. Inspect the site, and if you cannot do that, don't assume anything. You cannot duplicate exactly a previous situation.

"To develop, you have to understand a recipe. You start with an idea to make A and B, and then when you have created an entity you respond to the food as it takes shape. When you become so familiar with it that you have it in depth, you adjust to the feel of it. You know it so well; you can do this and not do that and finish it with the proper result for two hundred. You will know it well enough to adjust for moisture, for dryness, for an oven too hot, or a dinner too late. The base product will feel right to you, and you will be able to finish it with the proper results in a variety of conditions. Catering is not a question of self-consciously expressing yourself. Your craftsmanship will do that."

When I asked Jacques Pépin what he still found difficult in the business, he said: "Finding the best—the best produce, the finest quality fish and fowl—I am always on the lookout for the most excellent ingredients to use." In answer to what he is still learning: "It never stops. On all my trips to other countries I observe new combinations, additional traditions and techniques. I am always open and curious." And what does this stellar and gracious chef, who could eat anything, anywhere, eat on those rare occasions when he eats alone? "Most of the time I choose soup or eggs." We can only imagine how delicious they are.

The following recipes by Jacques Pépin come from a book that has been in every kitchen that I have had since it first came out as *La Technique*, published by Wallaby/Pocket Books. A version of this recipe appears in *Jacques Pépin's Complete Techniques* (New York: Black Dog & Leventhal Publishers, 2001), and is used with the permission of the author.

Mayonnaise

Mayonnaise is perhaps the most useful cold sauce in the world. The word may come from the medieval word *mayeu*, meaning egg yolk, or, according to *Grimald-de-la-Reyniere*, from the verb *manier*, meaning to knead. Mayonnaise lends itself to an infinite number of variations. Mayonnaise is usually served with cold foods such as hard-boiled eggs, cut vegetables, salad, cold fish, shellfish, cold meat and *pâté*. (Its sister, hollandaise, made with egg yolk and butter, is served warm with fish, eggs, and vegetables such as asparagus, broccoli, and the like.) In French cooking, when the ingredients of a particular salad are bound with mayonnaise, it becomes *mayonnaise de volaille* (chicken salad), *mayonnaise de homard* (lobster salad) and so on. Though according to classic French recipe books, mayonnaise is not made with mustard, I have rarely seen it made without. Mayonnaise made in the food processor or blender will keep longer when refrigerated than the handmade counterpart because the elements are more finely bound together.

Mayonnaise can become *sauce verte*, a green sauce made with mayonnaise, watercress, tarragon, parsley, and spinach; *sauce gribiche*, mayonnaise with hard-cooked eggs, French sour gherkins, capers, and shallots; *sauce tartare*, mayonnaise with parsley, chives, chervil, and sour pickles; *sauce la Varenne*, mayonnaise with a puree of fresh mushrooms; *sauce russe*, mayonnaise with fresh caviar; and of course, the well-known *aioli*, known as the butter of Provence and made with a very substantial amount of pounded garlic and olive oil. Of course, mayonnaise can be done with olive oil (the best is a virgin oil), or peanut oil, or a mixture of both; it is just a question of personal taste. Buy vinegar of the best possible quality, such as *vinaigre d'Orléans*. Use good mustard. The quality of the ingredients is sine qua non to the end result. Be sure that the ingredients are at room temperature. If the oil is too cool, the mayonnaise will definitely break down. If kept refrigerated, the mayonnaise must come to room temperature slowly before it is stirred or it will break down.

-Jacques Pépin

Mayonnaise

YIELD: 2½ CUPS

2 egg yolks

1½ teaspoons Dijon mustard

1 tablespoon tarragon or wine vinegar

Dash of salt

Dash of freshly ground white pepper

2 cups oil (peanut, olive, walnut, or a mixture)

1. Place all ingredients except the oil in a bowl and stir with a wire whisk. Add the oil slowly, whisking at the same time.

2. Keep mixing, add in the oil a little faster as the mayonnaise starts to take shape.

3. Consistency of the correct mayonnaise is slightly looser than store-bought).

4. To serve, scoop the mayonnaise into a clean bowl, being careful not to smear the sides of the bowl. (Place the mayonnaise in the middle of the bowl.)

5. Smooth the top with a spatula by turning the spatula in one direction and the bowl in the other direction.

6. When the top is smooth, move the spatula in the same circular and reverse motion, going up and down to make a design on the surface.

7. With your finger, push out the mayonnaise left on the blade of the spatula in the center of the design.

NOTE: When the oil is added too fast, or when the ingredients are too cold, the mixture breaks down. It looks like a broken-down custard. Mayonnaise can be put back together with egg yolk, mustard, vinegar, or a small amount of hot water. Place 1 teaspoon of vinegar, if vinegar is used, in a clean vessel. Add I teaspoon of the broken sauce and whisk thoroughly. When smooth, add another teaspoon of sauce, then another, and when the mayonnaise starts to hold together, you may add the sauce at a faster pace.

For another method, place the vinegar or hot water directly into the broken mayonnaise in place along the edge of the bowl. Using the tip of your whisk, without getting too deep into the mayonnaise, mix the liquid with the top layer of the broken sauce until you see that it is getting together. Keep mixing, pushing your whisk deeper and deeper into the mayonnaise. Then, whisk larger and larger circles until all of the sauce is back together.

Puff Paste Cheese Straws (*Paillettes* and *Diablotins*)

Paillettes and diablotins are cheese straws; the first are flat strips and the others are twisted. You can serve them with consommé for a very elegant first course, or with cheese or drinks. If you have the time, it is preferable to roll the dough out the day before and let it relax in the refrigerator overnight. This will reduce shrinkage and irregular puffing.

YIELD: 36 STRAWS

1 recipe Fast Puff Paste (recipe follows) or thawed frozen puff paste

1 egg, beaten

¾ cup grated Parmesan cheese

¼ cup sweet Hungarian paprika

1. Preheat the oven to 425°F. Line baking sheets with parchment paper.

2. On a lightly floured board, roll the dough out ⅛ inch thick. Brush the surface of the dough with the beaten egg. Mix together the Parmesan cheese and paprika. Sprinkle the mixture on top and rub so that the whole surface is covered. Turn the dough upside down and coat the other side with the mixture. Fold the dough in half. Cut into strips about ⅜ inch wide. Unfold the strips.

3. Leave the dough flat or, to make twisted cheese straws, place one hand at each end of a strip. In a swift movement, roll the strip forward with one hand and, at the same time, roll it backward with the other. The strip will be twisted into a corkscrewlike spiral.

(continued)

4. Place the strips, whether twisted or flat, on a wet or parchment-lined baking sheet. To prevent the strips from shrinking during baking, smear the ends onto the parchment so they stick and hold the dough stretched.

5. Bake for 7 to 8 minutes, or until nicely browned and crisp. Trim the ends off and cut the strips into 4-inch sticks.

Fast Puff Paste (*Feuilletage Rapide*)

When in a hurry, you can prepare a fast puff paste in one hour at the most, and use it right away. It is quite satisfactory in most instances, except for vol-au-vent (patty shells). The dough does not develop quite as uniformly and is not as flaky as the classic dough described in *La Technique*, but the differences are small and apparent only when the doughs are compared side by side.

YIELD: 2 POUNDS

3¼ cups plus ¾ cup all-purpose flour

2 cups (1 pound) cold unsalted butter, cut into fine dice

1 teaspoon salt

1 cup cold water

1. Mound the flour on a work surface. Make a well in the flour and place the butter and salt in the center. Using a pastry scraper, cut the butter into the flour. Add the water and rapidly combine all ingredients into a mass. Do not knead the dough. At this point, the dough will look very lumpy (the butter will still be in pieces), but it should hold together. Flour the working table generously. (This dough requires more flour during the rolling than a conventional dough.) Roll the dough into a ⅜-inch-thick rectangle.

2. Brush the flour from the surface and fold one end of the dough to the center of the rectangle.

3. Fold the other end in. Both ends should meet in the center. Brush again to remove the excess flour. Fold the dough in half.

4. You now have one double turn that gives you 4 layers of dough. Give 2 more double turns—a total of 3 altogether. This is the equivalent of 4 to 5 single turns, enough for a fast puff paste. If the dough does not become too elastic, the 3 turns can be given consecutively.

Jason Scholz, Chef

High Cotton, Charleston, South Carolina
Maverick Southern Kitchens

"It doesn't change much, even as your professionalism grows, but certainly starting out, forget about your social life, holidays and family activities. Don't expect to get rich any time soon. Keep a notebook and write it down, because whatever it is, will escape your mind. Exercise; you need to keep in shape, run, lift weights, catering takes a lot of stamina."

Chef Scholz's food is simply scrumptious, and the special events he caters are as relaxed as they are memorable. As part of a tasting I have the duck hash made with Vidalia onions, in puff pastry, with a vinaigrette of pecan oil, sherry vinegar, and pecans, which is a signature dish. I also nibble at crab crepes, oysters in buttermilk batter, corn pudding, and buttermilk–blue cheese grits. One mouthful is better than the last.

"I grew up in the Midwest," says Scholz. "My mom had a small catering business. I prefer to use straightforward ingredients and to prepare them so that everything on the plate is recognizable. I grew up eating a lot of meat and still enjoy cooking it. I learned charcuterie and pâté. Charleston developed my taste for local seafood. I accompany everything with the freshest vegetables and salad. We have developed dialogues with farmers, ranchers, fishermen, and purveyors of the freshest ocean fish and seafood, vintners, and distributors. The grits and grains are from Morgan's Mill, a small local company."

Some baked goods are made in-house, while others are baked by Ambrosia Bread and Pastries, also owned by the Maverick Group. Chef Scholz has also developed such a good palate for wine that when Mondavi Vineyards held a tasting dinner in Charleston they asked him to pair the food with the wine. The group reported that "Every dish made the wine better." Dessert was white chocolate mousse with peach-buttermilk sorbet topped with toasted oatmeal and served with a Moscato d'Oro '99.

Scholz explains, "Catered events are primarily for area residents, but many groups choose us as a destination. They might want something traditional or regional. Often, they choose crab and corn soup, mahi mahi with shrimp, and a cobb salad. For large events, we have chefs working at manned stations, oyster and clam shucking, passed hors d'oeuvres. Practice consistency and cleanliness; you have to look good, and everything has to look as good as it tastes. For buffets, replate frequently so that food doesn't look picked over. Keep it fresh and looking fresh as long as the event lasts."

As for his advice for beginners: "It doesn't change much, even as your professionalism grows, but certainly starting out, forget about your social life, holidays, and family activities. Don't expect to get rich any time soon. Keep a notebook and write *it* down, because whatever *it* is, will escape your mind. Exercise! You need to keep in shape, run, lift weights; catering takes a lot of stamina. Get good knives. I still have most of the first Sabatiers and Cutcos I started out with. Develop your own taste. Infuse oils and vinegars so that tastes resonate. Eat and cook food you've not tried before." Chef Scholz says that the beginning caterer's biggest mistake is this: "They don't listen to the client. You have to listen to the client. Everything they want, they should get."

Scholz started with the Maverick Group under the direction of chef Frank Lee at the Maverick Group's Slightly North of Broad, where he learned the benefits of daily meetings and a lot about southern cooking. Then he did a stint at the group's Slightly Up the Creek, on Shem Creek in Mt. Pleasant, where catering is often outdoors, on the deck. Beaches and boats have also been the scene of many of their memorable events. The year-round business is local, but at vacation and holiday time visitors often want to throw a party with a short window for planning. Happily, everyone seems to want dishes like pan-fried crab cakes with green tomato relish and a side of grits with shrimp and andouille sausage, dressed with sautéed red and green onions and tomatoes. The guests also enjoy the Shem Creek Sunset (pineapple juice, dark rum, and grenadine) and for dessert, a Georgia peach cobbler.

Chef Jason Scholz's Charleston Crab Soup

YIELD: 20 CUPS OR 10 BOWLS

4 cups (2 pounds) unsalted butter

2 large onions, finely diced

8 stalks celery, finely diced

4 teaspoons salt

2 cups flour

4 quarts water, heated

2 quarts milk

4 cups heavy cream

2 pounds lump crabmeat, picked over

2 teaspoons ground mace

6 ounces any sherry

Salt to taste

Melt the butter in a soup pot over medium heat. Add the vegetables and sauté for 10 minutes, or until soft and transparent. Stir in the flour and cook, stirring, for 3 minutes. Stir in the hot water, pouring steadily. Add the milk and whisk vigorously. Stir in the cream, crabmeat, mace, sherry, and salt.

High Cotton Blue Cheese Grits

SERVES 20

3 cups heavy whipping cream

3 cups water

1½ cups (¾ pound) butter

1½ cups stone-ground yellow corn grits

6 ounces buttermilk blue cheese

Salt and freshly ground pepper

In a large saucepan, combine 2¼ cups of the cream, the water, ¾ cup butter, the salt, and pepper. Bring to a boil. Remove from heat and slowly add the grits using a heat resistant spatula or wooden spoon. Stir for 3 minutes, then cover and let stand for 20 minutes. Stir in the remaining ¾ cup butter and ¾ cup cream, then the cheese. Add salt and pepper to taste. Serve garnished with sweet pepper relish and chives. Enjoy!

Jim McMullen, Owner
Stephen Rowan, Executive Chef

Jim McMullen's Catering, New York, New York
Annie's Restaurant, New York, New York

"It's not about being creative, it's about organization. Thinking about diverse things at the same time—can the glasses be washed and reused or do you have to have an enormous amount of them? Do the waiters have their own gloves? How will everything be transported? When, and in what order? It takes serious management skills. Everything has to work. It's a second cousin to the restaurant business, not immediate family."

—*Jim McMullen*

For those restaurateurs who are thinking about entering the catering business, Jim McMullen is the exception that proves the rule. A successful fashion model in New York, he decided to open a restaurant on the Upper East Side of Manhattan in 1975, with $20,000 and no experience. McMullen wanted to go into a business, and says he chose the restaurant business somewhat arbitrarily only because he knew people in the field. He had never before worked in a restaurant and was barely familiar with what the back of the house looked like. "I was a yo-yo. A fortunate yo-yo."

One with uncommon common sense, too. He says that he started with simple food, like hamburgers and chicken potpies. "People's palates weren't sophisticated then. Now, dozens of cuisines later, everyone is back to comfort food. People started wanting private parties, and since I had a large kitchen and a dining room I could close off, I was soon catering on the premises regularly. As requests grew, I bought a building down the block in which I opened a large off-premise kitchen devoted to catering, with a banquet manager, a catering chef, and a staff. The wait staff are usually people who have worked in the restaurant, so there is a relaxed spirit."

McMullen contrasts the fixed menu of a restaurant with what he thinks of as the almost unlimited possibilities of catering. "Equipment is extremely important. For parties in the neighborhood, food can virtually go from oven to event. For events farther afield, the service staff must be equipped to cook off-premise at any function. Most restaurants are asked to cater. And restaurateurs must ask themselves if they have a large enough kitchen and storage space to do catering without closing their restaurant. What can they deliver that will please clients who may be expecting the same things they have eaten in the restaurant? Kitchens are getting smaller and smaller as rents get higher, and each square foot has to produce income. A restaurateur might consider renting another kitchen or even a clean storage space where off-premise equipment can be stored.

"It is easy to lose money catering, as it is very labor-intensive in different ways from the restaurant business, and you can't go to the client a few days before their event and tell them you have to double the price. You have to have an organized mind. I catered my own wedding for six hundred people under a tent on Sutton Place.

"It's not about being creative, it's about organization. Thinking about diverse things at the same time—can the glasses be washed and reused or do you have to have an enormous amount of them? Do the waiters have their own gloves? How will everything be transported? When, and in what order? It takes serious management skills. Everything has to work. It's a second cousin to the restaurant business, not immediate family. Also, because it's a special event, people want everything in its place. That's what they remember. They are not as forgiving as they are in a restaurant. I was lucky, but I would advise someone getting started to get a job as a waiter with a substantial caterer and see how it works. If they can, they should work in the kitchen. Be prepared for a long haul getting steady work.

"Getting started is a long selling job, and you have to be out there working at getting clients. Publicists are expensive and never guarantee results. Someone might want to consider going into partnership with one and see how it works if there is a vested interest in the business. Going to conventions and networking hasn't been the way for me. I didn't find people too eager to share. That's changing now; it is getting better, but early on when I started it people were not as open.

"I always knew I wanted to run a place where other people wanted to eat. If that coincided with my taste, fine, but the moment you cease to be objective, you lose something. I have been through various cuisines as people wanted to try different things, but I always kept old standards on the menu. I like taking a somewhat traditional, moderate tack that has a broad base, even though people are more sophisticated than when I started. I prefer to cater that way, too. I do some really large parties, but I prefer a group of up to four hundred, because each service can get more attention. The catering business can lose money. You can really get your head handed to you if you don't figure it all out ahead of time. You can't tell the client you didn't cover your expenses; they'll laugh you to court. The main reason for success is the ability to grow and develop. Evolve a concept, but be there to please. There are food swings, but the base remains the same."

After twenty years, Jim McMullen sold the original Jim McMullen's. He opened a new restaurant down the block and named it Annie's, after his grandmother. It is a truly welcoming family restaurant with adult-oriented quality and service. Steve Rowan, the executive chef for both Annie's and Jim McMullen Catering, has one of the most straightforward approaches in the business. He is concerned with quality ingredients and purity of tastes.

Steve says: "The greatest advice that I can give to a new caterer is don't be afraid to adapt or improvise. We were once scheduled to hold an outdoor corporate affair during an April shower. We set up tents just in case. Of course, it came down—it poured for twelve hours that day and even the tents had three inches of water in them. We quickly set up in the company's office furniture warehouse. The food was good, and no one seemed to mind. Having grace under fire was key!"

Steve Rowan's Mini Crab Cakes with Tarragon-Mustard Rémoulade

YIELD: 3 DOZEN MINI CRAB CAKES

1 pound lump crabmeat, picked over

3 slices white bread, crumbled into ½-inch bits

1½ tablespoons Dijon mustard

1 teaspoon Worcestershire sauce

¼ teaspoon cayenne pepper

1 tablespoon Old Bay Seasoning

4 tablespoons parsley, chopped

1 large egg, beaten

2 medium shallots, minced

3 tablespoons mayonnaise

Grated zest of 1 lemon

Salt and white pepper to taste

Vegetable oil for searing

Tarragon-Mustard Rémoulade (recipe follows)

1. Preheat the oven to 350°F.

2. In a large bowl, combine the crabmeat and bread bits.

3. In a medium bowl, mix together the remaining ingredients, except the oil and sauce. Add to the crabmeat mixture and stir to blend.

4. Using about 1½ tablespoons per cake, form into patties the size of a half-dollar.

5. Heat the oil in a large skillet over medium heat, and pan-fry the cakes for 1 minute on each side. Transfer to paper towels to drain.

6. Serve now, or reheat in a preheated 250°F oven for 10 to 15 minutes. Pass the sauce alongside.

Tarragon-Mustard Rémoulade

YIELD: ABOUT 2 CUPS

1½ cups mayonnaise

3 tablespoons Dijon mustard

2 tablespoons Pommery mustard

1 large shallot, minced

10 small cornichons, minced

2 tablespoons minced fresh tarragon

In a small bowl, combine all the ingredients and blend well.

McMullen's Catering Chocolate Phantasm (Flourless Chocolate Torte)

YIELD: 3 TORTES

1 pound semisweet chocolate, chopped

1 pound unsweetened chocolate, chopped

2 cups (1 pound) unsalted butter, chopped

1 cup water

2 cups sugar

2 cups light corn syrup

10 large eggs, beaten

Whipped cream and sliced fresh strawberries for serving

1. Preheat the oven to 350°F. Line three 10-inch round cake pans with parchment paper.

2. In a double boiler over barely simmering water, melt the chocolates and butter. Set aside to cool.

3. In a small saucepan, bring the water, sugar, and corn syrup to a boil. Reduce heat and simmer for 5 minutes.

4. Mix in the eggs and whisk briskly until shiny and smooth.

5. Add the chocolate. Blend thoroughly.

6. Divide the batter among the prepared cake pans. Bake for 25 to 30 minutes, or until surface springs back when touched lightly. Remove from oven and let cool. Serve with whipped cream and sliced strawberries.

Joe McDonnal, Partner/Owner, Executive Chef
Virginia Wyman, Partner/Owner

The Ruins, Seattle, Washington

"Above all, keep it simple at the time of food service. There is nothing worse than a catered meal that has been too ambitious in the execution and sloppy in the presentation."
—Joe McDonnal

Joe McDonnal's energy and good nature are apparent as he talks about his first business, Market Place Caterers in Seattle, which he owned for twenty years. He first worked as a florist and floral designer, which meant decorating for parties where he got to see the creative work going on in the kitchen. The more he did flowers, the more interested he became in food and cooking. Since he was living in New York at that time, McDonnal started taking the Thursday evening classes offered by James Beard, Dione Lucas, and other famous cooks who shared their skills in a hands-on learning situation with small groups.

His next step was Italy, where he was a chef in a restaurant outside Florence for a while, then back to New York and then off to Spain for a "brief trip" that lasted nine years. After two years there, he opened a restaurant, and then, he says, "It was the classic seven-year thing, seven years and one day. I was not just homesick, but all that sun was too much, and all that noise.

The perfect antidote was the beautiful Northwest, where he went to visit his mother. After spending some time with an uncle, who was also a fabulous chef, McDonnal decided to stay.

He opened a small catering business, because he thought it would be more fun than a restaurant.

"It's not the same room, the same china, the same menu all the time. Catering offers a wonderful challenge and variety, in a loft, under a chestnut tree, and in the wonderful private houses and gardens of Seattle and its environs. When you work for a celebration, you bring the romance back to eating. You don't get to do that in a restaurant, where things have to be more controlled and people are counting calories.

People are starting to be afraid of the contents of the food they eat. Awareness is one thing, but fear?

"When clients contact me, we talk. Then I say I'm interested, and they say they're interested. I listen really carefully, because I know I have to make it logistically workable. We get off the phone, and I use my design imagination. I visualize a floor plan, the decoration, sometimes even the entertainment. Often, the menu is the last thing. Then I call the clients and say, 'Yes, I can do it. It will cost about x number of dollars.' They take a deep breath and say yes, or no, thank you. We meet and finalize the details. It should go smoothly and not take too long, but if the clients take six hours to select linens, it is your duty to spend the six hours pleasantly. From start to finish, you are building a future memory, and the dinner is only part of it. From first take to getting the bill, the clients should be so thrilled with what you do that they are happy to pay the bill. Making people happy is a personally rewarding way to spend my time. I have stacks of mail. It's wonderful. I like it all.

"Seattle is very beautiful and filled with gorgeous gardens. Some are modest gardens that become very exciting in the summer. We do a lot of dinner dances, which are sometimes sumptuous, and private parties where people like to dress up and enjoy a casual elegance that is never conspicuous. Everyone remembers a party a few years ago for twenty-four people in someone's home. One room was set up as a small theater with a Steinway piano, and when people were seated, Ella Fitzgerald walked in. That's a memory."

He emphasizes that you need a team. "The people in the office are equally important. Everything comes to a screeching halt if the wheels on the truck are not in first-rate condition. Bills have to be paid and submitted in good order. You need service people who know your style and understand how you want the event to function. They are your real public relations division. From the minute clients get to the door, everything that happens and everyone they speak with is part of a special occasion.

"We have two vans and do menus that can be delivered hot or cold from our kitchen, or prepared off-premise. So much depends on what you can do at the last minute. It is physically hard work. There is no separate moving company, no separate sanitation crew. A lot of the work is as unglamorous as you can get. The hours are hell. Eighteen-hour days are not unusual when you are busy. And you have to take the work when it is there and deliver without compromising quality. Forget holidays, except for maybe St. Swithun's Day—you're working. Forget dinner with family and friends—you are busy until one in the morning, working while others play. It's quite a rush, and sometimes your alternatives for recreation are very limited and companionship restricted. You really have to figure out how to deal with the stress of work and how to make time for family and friends."

There are few personal/professional partnerships as successful as the one between Joe McDonnal and Virgina Wyman. They complement each other and bring their considerable experience, expertise, and enthusiasm to a unique and exciting way of presenting food to the public. It takes a lot of effort to excite pros. Joe was the one who catered the legendary reception for Joan Mondale when she was head of the National Crafts Council. He created mounds of clam-shell dunes on which were presented astounding clam pies.

Their creative vision has led to a private Seattle dining club, The Ruins. Everyone in Seattle wants to eat there. There are three kitchens with separate staffs with cross-over skills: an abundance of people, ability, and enthusiasm. For décor, Virginia and Joe pooled their antique and artifact collection: a white carousel horse, a huge prop elephant that raises its trunk, a grand piano, and for quieter moments in front of the fireplace, their rare-cookbook collection. The club has a reasonable initiation fee and nominal annual dues. There are over a thousand memberships. Catered events, on or off premises, are for members only. That way you have a fighting chance of finding them free for an event. It is a very personal vision that they share.

It is situation whose time has come for Joe and Virginia. A place where people would begin recognizing each other, where the guests could really feel at home, but with better food and service.

When I ask Joe what his biggest reward is he says, "I still love doing what we do." Clearly everyone who hires them loves what they do as well. As far as giving newcomers advice, he is very clear. "Above all, keep it simple *at the time of food service*. There is nothing worse than a catered meal that has been too ambitious in the execution and sloppy in the presentation. Keep recipes with a large number of unrelated ingredients to a minimum; just straightforward and simple food. Cannelloni alla Fiorentina, for example, is very suitable for a catering job, because (though it takes many ingredients) it is all made ahead and simply baked on site. It is, of course, not simple of procedure, but the flavor is very sophisticated, and straightforward. It is extremely good."

Spoon Bread from The Ruins

YIELD: 10 CUPS

2 cups buttermilk

2 cups milk

½ cup white cornmeal

½ cup yellow cornmeal

1½ teaspoons salt

4 large eggs, separated

1 teaspoon baking powder

¼ cup (2 ounces) unsalted butter

1½ cups grated sharp Cheddar cheese

1. Preheat the oven to 400°F. Butter and warm a 10-cup soufflé dish.

2. Combine the buttermilk, milk, cornmeal, and salt in a saucepan. Cook over medium heat, stirring constantly, until the mixture comes to a full boil. Remove from heat. Whisk in the egg yolks, baking powder, butter, and cheese.

3. In a large bowl, beat the egg whites until stiff but not dry.

4. Fold the egg whites into the cornmeal mixture. Pour into the prepared soufflé dish.

5. Bake for 45 minutes, or until a cake tester comes out dry. Serve from the soufflé dish with a spoon.

Joe McDonnal's Cannelloni alla Fiorentina

YIELD: 18 CANNELLONI

Filling:

2 small bunches spinach, stemmed and washed

1 pound whole-milk ricotta cheese

1 egg, beaten

1 clove garlic, minced

1 teaspoon salt

Few grinds of white pepper

½ teaspoon freshly grated nutmeg

¾ cup Parmesan cheese, grated

Béchamel Sauce:

½ cup (4 ounces) unsalted butter

½ cup all-purpose flour

8 cups milk

Salt, freshly ground pepper, and freshly grated nutmeg to taste

Pomodoro Sauce:

½ cup olive oil

1 cup finely chopped onion

1 cup finely chopped celery

1 cup finely chopped carrot

3 cloves garlic, minced

Two 28-ounce cans Italian plum tomatoes

2 teaspoons minced fresh basil

2 teaspoons minced fresh tarragon

Salt and freshly ground white pepper to taste

4 sheets fresh pasta, 5 by 12 inches

¾ cup grated Parmesan cheese

1. To make the filling: In a covered steamer over simmering water, steam the spinach until wilted, 3 to 4 minutes. Let cool, squeeze dry, and chop finely. In a large bowl, combine the spinach and the remaining filling ingredients. Stir to blend and set aside.

2. To make the béchamel: Melt the butter in a large saucepan over low heat. Stir in the flour and cook, stirring, for 3 to 4 minutes. Gradually whisk in the mild and cook, stirring frequently, until the sauce is thickened. Stir in the seasoning. Strain and set aside to cool.

3. To make the pomodoro sauce: Heat the olive oil in a large, heavy nonreactive pan over medium heat and sauté the onion, celery, and carrot until tender, about 5 minutes. Stir in the garlic. Remove from heat. Drain the tomatoes and reserve the liquid. Discard the seeds from the tomatoes and puree the tomatoes in a blender. Add the tomatoes to the sautéed vegetables; add the herbs, salt, pepper, and reserved tomato liquid. Place over low heat and simmer for about 20 minutes.

4. Preheat the oven to 350°F. Cut each sheet of pasta into four 3-by-5-inch pieces.

5. Place the spinach filling in a pastry bag with a 1-inch opening and pipe the filling down the center of each piece of pasta, leaving room at each end. Roll the cannelloni and seal the edges by pinching with your fingers. Gently simmer the cannelloni in a shallow pan for about 3 minutes. Using a slotted spoon, transfer to a bowl of ice water and let cool for a couple of minutes. If necessary, trim the edges with scissors.

6. Spread half of the béchamel sauce in the bottom of a lasagna pan or casserole large enough to hold the cannelloni side by side. Place the cannelloni over the béchamel sauce in one layer. Cover with the rest of the béchamel sauce and sprinkle with the Parmesan cheese.

7. Bake until the béchamel bubbles and the top is slightly browned, 15 to 20 minutes. Reheat the pomodoro sauce and serve alongside.

Linwood Dame, Owner/Executive Chef

Linwood's, Linwood Catering, and Due, Baltimore, Maryland

"If you think catering is for you, get a job with a caterer, learn from people in the business, and work the front of the house and the back."

I am sitting with one of the most relaxed people I have met in the food business. Linwood Dame is comfortable enough to have his young son keep us company as he eats his lunch. He excuses himself to say hello to regulars and to chat. It is, after all, lunch time at Linwood's. One of nine children in a family that almost never went out to dinner, Linwood Dame remembers his mother's coking with fondness and respect. The family ate together every night, and she made traditional "home-cooked" American food. Today, at Linwood's, the restaurant that also houses Linwood's Catering and its companion restaurant Due, you can find lamb chops, calf's liver, green beans, mashed potatoes, and bread pudding on the menu, along with fancier fare.

From the time he was a kid, Linwood's idea of fun was sharing dinner with friends and family, eating in or going out—even in college and the Coast Guard. Not surprisingly, he completed a two-year program at the Culinary Institute of America in 1982 and graduated with twelve job offers. He rejected hotels and chains, left Hyde Park on Friday, and started working Saturday night in Richmond, Virginia. He hasn't stopped working since. It was a forty-seat restaurant that did some carryout. In a short time, he had a percentage. Eventually, the place doubled in size and began doing off-premise catering. Linwood says this was a great time—hard work but fun. His father was a good businessman, and Linwood knew from the start that you need a good sense of business to be successful. When he married a TV reporter, he started looking to the future. He considered Washington, D.C., but genuinely liked Baltimore and wanted to build there.

Driving around one day, Linwood saw an office building in Owings Mills. He liked the location—the ten thousand cars up and down the road each day, the available parking. He checked the demographics with the chamber of commerce and saw that the population could afford a new restaurant and catering business. It is important to understand how a site is selected and good to see someone doing their homework. Linwood was confident that with five thousand square feet, a very comfortable 120 to 140 people could be seated comfortably, and with the charm of an open kitchen, who wouldn't want to eat there? The menu was designed in 1987, and fifteen years later, the basics are still there.

Another skill Linwood has is attracting people of all ages and interest to use his services. It is a skill to be able to do weddings, christenings, bar and bat mitzvahs, and anniversaries, and to also give full attention to galas like the opening of the Port Discovery Children's Museum, which featured a four-course seated dinner for fifteen hundred guests. Linwood's has catered many fund-raising events, including a seated dinner for the Baltimore Museum of Art, the Baltimore Symphony, and the Baltimore Zoo. They also have done both corporate and health-care events, such as the opening of the Acute Care Unit at the Anne Arundel Medical Center.

Most people like to boast of their gross sales, but Linwood says he is very aware of profitability factors and that sales don't always indicate profit. "You have to watch all the cost factors. You need a really good accountant. What do you buy, what do you rent? Most supplies are owned—not linens, though. Our trucks are custom built; some have separate hot and cold sections. They are very expensive, but we have to rely on them.

"Our catering receptionists are all detail oriented and do a thorough intake. They review it with the salesperson, who gets it and makes contact and sets up an initial person-to-person meeting, most of the time at the clients' home or office. Then a proposal is put together. The lead time can be anywhere from two weeks to a year, depending on the size and complexity of the event. If they accept the contract, we have another tasting for food and wine. We let the client know the availability of the wine they choose and then reserve enough for their event.

"I am always involved in the menu and the tastings. Whether I like it or not, people's tastes vary, but what is always necessary is a spectacular first and last course as well as signature breads."

I tell him that the bread is amazing. The baker makes artisan loaves from scratch. Another skill that Chef Dame has is putting together a great crew with which he shares the spotlight.

"A team is involved in the menus: tasting and checking out the responses. It isn't just a matter of whether I like it or not. Food interests are growing and changing. There is a little spicier direction: French-Asian cuisine, high protein, low carbs. And, of course, wine. Wine sales finally beat out liquor, even though prices have gone up. People are well traveled and well read—they expect a lot. We have twenty chefs and concepts and methods in flux. We are always reviewing what to keep and what to drop."

When I asked Dame for advice to newcomers in the business, he said, "If you think catering is for you, get a job with a caterer, learn from people in the business, and work the front of the house and the back."

As we walked around the back of the house, Linwood opened various walk-ins and freezers. In one walk-in was a woman in a heavy sweater preparing *oeufs en gelée*. That's dedication to a memorable first course.

A few days after the worst blizzard in Baltimore's history, I spoke with Dame's catering manager, Paula Devine, who said on one day of the storm there was an off-premise luncheon that the client was determined not to cancel. It took the catering director two hours to make what should have been a fifteen-minute drive to the catering commissary. Then, because the snow was too high for the Linwood's van, the food was loaded into her truck. With the help of three assistants, the director delivered, served, and cleaned up the whole affair.

The client said, "Thank you for braving the weather with a smile and an attitude so sincere it showed in your walk." Those are the clients who spread the word.

Linwood's Oeufs en Gelée

SERVES 20

13 cups strong chicken stock

10 envelopes unflavored gelatin

1 cup beef broth

½ cup sugar

1 cup ruby port

20 thinly sliced carrot flowers, blanched

60 scallion stems, blanched, trimmed to make stem and leaves

20 fully cooked poached eggs, cooled, and trimmed (20 egg-sized pieces of poached skinless chicken breast may be substituted)

1. To make the aspic: In a double boiler over simmering water, pour 5 cups of chicken stock and sprinkle with the gelatin. Stir gently, turn off heat, and let stand for 5 minutes to dissolve.

2. Meanwhile, in a stockpot large enough to hold all the liquid, heat the remaining 8 cups chicken stock, the beef broth, sugar, and port until it simmers. Pour the gelatin mixture slowly into the warm stock, stirring continuously.

3. Set 20 *oeufs en gelée* molds on 2 trays. Spray the molds with non-stick vegetable oil spray. Pour a layer of aspic into each mold and tilt until there is a secure layer. Place the trays in the refrigerator until the aspic is set. Keep the remaining aspic mixture warm on lowest heat.

4. Remove the trays with set aspic from the refrigerator. Dip the carrot flowers and scallion stems and leaves in the warm aspic and gently place on top of the set aspic in each mold. With a spoon, layer a thin bit of liquid over all and refrigerate again until firmly set.

5. Set the trimmed and cooled poached egg on top of each flower design. Gently fill each mold to the top with warm aspic. Chill until serving time. Unmold on mirrored silver trays.

Linwood's Chocolate Bread Pudding

SERVES 10

14 ounces bittersweet chocolate, chopped

1¼ cups (10 ounces) unsalted butter

¾ pound white bread, crust removed

1¼ cups heavy cream

1¼ cups ground almonds

1½ cups sugar

10 eggs, separated

4 ounces bittersweet chocolate chunks

Crème anglaise and raspberry sauce for serving

1. Preheat the oven to 350°F.

2. In a double boiler over simmering water, melt the 14 ounces chocolate and the butter. Set aside and let cool.

3. In a large bowl, soak the bread in the cream for 45 minutes, then break up any chunks with your fingers.

4. In the bowl of an electric mixer, beat the bread mixture until smooth. Add the almonds and beat until incorporated. Add the sugar and egg yolks. Beat until smooth, scraping down the sides of the bowl. Stir in the cooled chocolate mixture. Add the chocolate chunks and mix well.

5. Place the egg whites in a clean mixing bowl and whip with clean beaters until stiff peaks form. Fold the whites into the bread mixture.

6. Place in a well-oiled 9-by-13-inch baking dish, 2½ inches deep. Bake for 45 minutes or until firm and lightly browned. Remove from the oven and let cool. "We serve it with crème anglaise and raspberry sauce."

Due's Seared Tuna with Blood Oranges and Black Olive Oil

SERVES 1

6 ounces sushi-grade tuna

½ bulb fennel, trimmed and shaved

¼ cup kalamata olives, pitted

¼ cup extra-virgin olive oil

1 blood orange, peeled and sectioned

¼ cup microgreens

2 tablespoons olive oil

Juice of 1 lemon

Salt and freshly ground pepper to taste

1. In a blender, puree the olives with the extra-virgin olive oil. Season with salt and pepper. Set aside.

2. Heat an oiled grill pan or large sauté pan over high heat and sear the tuna for 45 seconds on each side. Remove from heat.

3. In a bowl, toss the fennel, microgreens, 2 tablespoons olive oil, blood orange sections, lemon juice, and salt and pepper to taste.

4. To serve, slice and stack the tuna in the center of the plate. Place the mixture of greens on top of the tuna stack. Garnish with the black olive oil.

Liz Neumark, President

Great Performances, New York, New York

"Nothing is done without a contract and a deposit. Beginners should not be shy about getting a deposit. That is what makes a contract and builds trust. There is a relationship that must be built with everyone: clients, staff, purveyors, vendors, and venues. None of those relationships work as one-night stands."

A few weeks after 9/11, I had occasion to be at a large covered pier on the Hudson River in New York City. It was a place where all the services were set up to help those who were grieving or searching for family members, those who had been injured, or those, like myself, who had lost the places they lived and worked. It was only after several long visits that I wandered over to the buffet. I honestly don't remember what I ate, but it was warm and delicious. I do remember that I had a roll and noticed that it was surprisingly first class. It seemed remarkable to me that any caterer could deliver steam-table food in that abundance— we're talking thousands of portions a day—and that good. There were various caterers providing other goods and services, but Great Performances was ready with no dress rehearsal to deliver day after day, weeks and weeks at a time, in very makeshift conditions.

In 1979, Liz Neumark started to organize wait staff into a temporary personnel agency in New York. She was a photographer, with friends and colleagues in the arts who needed supplemental income. The business grew, and by 1981 it was a full-service catering company. *Diversity* is too small a word to apply to Great Performances. From private residences to Grand Central Station, from boardrooms and artists' lofts, country fields and museums, to celebrate weddings, openings, holidays, charity galas, and commemorative occasions, they deliver deliciously, elegantly, appropriately, and seamlessly. Their respect for venues has earned them the right to cater almost anywhere the client wishes.

With high energy and intelligence, Liz Neumark has managed to snare some of the highest-profile catering jobs in the city. She has the relaxed, accommodating manner necessary for someone who is under pressure 24/7. As we sat and talked in her SoHo office, members of the staff kept coming in with samples of this and questions about that. Two of the dishes I had the pleasure of sampling were the lamb loin and the halibut that follow.

"We do at least a half-dozen projects a month," she says. "*Nothing* is done without a contract and a deposit. Beginners should not be shy about getting a deposit. That is what makes a contract and builds trust. There is a relationship that must be built with everyone: clients, staff, purveyors, vendors, and venues. None of those relationships work as one-night stands. As far as equipment goes, buy one-of-a-kind pieces that become signatures; the rest you can rent—tables, tabletops, seating, plates, and flatware."

The people Neumark hires often develop cross-disciplines and can pinch-hit for an event. There are twelve salespeople. "You need to feel well matched with the people you work with. If it's not the right fit, you won't be happy. It's always a collaboration. If I ever think of doing something else, I think: What would I have that I don't have here? I can even take my kids to school."

Neumark continues: "If you want to consider going into the catering business, work the back of the house, the front, roll up your sleeves. It is very demanding. Food is just part of it. There is a reason they say 'If you can't stand the heat, stay out of the kitchen.' We now have five hundred wait and service staff we can call on. The core works steadily: sales manager, operations manager, party manager, team captains. It's a people business, but you need organization. That's how we could respond when the Red Cross called us.

"We answered the phone on a Sunday night and rolled out three meal periods for two to three thousand people overnight for Monday. All that was based on previous relationships and experiences. We did have a little practice, though. Once we had a call from a famous ocean liner, which told us they had to turn around and be back in port in the morning. Could we be there with breakfast for three thousand? Of course, we did it. We just didn't know it would teach us the things necessary in a real emergency. These things give you a perspective in life. You stay balanced. Our handshake means something. We always want our integrity. And we always want to give something back."

Great Performances has opened a terrific *enotica*, a wine cellar called the Mae Mae Café adjacent to the head catering headquarters. This is a sample presentation.

Menu Suggestions

Panko-Crusted Prawn with a Tamarind-Citrus Glaze

Seared Nantucket Scallop in a Lemongrass Broth

Green Tea & Walnut–Smoked Chicken in a Savoy Cabbage Roll
with Gingered Yam

Roast Shiitake Flan with Frizzled Green Onion

Mustard-Crusted Seared Tuna on Bamboo with Raita

Pulled Duck Dumpling with Kumquat Chutney

Spicy Mongolian Beef on Baby Bok Choy with Crispy Leeks

Asparagus and Cucumber Roll with a Shiso Soy Dip

Shrimp Pâté on Daikon with Pickled Ginger and Miso Pecans

Thai Chili Soup with Scallion Toast

Sticky Rice Fritter with Spicy Cucumber Dip

Lobster and Mango Summer Roll

Seared Foie Gras on Lady Apple Chip with Caramelized Blackberry

Lobster Benedict with Hollandaise and Beluga Caviar

Asparagus Crepe with Lemon Devonshire Cream

Black Mission Fig with Honey Mascarpone and Duck Prosciutto

Daikon Flower with Beet Tartare and Garlic Skate

Pea Shoot Bales Tied with Chive with White Miso Dip

Asian Gazpacho with Cilantro-Jicama Cream

Carrot Soup with Asian Greens and Coconut

Shaved Fennel and Endive with Reggiano in a Sherry Vinaigrette

Jonah Crab with Mango and Avocado Salad

Grilled Chicken and Radicchio with Fresh Strawberries in an Aged
Balsamic Reduction

Sorrel Vichyssoise with Chive Blossoms

Open-Faced Grilled Panini: Heirloom Tomatoes Layered
with Opal Basil and Fresh Mozzarella

Fresh Turkish Figs Shingled with Taleggio and Arugula

Seared Colossal Sea Scallops with Pommes Anna, Pancetta Lardons,
and Caviar Crème

Lobster Risotto with Wild Asparagus and Coral Butter

Tahitian Black Rice Pudding with Coconut Milk and Pistachios

Honey Tuile with Lichee Nut Compote

Fresh Ginger Custard with Lemon Lichee Compote

Sweet Potato Indulgence with Coconut Crème Anglaise and
Cinnamon Crisps

Double-Chocolate Truffle Cake with Spice Crème Anglaise and
Green Tea Ice Cream

Coconut Tapioca with Kumquat Compote

© Asia Society greatperformances
212.727.2424

Lamb Loin with Truffled Mashed Potatoes and Asparagus

YIELD: 2 SERVINGS

3 ounces dried chanterelle mushrooms

1 12-ounce boneless lamb loin, silver skin removed

Salt and freshly ground pepper

1 tablespoon minced shallots

½ tablespoon minced fresh thyme

½ tablespoon minced fresh rosemary

3 tablespoons oil

2 russet potatoes, peeled and finely diced

4 tablespoons unsalted butter

½ cup heavy cream

¼ cup truffle juice (from canned truffles)

12 medium asparagus stalks, peeled

Olive oil, salt, and pepper to taste

1. Preheat the oven to 350°F. In a spice grinder or blender, grind the mushrooms to the consistency of dust. Pour onto a plate.

2. Rub the lamb with the salt, pepper, shallots, and herbs. Roll the lamb in the mushroom dust.

3. Heat the oil in an ovenproof sauté pan over medium heat and sear the lamb loin on all sides, about 1½ minutes per side. Transfer the pan to the oven and roast the lamb for 15 minutes, or to an internal temperature of 145°F.

4. To make the potatoes: Place the potatoes in a medium saucepan of cold salted water. Bring to a simmer over medium heat. Simmer until the potatoes are soft, about 15 minutes. Drain. Return the pan to low heat and shake the pan for 1 or 2 minutes to dry the potatoes. Place the potatoes in a ricer and puree back into the pan. Stir in the melted butter and heavy cream, then add the truffle juice. Adjust the seasoning with salt and pepper. Cover and keep warm in a larger pan of hot water.

5. To make the asparagus: Bring a pot of salted water to a rapid boil. Add the asparagus and boil for about 2 minutes, or until crisp-tender. Drain. Season with olive oil, salt, and pepper.

6. Slice the lamb and serve on warm plates with potatoes and asparagus. Drizzle with any remaining oil from pan.

Great Performance's Halibut with Bok Choy and Sticky Rice

YIELD: 2 SERVINGS

3 tablespoons olive oil

2 7-ounce halibut filets

½ bulb fennel, trimmed, chopped

1 quart orange juice

1 cup (½ pound) unsalted butter

Salt and pepper to taste

3 tablespoons grapeseed oil

4 heads baby bok choy, halved lengthwise

1 teaspoon chopped garlic

1 teaspoon chopped ginger

½ cup sushi rice

1 cup coconut milk

1 tablespoon fish sauce

1. Heat a small amount of olive oil in a sauté pan over medium heat. Add the halibut and sauté for about 6 minutes on each side, or until golden brown.

2. Combine the fennel and orange juice in a saucepan over medium heat. Bring to a boil, reduce the heat to low, and simmer until reduced by three-quarters. Remove from the heat and stir in the butter. Strain through a chinois. Adust the seasoning with salt and pepper. Set aside.

3. To make the bok choy: In a medium saucepan, heat the grapeseed oil (or other neutral oil) over high heat. Add the baby bok choy, garlic, and ginger and sauté for about 10 minutes, until tender.

4. To make the rice: Rinse the rice under cold water. Put the rinsed rice in a pot and add water to about 1 inch above the level of the rice. Cover and cook over very low heat until the rice is tender, about 20 minutes. Turn off heat and let stand, covered, for 15 minutes more. Stir in the coconut milk, fish sauce, and salt and pepper to taste.

5. Serve immediately on warm plates.

Peter Dent, Sole Proprietor/Chef
Allen Smith, Chef

Adobo Catering, Santa Fe, New Mexico

*"I didn't plan on a sole proprietorship, but that's the way
things turned out. There are advantages and disadvantages.
In some ways, it is simpler and clearer to be on your own,
but certainly there are times I would prefer to share some of
the rewards and challenges of the business. You can do that
with staff, but that is a bit different."*

—Peter Dent

"You can't really serve caviar in Santa Fe. Even on ice, it dehydrates quickly in the ninety-five-degree dry heat. Adobo has developed a contemporary Southwest cuisine that is a blend of the best of Central and South America, Native American with a touch of California and Texas. It's a lot more than corn, squash, and beans. At a recent celebrity dinner for sixty-five, the guests were raving about not only the enchiladas, rice, and beans but also the tortilla soup, which features crisp tortillas in a broth of chicken stock, tomato, onion, garlic, cilantro, and epazote, blended with heavy cream. Unfortunately, the flan collapsed on the long rocky road to the party, so the guests had to make do with fresh coconut ice cream."

Adobo does a lot of work for art galleries, cultural centers, and private parties in the homes and second homes of people from all fields who have a special feeling for Santa Fe, its history, and its landscape. One of their most interesting locations is an old abandoned turquoise mine. The hot, dry air means inventive menu planning: soups and terrines, grilled fish or fowl. A lot of the excitement in planning each function and seeing it through to a successful event is doubled because of the beauty of the surroundings.

"I am now the sole owner of Adobe," says Dent. "I started with two partners: Kevin Grenon, who moved on to other things, and Jonathan Horst, who I am very sorry to report died." Peter and Jonathan had met at Dean & DeLuca in New York, and each brought a good deal of culinary knowledge and experience to the business.

"I didn't plan on a sole proprietorship, but that's the way things turned out. There are advantages and disadvantages. In some ways, it is simpler and clearer to be on your own, but certainly there are times I would prefer to share some of the rewards and challenges of the business. You can do that with staff, but that is a bit different."

I asked Peter how business has grown and changed in the last few years. "There are more households with personal chefs. The population has grown, and so have the number of food services. We now do fewer small parties and more large ones. With so many restaurants, people will often host small dinner parties at one of them. Quite honestly, it can be more economical for a party of fifteen or twenty in a restaurant, especially if they order a set menu."

"Catering, of course, offers not only a conceptual difference from a restaurant, but also offers the attention to individual requests and personal service that cannot be equaled in a restaurant. Even in Santa Fe, catering has grown more competitive. We have been in business twelve years and still can't rest on our laurels. I now have a terrific chef, Allen Smith, who is from Texas via New York, where he taught at Peter Kump's Career program and ran an executive dining room on Wall Street."

Chef Smith also taught at the Santa Fe School of Catering. He explains: "Our clients are pretty sophisticated; most are from Los Angeles or New York. They bring their taste with them. We use the best of local ingredients and traditions and apply classic French techniques. We are pretty taste and style conscious, but we fit right into Santa Fe style, serving things like rabbit tacos with roasted local chilies. We'll serve nontraditional tropical fruits with duck enchiladas and a cherry chipotle and pistachio salsa."

Here are two of Adobo Catering's recipes.

Adobo Grilled Duck Breast Soft Tacos with Fruit Salsa

YIELD: 80 TACOS; SERVES 20

10 whole duck breasts, trimmed of all visible fat (reserve fat; see note)

80 fresh corn tortillas

Olive oil for coating

Salt and freshly ground pepper to taste

Mango or papaya salsa for serving

1. Light a fire in a charcoal grill, preheat a gas grill to high, or heat an oiled grill pan over high heat.

2. Lightly coat the duck breasts with the olive oil and generously sprinkle with salt and pepper.

3. Divide the tortillas into stacks of 10 and wrap each stack in aluminum foil. Place the packaged tortillas on the edge of the grill or in a low oven to warm.

4. Grill the duck breasts for about 4 to 6 minutes per side for medium rare.

5. Transfer to a platter, cover loosely with aluminum foil, and let stand for 15 to 20 minutes.

6. On a cutting board, thinly slice the duck and place in a rustic serving dish, with the tortillas in a napkin-lined basket. Or, place a few slices of duck breast in the center of each tortilla and fold over. Serve with fruit salsa alongside.

NOTE: Cut any trimmed pieces of duck fat into ½-inch dice and sauté over medium heat until golden. Using a slotted spoon, transfer the cracklings to a plate, sprinkle with salt, and use as a garnish for the tacos.

Mexican Chocolate Cookies

YIELD: 4 DOZEN COOKIES

7½ cups all-purpose flour

3¾ cups unsweetened cocoa powder

¼ teaspoon salt

4 level teaspoons ground cinnamon

¼ teaspoon finely ground pepper

4 cups (2 pounds) unsalted butter at room temperature

5 cups sugar

5 eggs

3 tablespoons vanilla extract

1. Sift the flour, cocoa, salt, cinnamon, and pepper into a large bowl. In another large bowl, cream the butter and sugar together until light and fluffy. Beat in the eggs and the vanilla, until smooth. Incorporate the flour mixture. The dough will be very stiff.

2. Divide the dough into 3 and form into 9-inch rolls 3 inches in diameter. Wrap each roll in plastic wrap and refrigerate until chilled, at least 2 hours.

3. Preheat the oven to 375°F.

4. Lightly butter and flour cookie sheets. (Silpat liners may be used.)

5. Place dough on lightly floured board and cut into ½-inch slices.

6. Bake 12 to 14 minutes, or until slightly firm to the touch.

7. Cool on cookie sheets for 10 minutes. Transfer to wire racks and cool 1 hour, or until thoroughly cooled.

8. When cookies are cooled, they may be kept in an airtight container for a week or frozen for up to 2 months.

Ronnie Davis, Owner, Director

Ronnie Davis Productions, a Division of Great Performances, New York, New York

"The job of the caterer is to make people happy. It is your charter to interpret what the clients want and extrapolate the specifics that let you deliver. You have to patiently show them how you can make what they want happen. Budget is another thing."

Ronnie Davis, formerly the owner and CEO of Washington Street Cafe, has a well-deserved reputation as a major problem solver.

Davis's grandfather, father, and uncle were caterers in Philadelphia, and he has known his way around a professional kitchen since he was five years old. He peeled potatoes and boiled eggs, bused tables, waited tables, and was a headwaiter at age sixteen. He honed his skills with a group of multiracial waiters in Philadelphia that traveled to hotels, celebrations, and Pullman dining cars. Davis says he learned that service is an art with great dignity. And because his father owned the business, he wanted to gain everyone's respect. He also earned a lot of his own money as a waiter by doing five parties a weekend when he was in school. At eighteen, he became a banquet manager for the Hilton. He then apprenticed with a fine chef.

He himself was the chef when he opened the Washington Street Café in New York City in 1980, and for several years he ran it as a restaurant and catering business. His catering reputation and event-planning abilities outstripped his restaurant. Making a choice, he kept the name but turned exclusively to catering.

In June 1999, Davis made a professional leap and joined Great Performances, one of the premiere corporate catering and events firms in the United States, as managing director. This move has allowed him more time and freedom to pursue his first love—event design and production. His first major event was assisting Mayor Koch in hosting six thousand delegates to the Democratic National Convention on the lawn of Gracie Mansion in 1980. Showing bipartisanship, he more recently produced the inaugural ceremonies for Senator Hillary Clinton and Mayor Michael Bloomberg.

"You have to ask yourself what your strength is and work from there. Learn what you don't know, even if you wind up hiring others to do it. Learn the back of the house, bus, wash dishes, see what happens to five hundred dirty place settings, track the sanitation, and clean up. Learn bartending—how to deal with liquor for five hundred. Learn about buying, checking orders, loading the food, getting the food to the location. How do you pack? How will it be transported? Will you be able to use a handcart, or do you have to carry it? Be a sous-chef. What does a head chef do at a party? Who administers it, sets it up, cleans up?"

"Appearance matters. Be dressed," he says, meaning a tuxedo, a wing-collar shirt, and black dress socks and shoes. That's for men and women.

To deal with details, Davis uses a function sheet on his personalized computer. It lists the date of the intake, the name of the client, who booked the job, where the event is to be held, the nature of the event, and the administrative needs, including licenses for liquor, parking, fireworks, and using a public place, as well as how much kitchen staff will be needed.

"Will more than one driver be necessary? Will a second driver have to park the van or take it to another location while the first delivers and maybe unpacks? What is the condition of the vehicle? What equipment is needed on the van? Will anyone meet them at the site?

"When interviewing potential clients, listen to what they want and don't judge. The job of the caterer is to make people happy. It is your charter to interpret what the clients want and extrapolate the specifics that let you deliver. You have to patiently show them how you can make what they want happen. Budget is another thing. Some clients have no idea how expensive each additional item or station can be. Not merely the ingredients but the preparation, the serving, and the cleanup. You will be well compensated, but you cannot dictate your taste or be all things to all people.

"You have an obligation to explain why you can't do something your client wants if you know it can't be done or that it is something you won't do. If your client still wants it, recommend they see someone else."

What sets Ronnie apart is his creativity and pioneering attitude. As a third-generation caterer, restaurant owner, and former chef, he delivers hard work and takes chances. Nothing fazes him. He stresses that as a caterer you must pay close attention to detail, so that you can be bold in planning events as large as the three thousand people he served at the Statue of Liberty, or a twenty-five-thousand-guest political event.

Being undaunted by scale allowed Davis to co-coordinate countless events relating to 9/11, serving those in need and celebrities alike. His advice to people starting out is always the same: "Be thorough; any detail can disrupt a major plan. Develop relationships you can count on and build on. Develop a reputation for being reliable; people are depending on you to deliver even more than you promised. It is very clear that what you must always do is pay attention."

Ronnie Davis Productions and Great Performances are deeply involved in New York's charity and not-for-profit community and work closely with organizations helping the homeless and children, as well as groups promoting a better quality of life in New York City.

Simon Andrews

Swamp Fox, The Francis Marion, Charleston, South Carolina

"Catering is pretty much a 'no excuses' profession. It takes a while to learn and accept that something will go wrong. The client doesn't want to hear that an oven isn't working. Bring an extra portable oven that you can crank up. Bring extra servings for the soup that someone spills. Think of it as 'what if' insurance."

When I visited him, Simon Andrews suggested that I sample some of his tomato soup with grilled-cheese croutons. The soup was surprisingly savory and scrumptious, and so was the rest of the food that Chef Andrews presented: deviled crab cakes with fried green tomatoes, peach glazed pork chop with collard greens. "Food has to be market fresh and well plated," says Andrews.

He also believes servers should be knowledgeable so that they can answer guest questions. Simon mentors students in Charleston who are studying at Johnson & Wales University and Trident Tech. Some of his interns are awarded credits by the University of South Carolina. He supervises them both at the back and front of the house, so they gain experience and confidence.

Born in Ireland, at the age of twenty-one Andrews moved to New York, where he began working in restaurants. Always interested in food, he rapidly became aware of the difference between good home cooking and the creative, crowd-pleasing food turned out by a professional kitchen. After graduating from the Culinary Institute of America in Hyde Park, New York, he returned to New York City to become a pastry chef. Then Andrews decided to travel south, and after a stint as the executive banquet chef at the Kiawah Island resort, he became the executive chef of the Swamp Fox restaurant at the Francis Marion Hotel in Charleston. The hotel is one of the few listed in the National Trust of Historic Places, and both the guest rooms and the event rooms have been splendidly restored.

In addition to running the restaurant, room service, and catered in-house events, Andrews has catered some of the most remarkable off-premise events in Charleston. He listens carefully to his clients and says, "Catering is pretty much a 'no excuses' profession. It takes a while to learn and accept that *something* will go wrong. The client doesn't want to hear that an oven isn't working. Bring an extra portable oven that you can crank up. Bring extra servings for the soup that someone spills. Think of it as 'what if' insurance. Also, use all forms of communication—radio, memos, e-mail, and phone—to keep in touch with the team."

Recently, chef Andrews sent me the following email:

When I think of "complicated catering" I am reminded of the times when I have multiple functions. For instance, some time ago I catered the opening of the Fort Sumter Visitor Center. This was a formal plated dinner with an hors d'oeuvres reception preceding. At the same time, I had a wedding for two hundred people, a reception with multiple chef stations at the Embassy Suites, a plated dinner for sixty, and a seafood buffet for 150 at the Francis Marion. There was a tremendous amount of coordination to be done on my part. I personally handled the Fort Sumter affair with a team of three cooks and ten wait staff. I made my sous-chef responsible for the wedding; I deputized a line cook and gave him the responsibility of the Francis Marion Hotel. That's a complicated day for me. All the menus were different.

The Fort Sumter deal required me to cook everything on site, but there was a problem: no kitchen facility. During the planning stages, I was okay with that, then I saw the room that they designated for "the kitchen"—it was the park rangers' office, complete with desks, computers, etc. Nothing could come out, because there was no room to put it. There was a small room off that one where the rangers had a microwave and a small table. That became the gardemanger, and all salads and desserts were constructed there. In the rangers' office, or "the main kitchen," I constructed a cooking area—lots of sterno sheet pans and portable butane ranges. Right inside the "main kitchen," I sectioned off an area with a ranger's desk to make the plating area and waiter pickup point. Just outside the room, we had enough space to create a wait station using boxes that I found, a sheet of plywood, and a little imagination. Every course was to be prepared, plated, and served as it was cooked.

I always think to myself that my brain is smarter than I am and I always listen to myself. My mind registers what it sees. For example, walking by a case of lettuce, my brain registers with me that it came in some time ago and should have been put away. I act on that. I notice everything that's going on and I am always thinking of my next move.

This is what we served at Fort Sumter:

Appetizer

Cold pickled jumbo shrimp
with an avocado and citrus relish and crispy leeks

Salad

Butter lettuce tossed in Champagne vinaigrette
and shaved Pecorino Romano

Entrée

Mustard-seared Colorado lamb chops
with a morel mushroom sauce and a bouchée of puff pastry
filled with a cold-water lobster ragout

Wilted spinach and a potato gratin with Asiago cheese

Cake with a raspberry coulis and berries

Fresh rolls and butter

Coffee service

We had a reception beforehand, outside with two full bars, hot and cold passed and stationary hors d'oeuvres, and an ice carving of the new Fort Sumter logo.

Passed Hors d'Oeuvres

Crostini with smoked duck rillettes and a hoisin barbecue glaze

Proscuitto-wrapped asparagus with honeydew melon

Blackened rare tuna on cucumber rounds with a wasabi aioli

Stationary Hors d'Oeuvres

Lavish display of fresh fruit and vegetables with imported and domestic cheeses, French bread, crackers, lavosh, pimiento cheese, and herb dips

Beef and chicken saté with peanut sauce and a teriyaki marinade

Miniature salmon and potato cakes with parsley and rémoulade sauce

Everything went as if it had been done at the hotel. The guests were blown away.

Stanley Poll

William Poll Caterers, New York, New York

"A new caterer has to learn not only skills and business but be prepared for a rollercoaster ride. I still have many new experiences, and occasionally one will feel surprisingly devastating. Even when you are very dedicated, you can't control everything."

Stanley Poll, who runs William Poll Caterers in New York City, jokes that catering à la carte requires the commitment of marriage without offering its benefits. You can be on the go twenty-four hours a day. "Your time is not your own—and that's almost entirely spent preparing meals and food for pickup and delivery only."

Stanley's father, William Poll, joined his brother's food business and opened a food shop in New York in the 1920s. In those days, many residents of the Upper East Side had full staffs—waiters, valets, butlers, and maids—but often not a large enough kitchen to prepare the food for large parties. The clients also needed large amounts of delicacies that Poll had the resources to supply. The clientele had sophisticated palates and appreciated quality food.

After World War II, domestic staffs were reduced, and more people worked outside their home. William Poll began to prepare frozen gourmet food that could be picked up on the way home. This innovation caught on with his customers. As his clients traveled farther afield to the Near East and Far East, Poll added dishes from these cuisines to his fresh-frozen line. The business gradually shifted to fresh prepared food. The Polls made dinner for the parties and special events of neighborhood people, and their business grew by leaps and bounds. The menu has expanded to sixty different dinners, though not all are available all the time. People from a tri-state area order their favorite meals from what still appears to be a small shop.

Stanley Poll stepped in when his father was thinking of selling and retiring. His expertise in advertising helps him to understand the market.

He advises people new to catering to do what they do well and create a market for it, rather than to compete against everyone.

"If you do a wonderful salmon, let that be your specialty. Build from there. Taking on A to Z is dangerous. If you make your base solid, you have something to build on. You need commitment, drive, and sustained energy. You also have to understand satisfying people's expectations—no changes at the last minute—and you have to be on time. Planes and trains can be late, but not dinner or, for that matter, coffee. People are driven by their appetite. They will wait hours at an airport without grumbling, but if their food isn't on the table within minutes, they feel free to complain. So whatever you are doing, you have to bring quality and timing. If you advertise, do it clearly. We advertise very modestly, and people are usually very pleased when they see what we deliver."

It is always a pleasure to speak to Stanley Poll because he is charming, warm, and sincere about his work. The business is still thriving after eighty years. This is a caterer who has specialized in providing not only specialty ingredients, but comfort food for his clients—whether it was trimming the crusts for Diana Vreeland's sandwiches or turkey loaf, mashed potatoes, and roasted vegetables for a celebrity family.

"These days, a lot of people are reassured by the basics. If they want something exotic, they will go out to dinner and feel adventuresome. Now when people entertain at home, they seem to prefer something low-key. The size of the parties has grown smaller and more intimate. It is as though people want to talk to each other more. Some of the pretense we were seeing for a while has diminished.

"A new caterer has to learn not only skills and business, but to be prepared for a roller-coaster ride. I still have many new experiences, and occasionally one will feel surprisingly devastating. Even when you are very dedicated, you can't control everything. You have to learn and apply all you know. Most of the time, it is exhilarating. You are providing food and events that will be in people's memories for a long time."

The following two recipes from William Poll emphasize tasty simplicity.

Lobster Fra Diavolo William Poll

SERVES 2

3 tablespoons olive oil

1 tablespoon minced garlic

½ cup white wine

¼ cup clam juice

1½ cups marinara sauce

Salt and freshly ground pepper to taste

2 tablespoons minced fresh basil

12 ounces cooked lobster meat

½ pound dried thin spaghetti

1. Heat the olive oil in a saucepan over medium heat and sauté the garlic until golden, about 5 minutes. Add the wine, clam juice, marinara sauce, salt, pepper, and basil. Add the lobster meat and simmer for 8 to 10 minutes.

2. Meanwhile, in a large pot of salted boiling water, cook the pasta according to package directions. Drain. Pour the sauce over the hot pasta and serve immediately.

Stanley Poll's Carrot Souffle

YIELD: 8 CUPS

1 pound carrots, cooked and pureed

3 eggs, separated

⅓ cup sugar

4 tablespoons flour

4 tablespoons unsalted butter, very soft

1. Preheat oven to 350°F. Butter an 8-cup soufflé dish.

2. In a medium bowl, combine the carrot puree and egg yolks. Beat until smooth. Stir in the sugar, flour, and butter until smooth.

3. In a large bowl, beat the egg whites until stiff, glossy peaks form. Fold into the carrot mixture. Pour mixture into the prepared dish. Bake for 35 minutes, or until puffed and golden.

Variation: To caramelize the soufflé, combine ½ cup packed brown sugar and ¼ cup melted butter. Pour over the top of the soufflé after 30 minutes and return to the oven for 5 minutes.

Sylvia Weinstock

Sylvia Weinstock's Cakes, New York, New York

"I have only one secret. I like my life and what I do, and I trust from that wondrous things will happen."

In Sylvia Weinstock's sunny Tribeca location, the phone never stops ringing. Without missing a beat, she takes each call with genuine interest and enthusiasm, pausing momentarily to confirm dates and times in a leather agenda. It is no wonder that many of her colleagues and clients have become friends. Always a successful home baker, when an illness kept her housebound she started making more elaborate cakes as a creative hobby, producing more than friends and family could devour. She took these to local restaurants, who bought as many as she could deliver. They started placing orders, and by the time she was better, she was in business.

After delivering a birthday cake a friend had ordered for a party at an elegant New York hotel, she called the banquet manager to see how he liked it. Impressed by both the cake and her professionalism, he ordered a cake for a wedding being held at the hotel, and the rest is cake history. She creates cakes for private and public events, museum and corporate affairs, and social and celebrity galas. Clients have been known to fly her and her cakes wherever their party is. Though many clients are celebrities, she says all her clients are special, and the cakes she delivers attest to that philosophy. Keeping her cake recipes simple and dependable, Sylvia Weinstock has brought the art of sugar decorating and sculpting to new heights. She developed a special sugar blend that can be made into flowers and other forms ahead of time. It can be manipulated by hand to make botanically correct flowers and stunning fanciful ornamentation. It sometimes takes two weeks to make the decoration for one cake. People not only eat the decorations, but take some home as souvenirs.

"Still, the most important part of the job is the interview," says Weinstock, "finding out what people's expectations are and translating them into what's doable. The cakes are, after all, for dream occasions, and people want nothing less than their dream satisfied. The purpose is to please the client, to deliver what they want. The next is the followup. Call the banquet manager or the client. Ask, did you like it? I really wait for that 'Yes.' It is important to me."

About specializing, she says: "We don't want to do it all. Our cakes are so labor-intensive that it would be hard to perfect them and pay attention to delivering an equally good meal."

Sylvia Weinstock says it is important for people starting out to know that they will have to put the business first, seven days a week, because it is service that is being bought and paid for. And, yes, a certain amount of tension and anxiety are a normal part of operating successfully.

"People are more sophisticated than when we started out. Now we do a cake that uses almonds, chocolate, and blood orange. As the business has grown, I have less private time. We make more and better samples to create designs with great individuality. Many couples are getting married at an older age today; they are more knowledgeable and making their own choices, which may be more daring and different from their parents. I spend time with them so that their event will have a unique look, feel, and taste. Groom's cakes are back in fashion, and those are fun. Smaller than the wedding cake, rarely made for more than fifty servings, they are often chocolate with silver design elements.

"We have used the same purveyors for years, Wills, across the street, for about twenty years. That helps quality and cost. We still have about sixteen on staff.

"I never feel competitive; there is only one Sylvia Weinstock. I know what I can deliver; if someone wants a 'knockoff,' they are welcome to it. I also am not a teacher. We don't take apprentices; we are a small place physically. I get ten calls a week from people who want to learn from me. Why would I do that? I hire a person who wants to work for me, not someone who wants from the start to be competitive. I tell them to go to work in any good bakery for twelve to fourteen hours a day six or seven days a week and see if they still like the idea.

"In the last couple of years, celebrations are often a little smaller than in the past, but the dynamics are the same. It is about the relationship with clients, the creativity and flexibility. We will fly cakes anywhere. A skilled staff member or I will accompany the cake, which is in parts that are assembled on location. I have only one secret. I like my life and what I do, and I trust from that wondrous things will happen."

William Henry IV, Executive Chef
Monika Henry, Food and Beverage
Manager

The Barony and the Westin Resort, Hilton Head Island, South Carolina

"Don't offer too wide a variety of wines and beverages. You want the client to feel good about his or her choice. If they are responsive you can steer them a little, but never disparage their taste."

—Monika Henry

I had the pleasure of interviewing Monika and William Henry in one of the most beautiful spots on the East Coast. They are one of the few couples in this industry employed at a comparable level by the same organization. It is a pleasure to see how they complement each other. They cater to people from all over the world who want to have an event in resort surroundings. There was a time when that meant certain limitations in what could be delivered. Now, with the aid of electronic communication and fast shipping, a well-trained staff with good equipment can cater to a variety of clients both on and off premise.

Monika Henry grew up in Hungary, where everyone in the family drank wine at meals. At an early age, she realized she had a palate and an appreciation of wine. She joined the Westin in 1995 as a supervisor and read all she could about wine as she tasted and tested. She urges people entering the business to use their imagination when savoring the flavors in order to find a vocabulary to describe them. She also advises asking others what they think so that you can broaden your personal tastes and extend it to your guests. "Keep asking questions of everyone. If you want to be involved in the larger world of beverages, go to school and take internship positions.

"When I was manager of the Barony Grill," she says, "I would sometimes taste wines with the customer and tailor the conversation to their experience and knowledge. This way you can encourage them within their own preferences, from sweet Zinfandel to a more subtle Riesling, fruity but less sugary. Never start clients from scratch, but build on their area of confidence. Develop a shared vocabulary. If the guest's taste is for something heavy, then talk peppery, berry, cherry, but with a smile. A lot of people don't want to worry about what they are drinking, and who can blame them?

"Over time, you develop relationships with distributors who will be your mainstay. Like everyone else involved in catering, you are in business. Not only will they give you good advice about delicious beverages, but also they will see to it that you have consistently fair pricing for wine and spirits. Your staff has to be well trained in selling and pouring as well as selecting so that cost control isn't undermined."

In South Carolina, liquor cannot be poured from quart or liter bottles. All "hard" liquor is sold in 1.7-ounce miniatures similar to those served on airlines. It is a state regulatory law, so pricing can be difficult, particularly for drinks made with several different liquors. "There is a lot of cleverness needed as well as some inventiveness. It is best to use only one mini of alcohol and one or more nonalcoholic mixes. For instance, a Long Island iced tea could cost a fortune, but we offer the drink with one alcoholic beverage and added flavorings from juice and syrups so that mixed drinks aren't astronomical."

Monika uses the word friendly often. She holds frequent meetings with her staff. Often, there are staff meetings with event and convention service managers, who are usually the ones who deal with the clients or their representatives.

"Always be gracious about your time, and if anyone wants to talk to you about his or her event—be available," says Monika. Never talk event planners into exceeding their budget; no one will thank you for it. Don't offer too wide a variety of wines and beverages. You want the client to feel good about his or her choice. If they are responsive, you can steer them a little, but never disparage their taste."

William Henry must have one of the best jobs in catering. Not only is he in charge of the food and food service for one of the most beautiful resorts in the country, but he also gets to spend the day with Monika Henry, his wife and colleague. Bill developed an interest in cooking in high school, and managed to arrange to leave school at noon and assist a chef for school credit. At sixteen, he was one of the youngest students to be admitted to the Culinary Institute of America. That opened a lot of doors, the best one being an internship at Pier House in Key West, an island resort on a smaller scale than his current location.

There, Bill learned to work under pressure and to appreciate what people on holiday expect. He says that you have to be willing to lead people—to take charge—and to always exceed the customer's expectations. He went on to learn abut larger volume at the Hyatt for a few years, then joined the Westin Hilton Head, taking a job as a line chef at the Barony. After six months, he was promoted to banquet assistant, then banquet chef, the executive sous-chef. Since 2000, he has been the executive chef. He is in his early thirties.

In addition to his culinary knowledge and skills, Bill has developed a good working relationship with staff. Communication and appreciation are high on his list of talents a good chef should cultivate. He has a daily meeting with staff and listens at least as much as he speaks. He makes it clear everyone is needed. The Westin is enormous, holding several events at once, both on and off premise, in a busy season. There are fifty-five fridges on the premises in various locations and a back-up generator. Bill does a lot of staff training himself, because he wants to raise the bar. As a result, the Barony is the only four-star restaurant on the island.

But Bill can deal with dinner for a thousand with ease. "It's in the rhythm," he says. "You have to conceptualize it. With enough stations cooking and plating, there is no reason people can't get food that is both delicious and hot." He doesn't push people, but for groups of hundreds, he does recommend his favorites: filet mignon and salmon, with a vegetarian option.

"Never say no," says Bill. "Catering is a matter of goodwill. Not just with obvious people like clients and employees, but with competitors and delivery people. During one storm we borrowed a few cases of wine from a competitor for an event. It was delivered by a local trucker we had helped out." He reads the questionnaires that are left for guests to fill out, "because I want to know what our clients think."

The Westin's goodwill extends to the community. Overages are given to a local "Second Helpings" and others are frozen for food bank pickup. A lot of smaller local social service groups are on their list too.

Here, Monika Henry has given us one of her catering menus that pairs food and wine selections, while Bill Henry offers his recipe for Frogmore Stew.

Chaine des Rotisseurs
Induction Dinner

February 9, 2003

RECEPTION

Passed Hors d'Oeuvres

Parmigiano-Reggiano Crisps with Goat Cheese and Truffle Mousse

Fingerling Potato, Osetra Caviar, and Chives

Ahi Tuna Tartar, Mango Wasabi, and Wonton Chips

Champagne, Chandon Brut Classic, NV

Classic Bellinis

DINNER

Appetizers

Roasted Honey Pecan Quail
with Carolina Grits and Papaya Reduction

Gloria Ferrer Pinot Noir, Carneros 2000

Fish

Seared Local Grouper and Foie Gras
with Braised Black-Eyed Peas and Country Ham and Micro Herb Salad

Artesa Chardonnay, Carneros 1998

Entrée

Rotissierie-Roasted Rack Of Venison with Savory Bread Pudding
and Essence of Red Wine, Figs, and Peaches

Simi Cabernet Sauvignon, Alexander Valley, 2000

Salad

Tangle Of Chef's Garden Greens with White Balsamic and White Port,
Aged Stilton, and Cinnamon-Flashed Walnuts

St. Supery Moscato, California 2000

Dessert

Raspberry-Chocolate Terrine

Smith Woodhouse Port, LBV 1992

Bill Henry's Frogmore Stew

You can double this recipe—everyone will want seconds, that's how great it is! Frogmore is another name for St. Helena Island, which is just up the coast from us by Beaufort.

SERVES 6 TO 8

½ cup (4 ounces) butter

1 onion, diced

½ head celery, diced

4 andouille sausages, cut into large dice

1½ cups all-purpose flour

½ ounce minced garlic

1 teaspoon dried tarragon

1 teaspoon dried thyme

2 tablespoons Old Bay Seasoning

¼ cup Worcestershire sauce

1 tablespoon Tabasco sauce

Salt and freshly ground pepper to taste

1 gallon crab stock or seafood stock

25 mussels, steamed and shelled

25 small shrimp, shelled

25 bay scallops

6 ears fresh corn, shucked and cut into quarters

3 pounds new potatoes, cut into wedges and parboiled for 10 minutes

Savannah Red Rice for serving (recipe follows)

1. Melt the butter in a heavy pot over medium heat and sauté the onions, celery, and sausage until sausage is cooked through, about 10 minutes. Stir in the flour and cook stirring, for 3 minutes.

2. Stir in the garlic, herbs, Worcestershire, Tabasco, salt, and pepper and cook for 2 to 3 minutes.

3. Whisk in the stock or broth. Bring to a boil and reduce heat to a simmer. Add the seafood and corn and simmer for 5 minutes or until cooked through.

4. Add in the parboiled potatoes and simmer until all ingredients are cooked through, about 5 minutes. Taste and adjust the seasoning.

5. Serve with white Carolina rice or Savannah red rice (recipe follows).

Savannah Red Rice

SERVES 6 TO 8

¼ cup bacon fat or vegetable oil

8 ounces andouille sausage, diced

1 onion, diced

5 stalks celery, diced

1 cup long-grain white rice

6 ounces tomato paste

4 cups chicken stock

2 tablespoons sweet Hungarian paprika

1 tablespoon dried oregano

1 tablespoon dried thyme leaves

1 tablespoon ground cumin

1 tablespoon chili powder

½ tablespoon garlic powder

Salt and freshly ground black pepper to taste

1. Heat a medium saucepan over medium heat. Sweat together the bacon fat, andouille sausage, diced onion, and diced celery.

2. Stir in the rice and tomato paste, then the herbs, seasonings, and stock.

3. Bring to a boil, reduce heat to a simmer, cover, and cook until the liquid is absorbed and the rice is tender, about 20 minutes.

Bourbon-Marinated Flank Steak with Onion Ragout from The Barony

SERVES 4

2 flank steaks (about 2 pounds each), trimmed of visible fat

2 tablespoons minced garlic

20 sprigs fresh thyme

1 tablespoon cracked black pepper

4 bay leaves

2 cups corn oil

½ cup Worcestershire sauce

½ cup bourbon

Onion Ragout for serving (recipe follows)

1. In a baking dish, mix together the ingredients except for the steaks and ragout.

2. Add the flank steaks, cover, and refrigerate for 24 hours.

3. Grill over an open flame or oven broiler to desired doneness.

4. Allow the steaks to rest for 5 minutes before slicing into thin strips against the grain. Serve with the onion ragout.

Onion Ragout

SERVES 4

8 medium-large onions, cut into julienne

1 tablespoon minced garlic

¼ cup vegetable oil

1 cup dry red wine

½ cup balsamic vinegar

1 tablespoon minced fresh thyme

1 quart veal or chicken stock

Salt and freshly ground pepper to taste

1. In a large, heavy pot over medium heat, sweat together the vegetable oil, garlic, and onions.

2. Stir in the wine and vinegar and cook to reduce by half. Add the stock and thyme. Cook to reduce by one-third. Stir in the salt and pepper.

4

Setting Up
Your Business

Sole proprietor is the designation of most start-up catering entrepreneurs. The good news and the bad news about this type of business are identical: The profits and losses are all yours. Until you decide what to do, you can simply open a separate bank account under your own name. If you choose a "business name," you can open the account under own name with an amended DBA, "doing business as" XXX Catering.

By far the most popular way to set up a small business is currently the S corporation. As with any situation demanding legal options, you must write a clear list of your intentions, needs, and questions, and have a lawyer experienced in catering review them with you. This is a good time to obtain the services of an accountant as well. Each decision you make carries federal and state tax, insurance, and legal liability ramifications. The general advantage of an S corporation is that your personal assets are not liable should your company run into credit problems. And although there is a lot more paperwork, you are taxed similarly to a sole proprietorship—that is, only on personal earnings. Though you may have up to thirty-five shareholders, all stock must be of the same class, and you must keep your books in time with the calendar year. Initially, your expenses are the small fees involved in becoming incorporated, company-name approval, and your corporate charter and seal. These fees, for a small start-up business, can usually be figured in hundreds, not thousands, of dollars, so it is generally well worth it. There are small annual fees, but they also help you think of your catering business as a separate financial entity, about which you can make goal-oriented decisions.

The C corporation is something your lawyer and accountant will advise you about if they feel your capital and business structure demand it. It requires full-blown corporate action and often cumbersome document and tax work as well as increased expenses. You may also want to ask your lawyer about an LLC, which is a limited liability corporation. This structure is gaining favor and has been approved by several states since the IRS said it was an acceptable corporate option. It may serve to give you both the tax advantages of a proprietorship and the liability advantages of a corporation.

Partnerships are rarely formed because they are structured as if each partner were a sole proprietor, with each subject to responsibility for the other. Sometimes, a limited partnership is chosen because it usually protects the investing partners from losing anything more than their original investment should a serious liability be incurred. Neither form of partnership is as generally useful for small businesses as forming a corporation.

The important thing is to ask a lot of questions of experienced people and organizations, and explain your goals as clearly as you can. Remember, even though you need, and the law requires, licensed professionals to perform certain legal and financial duties, you are the one who must shape a business you are happy with.

As mentioned earlier, the best way to learn the catering business is to work in all aspects of the field and see it firsthand. Take a course or two. Even though you may not do your own bookkeeping or accounting you should have an idea of your finances at all times. An excellent site for information that is very user friendly and a source of pertinent facts is the Small Business Administration. If you go on the Internet to www.sba.gov, you will get step-by-step directions for writing business plans and formatting your business profile and financial outlook. You may or may not use the SBA to start your business, but their guidelines will help you pay attention to the necessary financial details. You can also get an overview of the general state of business by logging on to sites such as the *Wall Street Journal,* which has links to many business resources.

Collecting Financial Information

One of the first things to do as you start to set up your office is to put together a personal financial resumé. It will help to establish your net worth, on which you can base your financial plan. Collect the following asset and liability information: house property, house contents, kitchen and office contents, investments, bank accounts, Keoghs, IRAs, personal assets and debts, outstanding loans, mortgages, unpaid taxes, and so on. These figures will give you a starting point. This is a place to be as realistic as possible, as your personal assets will probably be the foundation of your business.

Your next resource might be personal loans and credit from banks. Should you plan to seek loans from friends and family, this will usually be done only after you have had some experience and done a fair amount of research and development. In any case, you will be well advised to write up a letter describing the loan, the amount, and the conditions and time frame for paying it back.

Once you determine your operating fund, you will have to shepherd your assets well. Remember that an entirely off-premise small catering business is not one that venture capitalists will be interested in. Such an enterprise rarely shows enough profitability soon enough to pay back $4 to $10 per dollar of an investment within the five-year window that is their usual expectation. And rarely is the income or liquidity enough at any single point to reclaim the stake of investment bankers. Even after several years of being financially stable and maintaining good credit, it is unlikely that you will be able to raise an enormous new infusion of money. So overextending is a bad business plan.

For assets like a refrigerated truck or other equipment, the manufacturer can often be helpful in financing. Eventually, your business should have good enough credit to cover the need for expansion or new equipment.

If you are turned down for a loan to which you think you might be entitled, the Small Business Administration, which does not itself lend money, may consider guaranteeing your loan from the bank. They will arrange to guarantee a large percentage of your loan if it is approved. There is a cap on what they will do, so questions have to be very specific. A good description of your market, collateral, and payback plan must be presented with a solid three-year proposal, though the loan does not necessarily have to be paid back in that time.

When approaching a professional for capital, there is a ten-to-twenty-times better chance at success if the business has been operating for several years with some accomplishment and profit. You will get more attention if your story is one about a business that is ready to take off, rather than about one starting from scratch. As in catering itself, a lot depends on you. Investors want to hear a truly good scenario and projection about why you want a couple of hundred thousand dollars when your business only makes fifty thousand dollars a year. Show convincingly that this investment will turn your company into a million-dollar business, and people will listen. You will have to show a very good track record, personally and professionally, and offer a specific plan, whether it is buying banquet facilities, an old inn, or a food-processing facility.

In this situation, you yourself must be convinced that 50 to 75 percent of your business will be worth more than the 100 percent that you have now. Major investors want not only a higher yield on something risky, but often to be an active part of it. "Can I go deeper into debt?" and "Do I want to share my business with an investor?" are the questions to be asked twice each time you consider taking on bigger financial obligations.

Selecting Insurance

You will need some insurance as your lawyer advises you. When you are a small business, it is better to work with an insurance broker. Generally speaking, an agent gets bonuses from insurance companies for sales, and brokers earn most of their money looking out for your interests. Try to find a small brokerage house in your area and explain your needs. The big ones handle only really large accounts, and you will not be well served. A small brokerage firm can handle not only product liability, but general fire and theft, vehicle, and equipment, to say nothing of workers' compensation insurance, which is something that is required and regulated state by state.

Brokers shop around the insurance companies to see who is going to cover a risk in the best and most economical way. It is necessary to learn about all the insurance you are responsible for. Some people will not buy food from you without food insurance, and others will not let you operate on their premises without insurance for property damage. Most of the brand-name foods you use have Broad Form Vendors Endorsements attached to their own insurance policies, but it will be necessary for you to protect yourself. These days you cannot even leave samples at most places without a certificate of product liability. People have become more and more food conscious and aware of the relationship of food to health, and they are wary of food if they are at all unsure of its source and handling. Most people who have begun catering after years of cooking for friends, family, and other large groups resent this, but the professional network acknowledges the need for insurance and regards it as a necessary business operating expense and figures it as part of their overhead. It is not an area in which to be penny wise and pound foolish. Your thoroughness in researching this area will be well rewarded.

Given the enormous amount of food produced in this country, industry standards are remarkably high, and though you might fear a lot of risk, there are relatively few claims in this area. Some insurance costs will be an annual overhead amount, and others will be for specific jobs that have to be figured into your profitability analysis.

You might want cancellation insurance that protects both the host and the caterer for the loss of the deposit and the profit; usually there is a negotiable cap on what insurers will provide. There are also some companies that will insure a caterer on a per-event basis against the failure to produce promised services, like the band or a tent. Though some on-site compromises are made, a client can sometimes sue for general pain and suffering caused by a breach of contract.

The Insurance Information Institute is a nonprofit resource that will answer specific insurance questions: How do I insure this? For how much? What is the minimum I need to start? Their member companies get database news daily. They will direct callers to facts and figures that are guides to selecting coverage. As always in these matters, speak with your agent or broker and to your lawyer. Regulations have some variables, and you will need to make an informed and legally correct decision.

Kornreich/NIA Insurance Services is a company that has developed a program exclusively for caterers. A large business, even as a start-up, has more options than a small one, and often a young business does not even think about insurance until there is a snag that requires it. Speak with your lawyer. The program for caterers that Kornreich has outlined addresses this category and broadly analyzes it. There is some cost saving and buying strength in being part of a newly recognized insurance segment. The insurance industry is in great flux, and various plans from various companies will have to be reviewed. If you are stuck, Kornreich will work with your agent or broker, and if you do not have one, will suggest one in your area.

Setting Up Your Office

Most people would be surprised to see that many million-dollar businesses are run from spaces no larger than their bedroom. One of the advantages of starting an off-premise catering business is that you can begin at whatever level of investment you are comfortable with and achieve success. A desk, a table, a few chairs, files, shelves, and a reliable telephone, fax, and answering machine are enough for starters. Your computers and software will probably be your biggest initial office expense. From the start, you will want to be sure that the premises you are planning to use are legal for doing business. When you start out, your office will undoubtedly also be adjacent to your food storage and preparation facility. Make sure your licenses will go into effect right away. Be aware of the liquor laws in your state. They vary enormously and take a lot of looking into.

From the start, you want to develop a business data bank. Lots of scraps and notes are far too time-consuming and won't work for more than a week. Make it a habit to keep track of everything in the most organized way you can. It is practical to start out with a computer so you can start building correspondence and information files immediately. You will also want to make your presence known by e-mail, so that people can make inquiries from the start. This will also begin to build your client database.

A personal computer with the largest capacity of hard-drive memory storage is your best bet. A laptop with exactly the same software and formatting is helpful as well, since you may need to input and access information from various places. Personal digital assistants (PDAs) such as Palm Pilots are an excellent choice as well. A good printer and flatbed scanner and a digital camera will also be necessary. The camera will allow you to photograph dishes and locations to be shown.

Buy the best software available. For PCs, the Microsoft Windows XP Professional operating system is elegant enough for most needs. Word-processing programs abound, but in the long run it is best to use common basic software such as Micrsosoft Word for Windows. You can convert documents from almost any other word-processing program to Word format, and using popular software means it will be easy to communicate with others, have decent tech support, and obtain frequent updates. It also means it will be easier to find people who can work for and with you. Almost anyone you hire to work at the computer will have encountered both XP Pro and Word.

Keep one paper copy of important documents and back up your files to a disk, CD, or Zip disk daily. If you plan on producing your own menus and flyers, you might want a color printer, but it is not necessary, and you can always buy one later.

It is important that the printed materials that represent your business look professional. There are many software programs that will help you create decorative logos and letterheads. The expenses at stationers of such general office supplies as business cards, letterhead stationary, and labels with your logo that can go on presentation folders will be minimal. Most of the letters, forms, and reports that you need can be generated by your computer.

Keeping Track of Finances

With a minimum of paperwork, a little filing, and a good deal of patience, you can keep track of expenses, income, and profit. If you start out with a simple, clear system and make the time to keep it up to date, you will always know where you stand. Business is one place where you want your right hand to know what your left is doing. Whether you tend to be open-handed or tight-fisted, the paper trail you create will lead to a clear and comprehensive view of what your financial position is at any time.

There are many easy bookkeeping methods and computer systems that will help you (see below). A simple ledger with items entered as you pay or receive them will also do the trick. Keep separate files for cash receipts, rent, telephone, utilities, balanced checkbook stubs, and credit card statements. If you become too busy to do your own books, there are many freelance bookkeepers who will work one day or more per week or month. Ask your accountant what system he or she suggests for record keeping. You will be able to forecast your needs as you become able to separate your permanent overhead, various business outlays, and specific job costs. It is necessary at all times to have realistic information so you can get and give good value.

Your accountant will tell you what sales taxes are applicable in your region. You will probably also need IRS and state employer ID numbers and a resale number. Failure to acquire these can expose you to fines and penalties that will be more costly than paying correctly in the first place. And the stress reduction is enormous.

Using Computer Software

Computer systems vary from very user friendly to levels of complexity that require training sessions. By the time you contact the software companies listed here, the programs they offer will certainly have been upgraded. All software companies have people who will answer your questions. If you are one of those who thrive in the kitchen but are reluctant to get involved with computers, get over it! If you can, you may prefer to hire someone to set up and run your office, but computers are no longer an either/or option. Good software has enhanced communications and working conditions so that more jobs can be taken on and more employment created in the food-service industry, beyond fast food. Computers help with storing, filing, and tracking information. In addition to word processing, accounting, food inventories, and pricing, research on the Internet can lead to a variety of resources.

There are simple general business systems like Lotus, Quickbooks, or MYOB; you will probably want one that your bookkeeper or accountant is familiar with. Lotus's simplest bookkeeping system is 1-2-3. It will take a little learning, but Lotus offers written manuals and online support. It also comes with SmartSheets: preprogrammed invoices, agendas, accounts payable and receivable, network, and bank-balancing sheets. If you are purchasing only one system, this one makes sense because its popularity assures that you will find someone to operate it more than competently. It also has the capacity to be converted for use with a variety of systems. Most schools in your area will offer a few hours of instruction.

EATEC is a system with a particular plan for caterers that even start-up entrepreneurs can benefit from. The Catering System's main menu lets you enter an order and update it, do an event cost analysis, and keep track of equipment and beverage recipes suited for off-premise situations. It will also let you do catering accounting by opening client receivables as well as all categories of payables. These are keyed into both a standard accounting number, such as No. 2120 for accounts payable, and your in-house numbers as well. Suppliers are listed by name and category, produce, beverage, poultry, baked goods, paper, cleaning supplies, and so forth. It will let you balance several checkbooks and control petty cash. You can generate menus and recipes, then scale and price them. It also generates the nutrition information most people are interested in: calories, proteins, carbohydrates, various fats, cholesterol, sodium, and potassium.

EATEC is a system that can be used as simply as you want and grow with your business. It is DOS based, networkable, and IBM compatible. The general ledger worksheets can be handled by anyone who can distinguish a debit from a credit. Its catering features let you easily break events down into components that can be priced according to their details and put together for a client presentation. It is a good negotiating tool, because you can easily see what can be added, changed, or deleted. It also helps you generate several options that you can offer clients when they call for similar events like weddings or fund-raisers. It gives you the opportunity to offer fixed-price menus and allows you to set up beverage packages. You can quickly see the difference in equipment rentals for sit-down dinners and buffets.

CostGuard is one of the caterer's best friends. It is an effective software program that allows you to scale recipes and cost them in a consistent fashion. It offers a good deal of on-screen help. You can track inventory and vendors directly from food lists. It is interconnected in ways that tie in yields with the prices of ingredients. "Smart scaling" lets you see the recipe for any number, as well as costs and sales prices in the multiples that you will be using. It is satisfying to see a dollar amount. At the end of the day, it is dollars, and not percentages, that you take to the bank. You can also try substitutions, additions, or deletions in recipes and cost them out. You can generate any number of recipes, limited only by the size of your hard disk. You can combine recipes like sauces and dressings simply by calling them up into new ones. You can print recipes, with or without prices and notes, and generate shopping lists.

For people who put nutrition first, there is no better system than ESHA Research's Food Processor programs. For institutional caterers and people planning food careers that are nutrient based, or for people who wish to incorporate increasing amounts of recommended and researched analysis, the food list includes raw and cooked food like chicken breast with skin or without skin, and prepared foods like cheesecake or condensed cream of mushroom soup. It is compatible with IBM or Macintosh systems. It will calculate nutrients in single foods and recipes, or if you are packaging foods at all or even making samples, it will give measurements in both metric and standard household portions.

Dinesystems seems best suited for people who are combining food and fitness. It is a bit specific for a beginning off-premise caterer. But if you want to be aware of the integration of lifestyle, nutrition, and menus, it is an excellent program. DineHealthy4 lets you create a user profile that includes personal information as well as activity levels. It has a list of the number of calories burned in around two hundred different activities, including swimming (broken down into backstroke, fast/slow, breaststroke, fast/slow, etc.), in addition to the food values of almost six thousand items, with caloric and nutrient information of those commercially prepared and at fast-food franchises. It can analyze food choices and offer options to achieve goals.

The Caterplus systems by Caterware are designed by people with skills and experience in catering and computer software. It is satisfies caterers who need to work intuitively in a high-tech fashion. It does the most complicated tasks with great simplicity. Caterplus offers training programs to maximize use, and for a slight surcharge they will develop custom documents for you. Caterplus's Event Wizard integrates food, bar beverages, and rental labor and easily accounts for additions, changes, and deletions. It not only excels at account management, but it coordinates client profiles with event planning and food inventory, as it tracks all entries into a financial sheet. It can create reports and documents using its own format or let you substitute those you prefer, which means that you can integrate Word documents and interface Microsoft Office directly into the system, which makes communication simple. It has full Web integration as well as e-mail.

Caterease is a well-organized catering system with phone support and regular upgrades. It records information in various food-service activities. The Event Manager program has drop-down tools that let you add anything from photographs to subcontractors. The menu selections are priced, and food amounts can be changed with a click of the mouse. There are files for contact history into which you can cut and paste from other reports. It will track changes in dates and alert you to conflicts. It has staffing reminders as well as billing and payment charts. There is a limited customizable factor for each report so that they will be consistent, but you can tweak them to suit your needs.

5

Managing an Event from Introduction to Conclusion

This chapter leads you step by step through each stage of an event, including contracts and worksheets. It begins with interviewing, one of the most important parts of a caterer's job. From the interview you will learn exactly what the client wants. It's important to decipher not just the facts, but the spirit of the expectations that will have to be met.

You will hear a lot of flowery descriptions and breathless fantasies that will have to be translated into shopping lists, budgets, time schedules, labor, delivery, setup, serving, and cleanup. You will have to decide how much of a professional team is needed and how best to coordinate it. Most of the time, the client not only doesn't want to do the work, but doesn't even want to think of the work that has to be done. Magic is part of the calculation. Everything has to be presented in as gracious and reassuring a manner you can muster. Many caterers have a certain amount of stage fright all the time.

Whether you intend to deliver à la carte—that is, just the food— full service, or somewhere in the middle, the first large professional job you get will probably be a private party. You may not believe it now, but planning for one hundred people will soon seem like a simple task. The need for a relaxed sense of organization cannot be emphasized enough. It is your client's stress that you will have to deal with. He or she will fret and worry, because most private clients do not use caterers often, and usually it is for a special celebration that has emotional overtones. The client expects not only a wonderful time and a delicious meal, but fine memories, photos, and video opportunities.

Forget your desire for someone to hand you a blank check to create the meal of your dreams. It is your job to provide a service that pleases and suits each client. If you think you cannot deliver, it is better to say no than to do a shoddy job.

You will have to decide what area of the event to highlight. If it is a birthday party, a simple meal and an expensive cake might be in order. For a business lunch, the most expensive ingredients might be the main course, with just a light dessert. It sometimes helps to ask around for the going rate among other caterers. You don't want to create a conflict, and established caterers are not thrilled when you undercut them. By the same token, a newcomer simply cannot command the prices of well-known pros. Analyze the competition and attempt to be fair, as goodwill is important in the catering community. You want to deliver a truly professional product, and you don't want to commit to a price range you can't maintain. The odds are that if you can't deliver at the price your client wants, no one else will be able to either.

The client will undoubtedly want to know the per-person cost of the food. The easiest way to do this is to have a simple breakdown for the dishes you prepare most often, using average fair-market prices. The exact price may vary in pennies per pound from week to week, but to refigure labor costs each week would add more to the price of each item. Any radical changes will, of course, be reflected in your prices. This is where catering software for your computer is indispensable. In a very short time, you can put together various proposals with accurate figures.

The cost of prepared food is based on what it costs to prepare it in your kitchen or commissary. If your client wishes to pick it up at that point, you simply have to use your profit multiplier and write the bill. A general figure is times 4. Overhead staff time will be at least $10 to $15 an hour per person. When you factor wages, be sure that in addition to specific fees paid to you, your own time is never figured at less than double the minimum wage for any aspect of the work you perform. This sounds silly at first, but when you think that you will be planning and revising, comparison shopping, interviewing staff, scouting locations, and doing promotional and public relations work while not being able to earn other money at the same time, you will realize your business has to be cost efficient.

Pantry costs are figured either on a use-to-use basis—five cents a dish for salt and pepper, for example—or as part of your overhead. If the commissary pantry is stocked with staple items, you might try to keep a running tally of costs for the first year to get an accurate picture of what your must-haves cost and how best to be reimbursed for them. Often, a general pantry cost is best, because then the charge will be consistent.

Other kitchen expenses, like pots and pans and other cooking equipment, are factored in. If it is necessary to buy a new utensil for a specific event, the client cannot be charged for it, but it is figured in proportionally.

Here is one sample scenario: Someone who was a guest at a dinner party or perhaps a charity event you volunteered for has approached you to do a wedding party for about a hundred guests at their home and garden at 2 P.M. the afternoon of Saturday, June 15. It is now February, and you are free on that date, so you arrange to meet with the client.

Even though you may be meeting with a family that has to be pleased as a group, it is necessary to ascertain who is really in charge. Perhaps it is the bridal couple. Traditionally, it has been the bride's parents, but it might be the groom's, or both. If more than one person is involved, you will have ask them to choose a spokesperson. For social catering, your interpersonal skills will be your greatest preproduction asset.

Now you have the date, time, and nature of the event. It might save time to have the first meeting at the site of the party. Feel free to bring an assistant who will make a checklist of available prep, cooking, and warming utilities as well as cold storage while you are talking to the clients. It will be necessary to see how much can actually be cooked on site. Will professional pans fit in the oven and storage facilities? Where will the dirty dishes, glasses, and pots go? Busing and cleaning schedules and assignments are as important toward managing a successful event as shopping and cooking. Are there any special requirements, pets, children? Ask clients what can be used, from equipment to special serving pieces. Walk through the spaces, both back of the house and the party area. Ask if there are location restrictions. Ask about bathrooms, and if they need to be attended. Should a portable unit be rented? Is there adequate parking, and does the client want a valet? Will the client notify the police about the excess traffic and perhaps noise?

You will need to know the event agenda and general style. An advantage of meeting at a client's home or office is that you can get a feel for his or her taste and preferences: formal, casual, traditional, adventurous, quiet, noisy.

Will there be a ceremony? Is it the caterer's job to create the area for the service? Will the event be held rain or shine? Are tents required? Who will be there to grant access on site a day or two before and, if necessary, the day after the event? Will they be responsible for equipment left there before and/or after the event? Will you need to arrange for a private carter to remove the garbage, which has to be tied in heavy-duty bags, or will you take it back to the commissary to be disposed of?

What kind of food service is desired? Passed hot hors d'oeuvres and perhaps a service buffet with guests seated at set tables is one possibility that requires a minimum of wait staff. Sometimes a Russian service, where food is presented on a platter and a server puts the portion on each guest's plate, is used. Soup or a salad can be served this way while the main course is individually plated in the kitchen for American-style service. For your first big party, you might set up food at various buffet stations with servers at each large dish, in what is sometimes referred to as a modified British service.

Let's assume that, after much discussion, you select a menu that includes a large selection of hot hors d'oeuvres, cold platters, and a buffet of poached salmon with cucumber-dill sauce, naturally cured hams served with assorted chutneys and custom mustards, roasted mini-vegetables with lemon-mint butter, wild rice, a tossed field salad with edible flowers and house dressing. The bread baskets will contain herb and corn biscuits. There will be a stand-up cocktail hour with some hors d'oeuvre stations and some, fresh from the oven, butlered on trays. Wine, beer, and various soft drinks and waters will be at two bars, one inside and one outside. There will be a Champagne toast served on trays by the wait staff. Wedding cake, berries and cream, and chocolate truffles will be served for dessert. Coffee, both regular and decaf, as well as a variety of teas will be at an attended station after dinner.

A suggested staff for this party is: two for bar service, who will also set up, keep glasses filled during dinner, and help clear after the guests leave; a kitchen manager who is a good cook and will work in the commissary the day before the party as well, and will direct off-premises food flow; and a wait staff of three, who will help set up, pass hors d'oeuvres, serve buffet stations, and help clean up after guests leave.

The clients will take care of hiring the photographer and musicians and will set up the outdoor lighting. They want no tent but would like a small dance floor. Their colors are navy blue, orchid, and pink, and they would like small centerpieces on ten tables, but will order the bridal flowers themselves. They do not want assigned seats.

In off-premise catering, there are more consequences when a detail is overlooked or a glitch in equipment or product occurs. Backup is usually some distance away. The importance of planning and prepping cannot be overstated, especially at the beginning of your business, when each job will be in a new environment with a costly staff unfamiliar with each other and with the location. You must also rely heavily on your subcontractors. Most beginners think the only way to deal with this is to do everything themselves, but they are just delaying the inevitable. It is always better to start subcontracting early on, so that when you take on a large event you will know whom you can count on.

All financial discussions with clients must be put on paper. This includes not only estimated prices for the different variables discussed, but also the manner of payment. Deposits and cancellation fees must be included as well. This is another area where your computer and catering software have become essential.

It is reassuring to discuss all the small details with clients. What are the arrangements for staff meals? Will the musicians be eating, and where and when? Do the clients want to keep leftovers? Caterers traditionally remove leftovers rather than leave them with the clients, because they can no longer be responsible for the condition or maintenance of the food. If the clients want any remaining prepared food they must sign a waiver releasing the caterer from any liability for this food. They should also sign a waiver for any food brought to the event by themselves or their guests.

Think of the personnel needed. If you are the party planner and head chef, you will need a cook who is also a kitchen manager and an assistant who will shop and prep. Both of them can also tend primary buffet stations. Three waitpersons, two bartenders, and one buser will also help set up, clean up, and pack. You may also need a dishwasher. With rented equipment you probably just have to scrape and rinse, so with everyone pitching in, you can eliminate that job. Make a list and calculate the number of hours each person has to work; then add 10 percent for the estimate and a 20 percent gratuity. Properly briefed, with this kind of staff unpacking, kitchen prep, and setup should not take more than 2½ hours. The length of the event will be 3 to 4 hours. Cleanup, packing, and loading will take about 2 hours.

You will, of course, have to figure how many tables and cloths are needed for service stations. If none are available at the location, you will need at least 2 for the bar and 2 for hors d'oeuvres, which can be cleared and set up for dessert, and 3 for main courses. Since they are part of the environment you are creating, they should be dressed as prettily as the dining tables.

Most rental places also have side towels, aprons, and uniforms, too, if they are required. Check prices on the Internet and from the Yellow Pages. You might want to consider buying assorted chafing dishes and serving pieces, slowly building an inventory of commonly used dishes and signature items. Remember, though, that almost anything is available for rent, from any unit of china, flatware, and glassware to dance floors and potted palms. Clearly, prices of these will vary from neighborhood to neighborhood.

One of the most common errors of start-up businesses is forgetting that each and every item must be priced. Catering is a business of details: the fresh herbs for the soup, the price of the herbs, adding the herbs to the soup, and adding the price to the bill. This does not mean a caterer cannot be generous. In fact, it is a good idea to give a little something like an extra hors d'oeuvre or miniature muffin for the bread basket. List it on your bill as "No Charge," and your goodwill will be appreciated.

For our hypothetical event, ten centerpieces and some decorative table arrangements for the buffet tables must be ordered from a florist in the client's colors of navy, orchid, and pink, and be delivered to the location the morning of the event. Some flowers and leaves for dressing the food platters should be ordered as well.

When you begin calculating the price of an event, think of the basic cost of food and the price at which it leaves the commissary after being prepared. Also factor in beverages, labor, equipment rental, floral arrangements, transportation, disposables, office expenses, gratuities, and taxes, if applicable.

After the initial meeting, write the client a gracious, clear, and concise letter. Reiterate your discussion and offer only a few options. Describe what and how you will deliver, and offer a price estimate. If you yourself are not going to be present or will be there for only part of the time, specify who will supervise the event and make introductions early on. It may take a couple of additions and deletions, but on receipt of a signed confirmation letter, send a contract with additional sheets relating to menus and services. A 50 percent deposit should be required on signing the contract, with the balance due the day of the function. Make clear that revisions are permitted up to two weeks preceding the event. After that time, there should be a 10 percent error allowance for both client and caterer. Your catering software will enable you to document all correspondence accurately.

Calculating Amounts of Food

If you are catering an event like a wedding dinner, where a good deal of food is expected, remember the rule of thumb is a minimum of 1 and a maximum of 1½ pounds of food per person. Calculating approximately 20 ounces will leave plenty of leeway for various appetites. Quantity is your responsibility. Even frugal hosts expect volume. If they insist on pâté on a low budget, slice it thin and serve half an ounce on warm crostini on a bed of minced frisée lettuce with a mustard dressing. This way, 6 pounds of pâté will be more than enough. Instead of sides of smoked salmon, create a mousse of salmon, smoked salmon, and salmon roe, served in thumb-sized tartlets.

For 100 people with various hors d'oeuvres, 2 ounces of cheese per person is usually more than enough. That adds up to 12½ pounds. You might want to divide it into a selection: One whole wheel of Brie to be served baked with a hazelnut crust, and a half wheel each of Edam and white Vermont Cheddar to be served with seedless grapes. Two 14-

ounce goat cheese logs could be used in phyllo cups with sun-dried tomatoes and 1½ pounds blue cheese could be mixed with chopped toasted walnuts for mini pâte à choux puffs. Six baguettes will make about 200 crostini. To complete the hors d'oeuvres, add 2 big baskets of crudités with herbed yogurt dip served in hollowed round peasant breads, 200 caviar-and-cream-cheese pinwheels, 3 pounds of prosciutto and about 10 melons, 10 pounds of shrimp and dips, and miniature steamed dumplings and ginger sauce. Two 20-pound hams, three 10-pound salmon, wild rice and mushrooms, vegetables, mustards, and chutneys won't cost that much. Figure closely the costs of the flour, oil and vinegar, dips, sauces, and hors d'oeuvre ingredients, as well as cake, desserts, and beverages. Factoring at "times 4" after you make a detailed list will give you the food cost. This can be done with pencil and paper and a calculator, but it is a good time to start using your computer. If you are not accustomed to one, the awkwardness you feel at first will quickly be rewarded with the ease of success at repeated tasks.

Timing Is Everything

The pros all agree that there is no one set schedule that fits all events. You can arrange the outline and then fill in the blanks. Each event has to be done on a countdown basis after the initial strategy is settled on. Planning should take no more than one to two days for a complicated event. The key is the person in charge. If the event is on a Saturday, everything you need, except the bread, should be in the commissary by Wednesday evening or Thursday morning. On Thursday, all subcontractors and rentals that have been ordered earlier must be reconfirmed. Check with the client to make sure everything is ready on that end. If you have any doubts about staffing, this is the day to double-check.

When you are just beginning, you will have to work your calendar counting down from the date of the event. You need a plan and a specifically detailed checklist under your supervision. The responsibility for timing everything is up to you—the party manager—or the event executive responsible for a specific occasion.

Even Ridgewell's Caterer, which has been in business for over fifty years and has done presidential inaugural events, does not use a single formal schedule sheet. The company was started in 1928 by Charles Ridgewell, who came to Washington, D.C., as the British ambassador's caterer, and his wife, Marguerite, who had been on staff at the French embassy. Though they have done many inaugurations and everything from the Begin-Sadat peace treaty to the opening of Union Station, Ridgewell's practice and experience have taught them that particulars at different locations and at different times of the year vary. No uniform prefixed schedule is possible. Various catering software programs as well as simple business programs will help you make complex decisions as you compare components.

If you have put a reliable network of people in place and pay attention to orchestrating all the sections, your events will come together within 24 to 48 hours of the date. Catering is a business that shows its success at the time of delivery.

Sample Paperwork

Hampton Caterers
222 Ocean Street
Metropolis, USA 10011
Phone: 123-456-7890
Fax 123-456-7890
E-mail: fh@hamptoncatering.com
Website: www.hamptoncatering.com

CATERING CONTRACT

Date_____ Invoice #_____

Client_____ Client File # _____
Billing Address_____ Telephone (day)_____
E-mail _____ Telephone (night) _____
Host_____ Event_____
Location _____ Date of event _____
Time of event _____
Hampton coordinator_____ Type of function _____
Confirmed guest count _____ will be guaranteed by _____

Please note and initial. Client will be billed for guaranteed or actual count, whichever is greater.

EVENT SCHEDULE
Guests arrive_____
Bar and hors d'oeuvres (see attached)
Lunch/dinner (see attached)
Dessert/cake (see attached)
Music (see attached)
Special (see attached)
Conclusion _____

EVENT SERVICES

Event manager _____

Kitchen _____

Setup _____

Wait staff _____ Serving style_____

Bar service_____ Serving style_____

Hors d'oeuvres_____ Serving style_____

Meal _____ Serving style_____

Dessert_____ Serving style_____

Miscellaneous_____

SUBCONTRACTORS (SEE ATTACHED)

Cleanup_____

Overtime_____

The above is based on our agreed event plan, attached. Any client additions or changes at the event or 24 hours preceding the event may be billed at time and a half.

Event subtotal $ _____

Gratuities $ _____

Tax $ _____ (if applicable)

Total $ _____

Deposit $ _____ Due on _____

Balance $_____ Due on _____

Please sign this agreement and return with the deposit. Thank you.

For Hampton Caterers _____ Date _____

Client_____ Date _____

Hampton Caterers
222 Ocean Street
Metropolis, USA 10011
Phone: 123-456-7890
Fax 123-456-7890
E-mail: fh@hamptoncatering.com
Website: www.hamptoncatering.com

NEW ACCOUNT CREDIT FORM

Client_____   Owner_____

Address _____   Buyer_____
Telephone _____
Type of business_____ Year established_____
Referred by _____
Credit references _____
Bank _____
Account # _____
Telephone _____   Contact_____
Business references_____
1. _____

   _____
2. _____

   _____
3. _____

   _____

Comments:

Hampton Caterers
222 Ocean Street
Metropolis, USA 10011
Phone: 123-456-7890
Fax 123-456-7890
E-mail: fh@hamptoncatering.com
Website: www.hamptoncatering.com

EVENT PLAN

Date_____ Invoice #_____

Client_____ Client file # _____
Billing address _____ Telephone (day)_____
E-mail _____ Telephone (night) _____
Host_____ Event_____
Location _____ Date of event _____
Time of event _____
Hampton coordinator_____ Type of function _____

Notes:

Hampton Cateres
222 Ocean Street
Metropolis, USA 10011
Phone: 123-456-7890
Fax 123-456-7890
E-mail: fh@hamptoncatering.com
Website: www.hamptoncatering.com

MENU

Date _____ Invoice # _____

Client _____ Client file # _____
Billing address _____ Telephone (day) _____
E-mail _____ Telephone (night) _____
Host _____ Event _____
Location _____ Date of event _____
Time of event _____
Hampton coordinator _____ Type of function _____

WEDDING RECEPTION

Assorted Hot and Cold Hors d'Oeuvres

Miniature Rolls

Whole Poached Salmon

Sauce Mousseline

Cucumber-Dill Dressing

Fresh Fruit Salad on Bed of Mesclun

Crisp Duck à l'Orange

Wild Rice with Mushrooms

Asparagus Drizzled with Cream

Strawberries and Whipped Cream

Wedding Cake with Edible Gold Leaf and Flowers

Chocolate Champagne Truffles

Coffee and Tea

Open Bar

Mineral Water

Poured White and Red Wine

Champagne Toast

Notes:

Hampton Caterers
222 Ocean Street
Metropolis, USA 10011
Phone: 123-456-7890
Fax 123-456-7890
E-mail: fh@hamptoncatering.com
Website: www.hamptoncatering.com

MENU (with instructions for wait staff)

Date_____ Invoice #_____

Client_____ Client file # _____
Billing address _____ Telephone (day)_____
E-mail _____ Telephone (night) _____
Host_____ Event_____
Location _____ Date of event _____
Time of event _____
Hampton coordinator_____ Type of function _____
Waitperson _____
Maitre d' _____
Dress _____
Meetingplace_____
Arrival time_____
Staff meal provided _____
Mealtime _____
Probable overtime _____
Type of service course by course _____
Location of stations _____
Special meals_____

Notes:

Hampton Caterers
222 Ocean Street
Metropolis, USA 10011
Phone: 123-456-7890
Fax 123-456-7890
E-mail: fh@hamptoncatering.com
Website: www.hamptoncatering.com

KITCHEN MENU (attach to shopping list and recipes for kitchen file)

Date_____ Invoice #_____

Client_____ Client file # _____

Billing address _____ Telephone (day)_____

E-mail _____ Telephone (night) _____

Host_____ Event_____

Location _____ Date of event _____

Time of event _____

Hampton coordinator_____ Type of function _____

Notes:

Hampton Caterers
222 Ocean Street
Metropolis, USA 10011
Phone: 123-456-7890
Fax 123-456-7890
E-mail: fh@hamptoncatering.com
Website: www.hamptoncatering.com

MENU AND BEVERAGE PLAN

Date_____ Invoice #_____

Client_____ Client file # _____

Billing address _____ Telephone (day)_____

E-mail _____ Telephone (night) _____

Host_____ Event_____

Location _____ Date of event _____

Time of event _____

Hampton coordinator_____ Type of function _____

Menu approved by _____

Ingredients to be in commissary by (date_____)

Chef_____

Beverage controller_____

Are special liquor licenses required? _____

Wine and liquor provided by _____

Delivered to_____

Delivered by (date)_____

Setups provided by_____

Ice: Delivered ___ Available on premise ___ Storage needed ___ Available ___

Bartender(s) _____

Water: Bottled? ___ Available on premises? ___

Coffee: House blend ___ Espresso ___ Cappuccino ___ Decaf ___ Other ___

Special equipment needed_____

Refrigeration for milk needed _____

Type of service _____

Tea: Orange pekoe ___ Assorted herbals ___ Other _____

Cups and saucers required _____

Demitasse cups and saucers required _____

Glassware and stemware required _____

   On premise _____

   From commissary _____

   From rental _____

Are there adequate washup-for-reuse facilities on location?_____

Notes:

Hampton Caterers
222 Ocean Street
Metropolis, USA 10011
Phone: 123-456-7890
Fax 123-456-7890
E-mail: fh@hamptoncatering.com
Website: www.hamptoncatering.com

SUBCONTRACTORS

Date_____   Invoice #_____

Client_____   Client file # _____
Billing address _____   Telephone (day)_____
E-mail _____   Telephone (night) _____
Host_____   Event_____
Location _____   Date of event _____
Time of event _____
Hampton coordinator_____   Type of function _____

Notes:

Hampton Caterers
222 Ocean Street
Metropolis, USA 10011
Phone: 123-456-7890
Fax 123-456-7890
E-mail: fh@hamptoncatering.com
Website: www.hamptoncatering.com

IN-HOUSE KITCHEN PLAN

Date_____   Invoice #_____

Client_____   Client file # _____
Billing address _____   Telephone (day)_____
E-mail _____   Telephone (night) _____
Host_____   Event_____
Location _____   Date of event _____
Time of event _____
Hampton coordinator_____   Type of function _____

Notes:

Hampton Caterers
222 Ocean Street
Metropolis, USA 10011
Phone: 123-456-7890
Fax 123-456-7890
E-mail: fh@hamptoncatering.com
Website: www.hamptoncatering.com

IN-HOUSE SERVICE PLAN

Date_____   Invoice #_____

Client_____   Client file # _____
Billing address _____   Telephone (day)_____
E-mail _____   Telephone (night) _____
Host_____   Event_____
Location _____   Date of event _____
Time of event _____
Hampton coordinator_____   Type of function _____

Notes:

Hampton Caterers
222 Ocean Street
Metropolis, USA 10011
Phone: 123-456-7890
Fax 123-456-7890
E-mail: fh@hamptoncatering.com
Website: www.hamptoncatering.com

FUNCTION SHEET

Date_____   Invoice #_____

Client_____   Client file # _____
Billing address _____   Telephone (day)_____
E-mail _____   Telephone (night) _____
Host_____   Event_____
Location _____   Date of event _____
Time of event _____
Hampton coordinator_____   Type of function _____
In charge site inspector _____
In charge commissary kitchen staff _____
In charge location kitchen staff _____
In charge liquor staff (are licenses in order, ice, on premises, storage) _____
_____
Packing _____
Delivery driver _____
In charge setup staff_____
In charge subcontractors_____
Valet parking_____
Coatroom _____
Lounges _____
Other _____
Service _____
Maitre d' _____
Staff _____
Bar _____
Busing _____
Sanitation _____
Cleanup _____
Pack up to leave _____
Return driver_____

Notes:

Hampton Caterers
222 Ocean Street
Metropolis, USA 10011
Phone: 123-456-7890
Fax 123-456-7890
E-mail: fh@hamptoncatering.com
Website: www.hamptoncatering.com

EQUIPMENT NEEDED

Date_____ Invoice #_____

Client_____ Client file # _____
Billing address _____ Telephone (day)_____
E-mail _____ Telephone (night) _____
Host_____ Event_____
Location _____ Date of event _____
Time of event _____
Hampton coordinator_____ Type of function _____

Item	From Hampton Commissary	Available on Premises	Other

Notes:

Hampton Caterers
222 Ocean Street
Metropolis, USA 10011
Phone: 123-456-7890
Fax 123-456-7890
E-mail: fh@hamptoncatering.com
Website: www.hamptoncatering.com

SUBCONTRACTORS

Date_____ Invoice #_____

Client_____ Client file # _____
Billing address _____ Telephone (day)_____

E-mail _____ Telephone (night) _____

Host _____ Event _____

Location _____ Date of event _____

Time of event _____

Hampton coordinator _____ Type of function _____

Florist (see attached) _____

Bouquets _____

Boutonnieres _____

Centerpieces _____

Aisle _____

Altar _____

Tent _____

Wall _____

Column _____

Plants _____

Other _____

Platter garnish _____

Photographer (see attached) _____

Pre-event _____

Event _____

Music (see attached) _____

Band _____

Singer _____

Pianist _____

Instruments _____

DJ _____

Sound system _____

Other _____

Entertainment (see attached) _____

Emcee _____

Speaker _____

Magician _____

Performers _____

Fireworks _____

Other _____

Please note arrangements for meals and mealtimes:

Notes:
Hampton Caterers
222 Ocean Street
Metropolis, USA 10011
Phone: 123-456-7890
Fax 123-456-7890
E-mail: fh@hamptoncatering.com
Website: www.hamptoncatering.com

PREMISES

Date_____ Invoice #_____

Client_____ Client file # _____
Billing address _____ Telephone (day)_____
E-mail _____ Telephone (night) _____
Host_____ Event_____
Location _____ Date of event _____
Time of event _____
Hampton coordinator_____ Type of function _____
Apartment_____
Private house _____
Private garden _____
Public park _____
Hall _____
Chapel_____
Room_____
Tent _____
Historical site _____
Botanical garden _____
Requirements:
Wheelchair access to all rooms and lounges_____
Parking _____

SITE CHECK (hypothetical)
Equipment (2 tents, 1 floor, lights, no heaters needed, small dance floor),
heavy-duty extension cords, outdoor lights, speakers, microphone, piano,
tables and chairs

Notes:

Sample Rental List (Partial)

CHAIRS:
All Wood folding chair (camp) ....
Armchair...
Armchair—Tablet Folding, School type..
Baby booster chair ....
Bar stools..
Black fabric padded folding chair deluxe gold metal frame ....
Black plastic folding chair, plastic seat and back, Metal frame ....
Black Reception chairs.......................
Black wood frame, black padded seat
Blue upholstered folding chair, deluxe, Gold metal frame, padded seat and back..............................
Brown fabric upholstered deluxe, Gold metal padded seat & back.....
Children's chairs, 13" high with back
Gold fabric upholstered folding Chairs, deluxe Gold metal frame foam rubber, padded seat &........
Gold metal frame, Gold velour seat and back............................
Green upholstered folding chair, deluxe, Gold metal frame, foam rubber, padded seat and back ....
High Chairs.....................................
Reception chair, non-folding, spindle back Gold Frame, Green, Red, Gold or Black seats ....
Red fabric upholstered folding chair, foam rubber seat and back, Gold metal frame ....

TABLES:
Walnut Formica snack table ....
Super Bridge—30" × 30" ....
Banquet:
    4 ft × 30 in. wide—Seats 4 to 6..
    6 ft. × 30 in. wide—Seats 8 to 10 ....
    8 ft. × 30 in. wide—Seats 10 to 12 ....
Round Cocktail Tables, 24 in. Pedestal type base ....
30 in. Pedestal type base ....
    Round 36", Seats 4 (Bridge type) .
    Round 39", Seats 5 ....
Round 42", Seats 6..........................
Found 48", Seats 8 ....
Round 54", Seats 8 to 10 ....
Round 60", Seats 10.........................
Round 72", Seats 12.........................
Oval, 5 ft. × 36 in. wide, Seats 8 ...
Oval, 6 ft. × 36 in. wide, Seats 10 ..
Oval, 6 ft. × 48 in. wide, Seats 12 ..
Oval, 7-1/2 ft. × 54 in. wide, Seats 14 ....
Special, 4 ft. × 24 in. wide ....
    6 ft. × 18 in. wide ....
    6 ft. × 24 in. wide ....
    8 ft. × 24 in. wide ....

SPECIAL DISPLAY TABLES:
1/4 Round Sections, 4 sections make 10 ft. round table with cut out in center ....
1/2 60" Round Table for display .....
Risers: 4 ft. × 12 in. × 12 in. ....
Risers: 6 ft. × 12 in. × 12 in. ....
6 ft. Formica top table.....................
8 ft. Formica top table.....................
Set of rubber Wheels for any table ...

BARS:
2-1/2 ft. Bar ....
4 ft. Bar ....
6 ft. Bar ....
Deluxe Rolling Bar ....
Bar Rubber Mat ....
Bar Stools ....
Wine Steward's Key on gold-plated chain ....
Cocktail Shaker, stainless steel, complete..

DANCE FLOORS—INDOOR:
Rola-Flor, 10 ft. × 10 ft. ....
Rola-Flor, 10 ft. × 20 ft. ....
3' × 3' parquet sections...................
Bandstands, runways, speakers' platforms, dance (tent and canopies to order) ....

CHINAWARE:
Dinner Plate, Cake and Salad Plate, Bread and 1 Deep Dish Dessert, Cup, Saucer, Demi Cup and Saucer, Bouillon Cup, Soup Plate
Gold Band ....
Silver Band ....
White China, swirl edge (limited qty.) ....
Black octagon ....
Masterpiece translucent china, all white ....
Platinum rim with floral design (limited qty.)................................
Kosher, new china ....
Ginon thin scalloped gold band (limited qty.)................................
French Imported Glass dishes / (may be used for Kosher) ....
Tea & Toast Sets—China ....
China Bowl—Extra Large ....
China Platters 16"...........................
China Platter—Extra Large ....
China Gravy Boats............................
Tea & Toast—Glass..........................

GLASSWARE:
Hi-Ball Whiskey (shot) Glasses, Juice, Old Fashioned Fruit Sherbet..
Punch Cups, Ash Trays ....
Old-Fashioned Beer Mugs, Parfait, Iced Tea Glasses ....
Coffee Mugs, white milk glass or white china ....
Double Old-Fashioned or Double High Ball ....
Glass Pitcher ....
Fruit Supreme..................................
Glass Ice Bowl ....
Glass Ice Bowl, Large ....
Nappies...
Nappy underliner ....

STEMWARE:
Pony, Brandy Snifter, Liqueur, Cordial...
Cocktail, Whiskey Sour, Wine, Manhattan or Stemmed Sherbet ....
Champagne, Water Goblets ....
8 or 10 oz. Continental Wine or Irish Coffee ....
Solid Stem Imported Stemware, Queen Mary Imported Design ......
French Imported Crystal ....
Jumbo Wine Goblet, 17-1/2 oz. ....
Tulip Grande Wine ....
All Purpose Stem Goblet ....
Tulip Champagne ....
Flute Champagne—Crystal ....

SILVERWARE:
Knife, Dinner Fork, Salad Fork or Cake Fork, Teaspoon, Oyster Fork, Butter Spreader, Demi-Spoon, Iced Tea Spoon, Soup Spoon ....
Rogers Silverplate (American Lady) .
King George Silverplate ....
Deluxe Silverplate, Chalfonte (for formal dining) (limited qty.) ....
Stainless Steel.................................
Silverplate Serving Spoons or Cold Meat Fork ....
Cake Server ....
Kosher (New Silverware)...................
Gold Flatware ....
Gold Serving Spoon or Fork ....
S/S Serving Spoon or Fork ....
Bowls, Revere:
    5" ....
    7" ....
    10" ....
    12" ....
Bread Tray, Silver ....
Bud Vase, Silver ....
Butter Dishes, Silver ....
Cake Knife ....
Cake Server, Silver ....
Cake Stand, 13 in. round 8 in. high .
Cake Stand, 2 tier, 2 Separate ....
Cake Stand, 3 tier, 3 Separate graduating stands ....
Candy Shells, Silver ....
Carving Knives ....
Carving Sets, Knife, Fork ....
Casserole—Electric ....
Cigarette Urn, Silver.........................
Champagne Bucket, Silver ....
Champagne Stand with Wine Cooler, Silver ....
Cheese Knives ....
Coffee Server, Silver ....
Coffee Server, Silver Deluxe ....
Cookie Stand (Compots), Medium...
Finger Bowl with Liner, Silver ....
Fish Knife or Cheese Knife (Individual) ....
French Servers ....
Fruit Bowl, Oval, Silver ....
Fruit Knife, Silver ....
Gravy Boats, Silver with underliners .
Gravy Ladle, Silver ....
Gravy Boat, underliner, Silver...........
Ice Bucket with Cover ....
Ice Tongs.......................................
Ice Buckets, Plain, Silver ....
Lazy Susan, 3 Tier tid-bit dish type ..
Lazy Susan, 5 compartments—flat revolving, 18" diameter, 3" high ....
Lemon Trays, Silver..........................
Mint Stand, Small, Silver ....
Mint Stand, Large, Silver..................
Nappy Dish with Liner, Silver (quantity limited).........................
Punch Cups, Silver ....
Party Scale, Silver ....
Relish Dishes, Olive, Celery, Pickle ..
Salad Dressing, 3 Dip ....
Salt & Pepper Shakers, Silver............
Silent Butler, Silver..........................
Server, Oval Glass Liner ....
Soup Ladle, Silver............................
Soup Tureens with Ladle and underliner ....
Spoon or Fork, Serving ....
Serving Spoon or Fork, Long Handled, Deluxe ....
Sugar Tongs ....
Sugar & Creamer, Silver ....
Tray for above, Silver ....
Tea Kettle, Swinging, Silver ....
Vegetable Dish, 2 Compartments .....
Water Pitchers, Silver.......................
Wine Cooler and Stand (Chrome) ....
Wine Cooler—Top Part of Above (Chrome) ....
Wine Cooler, Silver—Top Part of Champagne Stand ....

CHAFING DISHES:

Silverplate, Canned Heat
  - 2 qt. round.................................
  - 2 qt. Deluxe 2 comp. sc ....
  - 3 qt. rd. deluxe chafer with pyrex liner ....
  - Extra liner for 3 qt. chafer.............
  - 3 qt. square chafer........................
  - Twin Silver chafer, each pan 2 qt ..
  - 1 gal. round ....
  - 6 qt. round deluxe.........................
  - 7 qt. round deluxe.........................
  - Oval Chafer, Alcohol Heat ....

Stainless Steel, Canned Heat
  - 1 gal. oblong—1 compartment ....
  - 2 gal. oblong—1 compartment ....
  - 2 gal. oblong—2 compartments ....
  - 2 gal. oblong—3 compartments ....
  - 1 gal. oblong—1 compartment—Electric ....
  - 2 gal. oblong—1 compartment—Electric ....

Stainless Steel Marmite Dish.............
Extra Food Pan for Chafing Dishes ..
Extra Water Pans ....
Crepe Suzette Pans ....
Recharde Lamps ....
Food Warming Lights ....
Fondue Sets ....
Extra cans Canned Heat ....

SERVING PIECES, CHINA & GLASS:

Ash Trays, Glass ....
Ash Trays, China ....
Bud Vase, Glass ....
Bud Vase, Crystal ....
Carafe ....
Candlestick, Glass ....
Celery Dish, Glass ....
Fish Platter, Glass, Small ....
Fish Platter, Glass, Large ....
Oil & Vinegar Service (Cruet)..........
Gravy Boats, China..............................
Ice Bowls, Glass ....
Olive Dish, Glass ....
Platters, China ....
Relish Dish, Glass ....
Salad Bowl, China ....
Salad Bowl, Glass, Large ....
Salad Bowl, Silver Rim.......................
Salad Bowl, Large Glass French Crystal...
Salad Bowl, Plastic, Individual.........
Salt & Pepper, China ....
Salt & Pepper, Glass ....
Salt & Pepper, Crystal ....
Shrimp Server, Glass, Silver Liner ....
Sugar & Creamer, China ....
Sugar & Creamer, Cut Crystal Style .
Sugar & Creamer, Glass......................
Vegetable Bowl, 2 comp. China ....
Vegetable Bowls, China....................
Water Pitcher, Glass ....
Water Pitcher, Crystal.......................

COFFEE POTS:

7-Piece Silver Deluxe Coffee and Tea Set—Tea Pot, Coffee Pot, Sugar, Creamer, Waste Bowl Tray, Deluxe Urn—30 Cup ....
5-Piece Silver Tea and Coffee Service—Coffee Pot, Tea Pot, Sugar, Creamer and Tray ....
Coffee Makers—
  - Percolator, Electric, 30 Cup ....
  - Percolator, Electric, 48 Cup ....
  - ?????, 55 Cup Stainless Steel Deluxe...

PUNCH SETS & FOUNTAINS:

Punch Set—Silver Deluxe—Consisting of Bowl on Pedestal, Long-Handled Ladle, and 12 Silver Punch Cups on Silver Tray ....
Punch Bowl, Silver, Ladle, 3 gal. No Cups ....
Punch Bowl, Silver, Ladle, 5 gal. No Cups ....
Punch Sets, Glass Bowls, Silver Ladle and 12 Glass Cups—2-1/2 gallon Bowl....................................
Punch Sets, Crystal Bowl, Silver Ladle and 12 Glass Cups...............
Punch Fountain, electric, 3 gal. ....
Punch Fountain, electric, 5 gal. ....
Punch Ladle, Silver.............................
Punch Cups, Glass (extra) ....
Punch Cups, Silver (extra) ....
Base for Glass Bowl ....

6

The Staff and Subcontractors

In the catering business it is essential to know how to do it all, even if it's impossible to do it all yourself. If you do not know how long it takes to clear one hundred settings, set up a Champagne toast, pack up the commissary, and load the truck, it will be difficult to know what to expect from the people working with you. It is easy to underestimate the actual time it takes to get a job done. Caterers often work under pressure of time in makeshift conditions, so compatibility as well as experience and stability is part of the job description for both staff and subcontractors.

Good teamwork between office, kitchen, and service staffs is essential for a pleasant and productive workplace. Often, people will have to be cross-trained. Even office staff must be service-oriented and relate well to people. Positive and cheerful people, who are solution minded, are as important in the office as at an event. Anyone who picks up your telephone is part of the selling team. Office flexibility will be as important as kitchen flexibility. Ideally, you will surround yourself with independent people who are team players.

From the start you will have one or more full- or part-time employees. Under current rules, anyone you are paying $100 or more a month would almost certainly be classified as an employee and must be treated under IRS considerations. If you call the IRS, you will eventually reach a representative who will tailor an information packet to your needs. For example, IRS Publication 15, Circular E, defines who is an employee. The IRS also has guidelines for self-employed, independent contractor, and consultant tax requirements. It is always useful and necessary to speak with your accountant about these things, but it helps to know what to expect.

The law requires you to know whether people in your employ are citizens. You must see proof of residency or other papers, such as a green card, that entitle them to work in the United States. You are also obliged to make sure you are in compliance with child labor laws. The youngest age for full-time employment in most states is sixteen unless special working papers are supplied. There are minimum wage and overtime rates for the food-service field that must be honored. Disability and unemployment insurance are also regulated. Attention to what may seem at first like many nuisances will save a lot of grief and money in the long run.

The IRS, the Department of Labor, and the Small Business Administration will all assist with information. Of course, your lawyer, accountant, and business consultant are also sources of advice on compliance in these areas.

Workers' compensation is an insurance policy that virtually all states require, much the way auto insurance is mandatory. It is an insurance policy that you can get from a private carrier or from a special state agency acting as a carrier.

Caterer Staffing

The kitchen staff may at first simply assist you or complement your skills. But if you yourself are not going to be the chef, your first hiring task will be to find a chef. Usually you will know one who is willing to work on a per-job basis. It is, however, best to get a commitment for three or four days a week when you are starting out.

If you are acting as chef, then you might consider hiring a good sous-chef or someone from a culinary school who has done some internships to give you support. It is not until you have grown your business that you can afford to hire inexperienced people who need training.

Depending on the size of the job and your baking skills, you may choose to buy breads, rolls, and pastries from an outside source. Hiring a good baker who will work on a part-time basis is an alternative. If you prefer not to bake, it is handy to have someone who will. Hiring a baker who is willing and able to prepare main dishes is, of course, another option. You do want someone with professional experience, so that you can look away occasionally.

The value of the wait staff cannot be overemphasized, since it is often the service that makes or breaks an event. From the start, you have to treat the staff like the professionals they are. No matter how good the food is or how beautifully it is plated, if it is not served in a pleasing, expert way, the guests will not have a good time. Until you develop your own Rolodex, the best sources are agencies, universities, and culinary schools.

When you are just starting, you may ask wait staff to help pack the food, pick up the rental items, and prep when you get to the location. They will probably arrange tables and chairs and set the tables, too, to say nothing of cleaning up and returning everything. Some of the people you hire may work twelve hours straight, so it is important to discuss overtime not only with your client, but with the staff as well.

Bartenders, people who know not only about wine and liquor but serving portions and the appropriate law, have the right and the obligation to refuse to serve a minor or someone who has obviously had too much to drink. Under almost all circumstances where a guest has had one drink too many, the bartender should speak with the party manager, or in their absence, the host, and tactfully but firmly tell them that a guest needs transportation home. There are reported cases in many states where the bartender and the bar owner have been found liable for injuries caused by a drunk driver.

Production assistants do food ordering and shopping, stocking and inventory, propping and packing. Choose someone energetic, intelligent, and beginning a food-service career.

The office team includes at least a part-time bookkeeper to make sure client bills go out and bills and taxes are paid. When your business takes off, you might want the pleasure and luxury of hiring someone full-time to handle correspondence, work charts, orders, and some phone work so that you can come and go freely. It is important that when someone other than yourself answers the phone it is with the same inviting warmth you would use. Client contact comes first.

Buspersons not only clear tables and fill coffee cups, but also help replace serving dishes, coffee urns, and so forth if it is too large a party for the wait staff to do so.

The cleaning staff holds essential positions, which must be filled with as much care and respect as any other, because your business license depends on it. Everything has to be cleaned all the time, not just pots, dishes, and appliances, but walls, floors, and bathrooms. Even the office and vehicles are held to a higher standard than in other businesses when you handle food. It is also possible to hire the same people to do cleanup off premises as well.

Drivers need to have a commercial driver's license and be familiar with local rules and regulations. You might hire a driver and a vehicle, but then you must be sure the van is used only for food because it must be clean and free of chemical odors and other pollutants that would affect food. Is the driver doing only dropoff and pickup, or is he or she part of the off-premises team? You are responsible, so the driver must inform you of any maintenance or repairs that are necessary.

When you want to expand your business you may want to hire a staff salesperson who can also help manage events. Choose someone who has had experience selling food services and can reflect your particular abilities and product to represent you to potential clients. This person should also reflect your own sense of social etiquette and your interpersonal skills.

A party manager or account coordinator is an asset when your business grows, or during a busy season like the month of June, when there are frequent weddings and graduation parties. The manager is the person you will introduce your clients to after they have contracted the event. He or she is the liaison person for all questions the clients have, from the color of the linens to the size of the plates, the photographers, and the location and menu. The manager creates work schedules, determines the staff needed, and fields any problems. The party manager makes sure everyone is on time and may be the one who goes to the location for the duration of the event. The party coordinator may be given a fixed percent of the income from an event that he or she has been in charge of.

Your own management skills will grow as you need them. Offer competitive wages, gratuities, and pleasant working conditions, and you will more than compensate for lack of experience as an employer. Communicate clearly about tasks, breaks, and meals, and never be too busy to listen. Rehire the part-time and independent people you enjoy working with in order to establish a positive working relationship that builds confidence.

In catering—especially in a new, small business—people have to be flexible about tasks. A buser may also be the parking valet, and the wait staff may help take coats. Everyone helps to pack up and leave the premises. Your pre-event function sheet will spell this out. Each employee should receive a schedule of what his or her duties are before the start of every function.

General safety rules have to be in effect at all times to prevent accidents. All employees should know where the first-aid kit is as well as the fire extinguisher. Not only is this sensible, but it is required by law. Employees are protected by the Occupational Safety and Health Administration (OSHA), whose regulations cover things like no-smoking rules, fire alarms and extinguishers, and the proper storage of knives and flammable material. It is best to check on their requirements.

Employee perks, like transportation, parking, and meals, can often be spelled out. Most of the time, gratuities are simply added to the bill and divided among the staff. Many places have a policy of individual gratuities being pooled and shared as well.

Dress codes are important. Nothing and no one can be clean enough. Even the illusion of dirt worries people. In addition to food sanitation, which is very specific, everyone working has to be sure their persons and clothes are very clean. Tuxedos, black and white, or a color and white classic clothes are the standard attire for servers. The traditional kitchen whites, abundant aprons, side towels for food preparers, and skirts or pants are variables depending often on regional tastes. Generally, the kitchen staff is provided whites when they are prepping and cooking off premises, and the wait and bar staffs supply their own clothes, but there are no fixed rules. There is no need to be rigid about wardrobe, but staff should be pleasantly and identifiably dressed.

A minimum of the simplest jewelry is okay, but heavy stuff or anything dangling is dangerous, and it gets very hot when you reach into an oven or stand over a steam table. There is nothing to be done about guests who wear scents that overpower food aromas, but staff should never have more than a touch.

There are a few no's: no smoking, no gum chewing, no drinking, no lateness, no contagious illnesses, no open cuts or sores, and no colds. And no long chats with the guests, although most events are not so formal that pleasantries are not exchanged. Even among themselves, the staff should keep public conversations brief, so that the guests feel they are the ones getting the attention.

In any task-oriented situation, the goal is to find mutually beneficial solutions, to delegate work, and to maintain customer satisfaction. Accurate information and clear intentions will prevent most conflicts. If you perceive performance problems, it is your responsibility to address them and assess the facts and feelings of the matter at hand. Techniques of self-discipline and conflict management will emerge as you coordinate everyone's contributions. Communication, commitment, and a little compromise go a long way. The buck stops with you, and sometimes listening to complaints and constructive criticism comes with the territory.

There is a show-time element to catering, so roles have to be assigned carefully and performed punctually and graciously. Clearly, the staff has to be supportive of each other, collegial rather than competitive. By the same token, your staff should never have to put up with embarrassment or abuse. You or the event manager will have to be the diplomat and handle negative situations in support of anyone working for you.

7

Choosing a Location

One of the delights of catering is that in addition to hotels and reception halls, any site is a possible location. Not only private homes and gardens, but parks, museums, historical mansions, corporate headquarters, ballparks, renovated train stations, and trains and boats can serve as wonderful settings for your events. Even abandoned mines, bridges, rooftops, and schoolyards all can serve, morning, noon, or night, as dramatic alternatives. Catering is done on movie sets and opera stages, in airplane hangars, public libraries, and town halls.

Most large events done by start-up caterers are basically stand-up, even when there are tables and chairs for the guests. Since service is circumscribed, it is the setting that will create the pleasurable environment that all partygivers and partygoers expect.

The design of the site is often the caterer's job, and the first impression the guests have of an event. Food presentation must be inviting at each station. Your food standards must be reflected in the quality of the ambience you instill. Decor and moods are not substitutes for delicious food in the proper amount, but they do enhance anything served.

Style is personal, but in catering it has to be a consensus. Your clients do not want to walk into an event they are hosting and wonder where they are. If it is a very large party, it is best for you to have a few samples of colors and a few sketches or photographs. Until you develop your own photo file, these can be gleaned from magazines. Refer to them in your confirmation letter and, if possible, have a floor plan or sketch of the arrangement you have in mind.

The atmosphere contributes greatly to how much enjoyment people have. One or two unique touches are often enough. Mainly the task is to harmonize the occasion, the setting, and the food. Decor can be selected either to turn a neutral space into a specific theme or to enhance thematic surroundings.

If you are not familiar with the site, do not make any assumptions. Check it out first. There may be features over which you will have no control. Though you cannot have a backup location, you can have backup equipment. Portable equipment and decor can be delivered almost anywhere, for a price. If there is a potential difficulty for a complicated event, make sure someone is in charge of the equipment. They should confirm delivery, make sure it is operational on location, and supervise its maintenance and return. The commissary must be functional at all times and geared up for special events to coordinate with the event location. Catering is a one-opportunity occasion, so a missed detail has a ripple effect. Even the most good-natured client will have zero acceptance for excuses.

It is the job of the account manager to visit the site of the selected location and walk through the facility, sometimes with a digital and/or Polaroid camera and tape measure, taking notes and making sure what is actually there. It is also necessary to find out when the area will be free for setup and by what time you must have everything cleared out. In addition to the party area, kitchen, washroom, coatroom, and social area, questions about smoke detectors, fire exits, emergency lights, insurance and security, access, parking, zoning, permits, and liabilities must be answered. Is there wheelchair access to both the dining area and the washrooms? Are elevators usable at all times?

Off-premise catering is an exercise in creative hospitality. Your client is expecting a high level of pleasure, which you must build with nuts and bolts like organizing supply and waste management routines and delegating on-site tasks to reliable people. Performance-oriented schedules will lead to very productive relationships with staff and subcontractors. Your computer software will help you keep track of everything. Be sure to have copies of everything related to your event with you. A laptop or a palm device is often helpful.

The technical aspects are the same whether you serve New Mexican or northern Italian specialties. Whether the theme is ultramodern, nostalgic, personal, public, relaxed, formal, tent, or ballroom, food must be delivered, prepared, served, and removed. Clean dishes have to be plated and dirty ones washed. The person in charge of admission to the location and a second emergency person must be listed on worksheets so that the building and grounds are accessible the day of the event and the day after.

The directions to the setting must be clear and parking must be available. If there is not an easily accessed parking lot, insured valet parking services can supply bonded uniformed personnel to parties. They will do everything related to parking that a large event requires. Since they give the first and last impression of service, capable professional service is important. Valet services know whom to call about police permits, and they have good rapport with people who handle traffic. It is well worth hiring them, as they will accept all liability and are aware of various conditions that prevail in both urban and suburban locations. They will look at the site and determine the best way to handle the traffic.

Remarkable places are available to stage events. In the directory section at the back of the book, you'll find a list that is only an indication of the fun you can have choosing a site for your event. Event planning is an increasingly important part of catering, and developing a good relationship with people at the locations that you want to use is very important. Also, you must ask questions directly. Some venues want not only proof of insurance and references, but also a deposit and in some nonprofit cases a donation.

8

Nonfood Supplies

A restaurant, once outfitted, is more or less a done deal, but caterers regularly encounter situations quite different from previous ones and have to set up and oversee an event in an environment over which they have little control. While the possibilities for creativity are endless, the means are not. Because of the higher impact of any glitches, the quality or performance of nonfood supplies can make or break a party.

What is trendy is easy. A few accent pieces and colors can set a mood. Presentation platters, flowers, lights, and what is generally called ambiance have to be gracious but not so pretentious that they make people uncomfortable. Commodious tables and comfortable, affordable chairs are always welcome.

Outside suppliers are your best tool. Local rental companies will provide tables, chairs, and linens. Don't forget satellite tables for people to set down dishes or glasses they are done with, as well as one for gifts or presentations as the occasion warrants. The off-premise kitchen, however makeshift, must also have adequate prep and plating tables.

EQUIPMENT Restaurant and catering supply houses have commercial equipment: warmers, hot plates, and chafing dishes; warming, convection, and microwave ovens; and warming lamps and grills; as well as knives, sharpeners, and wooden cutting boards. Sometimes, the caterer just brings the prepared food, and it has only to be plated and served. Insulated food containers will keep food hot or cold.

If on-site cooking is necessary, you may want special-use items, such as electric skillets or woks, rice cookers, steamers, and/or deep fryers. Make sure you have hand-lift cabinets for food and a dolly for heavy loads. Ice containers and tubs may be needed. If you have specialties like pizza, you might want some pizza stones and paddles. Tea carts can be used for Spanish tapas and then for dessert. If the commissary is close to the event site, it might simply be more efficient to replenish the fully prepared food every hour or so.

It is a good idea to put together several site kits: a kitchen kit with a knife roll, a knife sharpener, scissors, twine, bamboo skewers, funnels, scrapers, pot holders, pastry bag, cheesecloth, spoons, spatulas, and tongs. A lemon zester and a juicer are handy, also. Immersion blenders or hand mixers are frequently essential, as are stainless-steel measuring cups, spoons, mixing bowls, colanders, and strainers. A few thermometers and timers as well as whisks, spatulas, and solid and slotted spoons should be organized so that they can do double duty off-premises. Pot holders, oven mitts, germicidal hand soap, detergent, extra aprons, and oversized towels can all go in a nylon duffle. Disposable products like aluminum foil, plastic wrap, paper towels, and tissues should be included. Also pack sealable heavy-duty garbage bags, and rubber gloves, both regular and heavy-duty, to deal with breakage, etc. Ecologically correct disposables, such as paper instead of Styrofoam, and biodegradable cleaning supplies are available.

Another useful site kit includes a first-aid kit and fire extinguisher, flashlight and batteries, heavy-duty extension cord, a staple gun, gaffer's tape, two- and three-pronged adapters, tape measure, level, pushpins, safety pins, needle and thread, hammer, nails, pliers, and Phillips and straight screwdrivers.

For packing, you might want bubble wrap, masking tape, sturdy moving-company cartons, flexible foam, and heavy-duty shallow flexible food containers for leftovers. Hard ones crack and are best for light things like salads, cookies, or crackers, while very flexible ones are useless because they distort and break their seal. Collapsible plastic crates help carry last-minute things.

DISHES AND SERVING PIECES Virtually anything can be rented. Before you start purchasing, experience will teach what items are most required for your clients' needs. For instance, rectangular covered chafing dishes, coffee urns, pitchers, and serving pieces for salads and bread in classically designed stainless steel will fit into almost any theme. Trays for hors d'oeuvres, serving, and busing, as well as stands for them, are often used. Standard six-ounce stemmed goblets for wine and coordinated water glasses might be worth owning.

When you rent, it is best to work with a 10 percent overage, for guests who bring guests, to replace items dropped, for returns to the buffet, or for drinkers who switch drinks more than expected. For a large, elaborate event, a more realistic figure is 25 percent over. It seems that the larger the party, the larger the percent of extra supplies that are needed.

The rental company will provide lists and work with you from the start. Selections of first-course plate, soup plate, dinner plate, dessert plate, cup and saucer, and demitasse cup and saucer are readily available. For flatware, the selections are made from salad fork, dinner fork, dessert fork, butter knife, cutting knife, soup spoon, dessert spoon, coffee spoon, and demitasse spoon. Serving platters and bowls, salt shakers and pepper mills, condiment holders, sugar and creamers, utensils, and special items are equally obtainable. From punch bowls to barbecue grills, there are companies that will deliver on time for the function you are planning.

Purchases of disposable plastic and paper items are often necessary, so you might want to buy certain things like plastic luncheon or dinner plates in bulk. Oversized napkins and sturdy flatware will be used for events where the service costs need to be kept low. Paper doilies line trays and platters effectively and can also be bought by the case. Cardboard separators used between layers of large cakes are also handy for platters of tea sandwiches and other finger foods.

LINENS AND UNIFORMS Linens are procured from the same house that rents the place settings. Beginning caterers usually rent all linens because each event is tabled and served differently for people with strong opinions about whether everything should be white, or a color, or combination of colors that never would have crossed your mind. It is also quite cost-efficient, considering the cost of maintaining them in a pristine condition and finding matching replacements. Order generously sized napkins and enough cloths for dining and serving tables. Extra linens are a necessity, not a luxury. They cover spills and are needed under chafers and trays and for servers. For buffets, sometimes double the amount of napkins are rented because guests leave them about and reasonably will not pick up an unknown one. Renting is such an important part of catering that many large catering companies have actually expanded into the rental business. They are quite happy to rent to the competition and work in very collegial ways.

What to wear? Fashion in the culinary world exemplifies the adage that the more things change the more they remain the same. For the most part, good-quality white chef's coats will get kitchen and food staff through most events, and tuxedo-style jackets are worn by wait staff at many traditional affairs.

Some men and women work in casual white linen jackets. Though white is so apparently clean, there are many situations where a uniformed look is inappropriate. When that is the case, discuss with your client whether simple white blouses or shirts and skirts or trousers will do. Safe and comfortable shoes are essential. For kitchen work, flexible clogs with rubber soles are almost universally liked, but there are many companies that make an informal dress shoe that is as safe as a pair of sneakers. The wait staff needs to be easily identifiable so they can be approached without hesitation.

Tents are often the solution to events held in gardens, both public and private. The most basic tents will shelter from sun and rain. They can be as plain and elaborate as the budget permits. Floors and dance floors are easily arranged, and heaters and lights can be installed. They should be professionally installed and taken down. Make sure that they are permitted on the grounds where the function is to take place. Runners and canopies can also be rented.

Caterers often function as consultants to their clients, and may be asked to hire and supervise florists, photographers, and musicians. More and more clients expect caterers to be full-service event and party planners. An event manager is a necessary part of the team.

FLOWERS There are florists everywhere who will work to order and deliver the arrangements you want directly to the event. As with all subcontractors, it is good to establish a good relationship with a single florist after trying a few so that you can get the selections you want with some special care. If the client has a florist they want to use, there is no reason not to. Begin by asking hotels and restaurants you like who does their flowers. Simple decorative accents are not difficult to make, and if you have a flair for it, an assortment of baskets with plastic liners and green florist's clay can be the basis for informal displays. If your area has flower markets or stalls, you can assemble refreshing arrangements at a good price. If kept in a cool place, they can be prepared up to twenty-four hours ahead of time. People have practiced by making gifts for friends and family. It is unlikely, though, that you will have time to take the flowers on. Check with floral designers, wholesalers, and florists to find the best in your area. Plants and even trees can be rented. Garnish flowers for platters and buffet stations can be ordered anywhere, but edible flowers must come from a reliable source.

DECORATIONS Displays and decorations have to be discussed in detail with the clients, especially if it is a corporate or cultural function that should reflect their taste. Clients will have strong feelings about the environment to which they are inviting guests. From a boardroom lunch meeting to a picnic in the park, restraint and good taste are always in order.

Will the clients supply the material and be responsible for setting it up? Will they want a theme decoration or a professional display? Special screening of films or videos are usually set up by the clients if needed, but once again the Yellow Pages will also provide you with even those resources.

PHOTOGRAPHERS Photographers are needed for many events. By and large, you will find them through networking. You want to know what a photographer's photographs look like before you commit him or her to your clients' once-in-a-lifetime occasion. Do not hesitate to look at portfolios when you make your choice. Be certain you understand your clients' specific needs and what they actually want to end up with. Photographs are very important to people, and you cannot be too careful in your selection.

MUSIC AND ENTERTAINMENT Generally, the clients make the selection of music and entertainment, but if you want to increase the services offered, you might listen to various groups, most of whom have tapes you can play for clients. It is also necessary to know if they have and will bring whatever instruments and electrical equipment they use. The size of the band is important as well. Some places cannot handle more than four people and their instruments. Musicians and entertainers may also be found through conservatories and colleges.

There are entertainers and supply houses that specialize in children's events and offer appropriate items. Most areas have companies that supply helium-filled balloons and deliver them. You can rent a helium tank from a resource in your area. Licensed fireworks can be arranged. In general, first-class fireworks are a thousand dollars a minute and are not to be suggested lightly.

Taking the Show on the Road

For locations away from the commissary, in addition to the specific food and equipment for the event, it is helpful to have several kits ready to go.

OFFICE KIT (BRIEFCASE)

Petty cash

On-site phone book

Emergency credit card

Business cards

Copies of licenses, permits, contracts, and worksheets

Local map

Digital camera and/or Polaroid

Cellular telephone

Small flashlight

Laptop computer and/or Palm Pilot

EMERGENCY SITE KIT (LARGE METAL TOOL CHEST)

First-aid kit

Needle and thread

Heavy-duty rubber gloves

Fire extinguisher

Safety pins

Pushpins

Fire extinguishing blanket

Staple gun and staples

Heavy-duty garbage bags

Two powerful flashlights

Paper towels

Matches

Mat knife and blades

Extra batteries and bulbs

Gaffer's tape

Pliers

Metal straightedge

Hammer, nails, and brads

Tape measure

Steam iron

Metal polish and cloth

Heavy-duty extension cords

Phillips and regular screwdrivers

Two- and three-pronged electrical adapters

KITCHEN KIT (NYLON DUFFLE BAG)

Knife roll and knife sharpener

Funnels

Germicidal hand soap

Whisks

Twine

Pastry bag

Detergent

Bamboo skewers

Tongs

Moisturizer

Solid and slotted spoons

Food thermometers

Extra aprons and towels

Solid and slotted spatulas

Can opener

Rubber gloves

Bottle opener

Sponges

Long-handled fork

Corkscrew

Plastic wrap

Lemon zester

Portable electric mixer

Aluminum foil

Juice reamer

Tissues

Stainless steel grater

Cordless immersion blender

Matches

Plastic tarps

Pot holders

Masking tape

Oven mitts

Assorted plastic bags and tubs

Grease pencil

Portable radio

Measuring cups

Measuring spoons

9

Food Safety
and Sanitation

This is arguably the most important chapter in the book. If food safety and sanitation is properly adhered to, you can focus on everything else. If it is not tended to, nothing else matters.

According to New York state law, a caterer is a person who prepares and furnishes food at a commissary that is intended for individual portion service at the premises of the consumer, whether such premises are temporary or permanent. A caterer is considered a food-service establishment operator and is required to perform in accordance with the statutes. A commissary is quite simply a place where food is stored, processed, and prepared. A copy of your state sanitary code is available and very helpful. Often the licensing requirements vary from county to county, and a good resource is your local board of health. You will probably need to take the twelve- to twenty-hour food-protection training course offered by many schools and frequently by the field services of your local health department. If it is difficult to get to a school, you can also do it by mail or online over the Internet. You or someone you work with will need a certificate stating that you know the sanitation laws required to be in a food-service business. The International Food Service

Executives Association offers online certification in food safety, as does the American Institute of Baking.

The basic guidelines have to do with cleanliness, but the specific routines of controlling bacteria and viruses have to be learned, because it is critical that they are done right. Sometimes, additional codes are amended, and you will have to stay alert for them. With an increase in the market for fish and shellfish, there are specific courses for the handling of seafood. There is now a Seafood HACCP (Hazard Analysis Critical Control Point) requirement if you are handling raw bars. It is a good course to take. You can do it over three days or choose a one-day intensive, and it is worth the effort.

ServSafe is a training and certification program sponsored by the National Restaurant Association's Educational Foundation. The program is nationally recognized as meeting the restaurant industry standard. It consists of eight or sixteen hours of classroom training in food safety topics such as basic microbiology, the importance of a comprehensive HACCP program, personal hygiene, sanitation, and pest control. ServSafe details how you can take charge of preventing foodborne illness through proper storage, preparation, holding for service, serving, and cleanup. Passing the test will be a great asset.

In New York state, for instance, it is now mandatory to refrigerate eggs between 35°F and 40°F. It has been discovered that even when the shell of an egg is not cracked, salmonella bacteria can multiply. Eggs stored properly will be fine for about one month. When cooking professionally, the best policy is to refrain from serving raw eggs, even in dishes like Caesar salad, mayonnaise, or eggnog. Eggs should be cooked within 2 hours of removal from refrigeration and served immediately after cooking. Egg-rich foods like custards, if refrigerated immediately, will keep for 3 to 4 days. When a recipe calls for cooking an egg mixture until it coats a metal spoon, the mixture will have reached the 160°F necessary for thorough cooking. Always use a food thermometer. The United States Department of Agriculture (USDA) recommends that eggs as well as meat, poultry, fish, and milk held at room temperature for more than 2 hours be discarded. Always check with your purveyor for "use by" information.

There are many places you can turn for up-to-the-minute information on food safety. The USDA Hot Line for Meat and Poultry (800-535-

4555) is available from 10:00 a.m. to 4:00 p.m. Eastern Time, Monday through Friday, and will answer specific questions about eggs as well. The Food and Nutrition Information Center of the USDA has a remarkable and diverse website library that is meticulously cataloged for your easy reference. They quite reasonably offer a disclaimer saying that inclusion in their files is not an endorsement by the USDA, nor do they ensure the accuracy of all information. They have sections for food-service management, nutrition and health education, food technology, and recipes. It is to your advantage to keep up with their listings because there are not enough hours in the day to seek out a full array of new information and run your business.

The Food and Nutrition Center, part of the National Agricultural Library located in Beltsville, Maryland, is also a treasure house of books, articles, and audiovisual material. They have an extensive research department that will help on a cost-recovery basis, but a lot of basic and bibliographical information is available at no cost. They will also try to assist you with answering specific food and nutrition questions. The Food Safety and Inspection Service has catering-oriented newsletters and other pertinent information on its website.

Universities publish findings that are very helpful. Dr. Dean O. Cliver led a team from the Food Research Institute at the University of Wisconsin that proved wooden cutting boards are actually safer than plastic ones, given they are both cleaned equally well. Plastic retains germs under cleaning conditions that will destroy them on wooden cutting boards. Plastic boards are twice as likely to continue transmitting germs.

Never let even the juices from raw meat, poultry, fish, or eggs touch any other food-preparation surface, utensil, or container. To avoid cross-contamination, wash not only the cutting board but also the knife, fork, spatula, and countertops after use. Wash them in hot, soapy water for at least 30 seconds, and occasionally use a mixture of 1 part chlorine bleach to 14 parts hot water. Do not reuse marinades or pour them into anything, like salads, that will be eaten uncooked. Do not even think of cutting salad ingredients on a board you have just cut a raw chicken on without washing it thoroughly first. Never put grilled chicken or meat back onto the plate from which it was taken raw. Check instructions on kitchenware and accessories for the appropriate cleaning agents to use. Baking soda solutions are still a good way to keep refrigerators free of mold. Dr. Cliver is now at the University of California, Davis, where he is a professor in the Food Safety Laboratory and World Health Organization Collaborating Center for Food Virology.

The U.S. Government Printing Office will send a free catalog in which you will find a large number of booklets that are a wellspring of food-handling facts and guidelines. For a nominal cost, you will be able to add them to your library. The American Frozen Food Institute is able to provide information in their area of expertise. All in all, there is a fine network in place for guidance and support.

It may seem awkward at first to address the personal hygiene of the people whom you select to work with you, but you have no choice. Avoiding the issue can have a negative outcome. It would, for instance, appear obvious that if anyone is ill, he or she should not be handling food, but the sad truth is that when people have personal and professional obligations they often overlook the obvious. You cannot permit anyone with even a cold to handle food, for very real reasons. As a matter of fact, anyone dealing with food publicly cannot even appear to be ill because it reduces confidence. In the catering business, you are responsible for your clients' comfort level, and their happy event is not the time to educate them on what is contagious and what isn't. Food handlers have to wash their hands constantly, and stay home with even a slight cold. Though viruses and bacteria can be carried by air, water, food, pests, and dirty equipment, the most common means of transmission are the hands.

Hair, clothing, and shoes, of course, have to be clean, and kitchen towels have to be changed frequently. Whether you use chef's jackets, casual wear, or unique expressions of personal style, everything must be immaculate and neat. Shoes should be comfortable, safe, and well maintained, whether you are just delivering the food or also setting it up and serving it.

The best and often the only way to deal with food contamination is to prevent it. The saying, "When in doubt, throw it out," never had more meaning. You can keep grains, cereals, sugar, flour, and dried beans, peas, and fruits at room temperature. Sugar and salt, herbs, spices, oils and vinegars, honey, and unopened preserves and jams don't need refrigeration either. They do have to be stored in a clean, dry place free of insects and rodents. They should also be shelved several inches up from the floor and away from the wall. Pantry items, including paper goods, should be checked from time to time.

The job of everyone in the food industry is to avoid contamination of food during storage, preparation, and service. You need to develop a prescriptive approach to food handling using personal hygiene and kitchen cleanliness as a basis.

People are a big cause of cross-contamination. It often embarrasses people to discuss the importance of hand-washing after toilet use. It is, sad to say, one of the biggest sources of food contamination. Basic hygiene will prevent carrying microorganisms from the bathroom to the food. Hands should also be washed often while preparing food to avoid transfering bacteria from raw food to cooked. If you are wearing gloves, either change them or wash your gloved hands frequently. Disposable gloves should be used for all food that is not to be cooked.

One of your best investments will be several food thermometers. Temperature control is the most successful way to manage food-borne illness. The rule of thumb is that any food needing refrigeration should never be at room temperature for more than an hour, a maximum of two, before serving.

Make it a principle to keep frozen food at below 0°F; cold food cold, under 40°F; and hot food hot at 165°F. The refrigerator temperature must be between 32°F and 40°F. Poultry, fish, and meat, including cold cuts and smoked meat, should be kept under 37°F; milk, butter, cheese, and eggs, not over 40°F. (Before serving, butter can be held for several hours at 50°F.) Most fruit, salad, vegetables, and desserts can do well up to 45°F. Whole citrus fruit, root vegetables, and squash are fine at 60°F to 70°F. Avocados, bananas, and tomatoes are best at room temperature. Cover and label everything—you don't want to contaminate cooked food with raw. Freezer temperature has to be between 0°F and −15°F for frozen poultry, meat, and fish, frozen fruits and vegetables, and ice cream and other frozen desserts. Make sure you have one thermometer in the refrigerator and one to test with.

When storing food, use shallow storage containers to present a large surface area, and place in the freezer or refrigerator as soon as possible. The idea of cooling hot foods to room temperature first is a dangerous idea left over from the era of iceboxes, when hot food would melt the ice, lowering the cooling efficiency of the icebox. Large-quantity food tasks have to be performed with an awareness of food safety. The danger zone is 40°F to 140°F. Defrost frozen food in the refrigerator, the microwave

Food Sanitation Procedures

1. Wash hands for at least 30 seconds with soap after using the bathroom.

2. Food handlers should not work when they have a contagious illness, even a cold, and any cuts or lesions should be well covered.

3. Keep workspaces clean.

4. Never let cooked food come in contact with raw poultry, meat, fish, eggs, or their juices.

5. Wash and rinse for 30 seconds any surface raw poultry, meat, fish, eggs, or their juices have touched, including your hands and knives.

6. Keep frozen food under 0°F.

7. Defrost frozen food in the refrigerator or microwave, and cook or serve within 1 hour.

8. Keep cold food under 40°F.

9. Keep hot food at an internal temperature of 165°F.

10. Transport and store hot foods hot and cold foods cold.

11. Serve food within 1 hour of removal from heat or cold.

12. Keep food storage and service areas free of insects and rodents.

13. Foods that have been left out for 3 hours are under no condition "leftovers"; they are trash.

14. Please note that it is necessary to keep up with current sanitation laws and health guidelines. The Internet is a great resource for this. Foodsafety.gov is one place to start.

(following the manufacturer's instructions), under running cold water, or cold water that is changed every 30 minutes. Cook within 2 hours.

Hot foods should be held at an internal temperature of 165°F until they are served. Of course, most foods have to be cooked at higher temperatures. For instance, safe cooking temperatures always mean internal temperatures from 160°F to 180°F for poultry. During boiling, baking, and roasting, bacteria and parasites, including the ubiquitous salmonella, are killed. A probe thermometer is your best tool. Usually, food is served well under the 2-hour holding limit. To maintain the temperature for occasions like buffet service, make sure the water in steam tables is 180°F, and the food served is at 165°F. If neither method is available, refrigerate or freeze immediately for future service. Mishandled food has to be discarded, so it is important to make sure all the people you work with understand the rules. Remember, there are many thousands of food-service establishments all over the world doing a remarkable job of providing safe meals with just a handful of regulations, but those are strictly adhered to.

Microwave ovens have become a part of the culinary scene. Safe installation, an attached probe, and a turntable are basic considerations for food safety. Glass and designated Pyroceram ceramic cooking utensils are preferred. Plastic should not touch food in the microwave, as the interactions of unapproved chemicals have not been fully analyzed yet. Avoid using leftover cold-storage containers in the microwave. Plastic wrap, which is often recommended to cover food containers in the microwave, should never touch the food. Follow the manufacturer's instructions and avail yourself of their 800 hotline number as well. There is still some trial and error in microwave cooking, but it can be a useful tool. Use both the attached internal meat probe thermometer for large amounts of food and your own meat thermometer if in doubt. Debone large pieces of meat or poultry, cover to hold in moisture, use mid-range levels for longer times to ensure thorough cooking, and turn and stir the food several times. It is often recommended that food stand to complete cooking time. Never partially cook and wait to finish. Never attempt to roast a stuffed whole chicken or turkey in the microwave.

An official at the New York State Department of Health, Sanitation, and Food Protection told me he had a terrific anecdote for this book: A private caterer in upstate New York had a party for sixty, and forty became ill. I thought that was no way to introduce a subject and that it was simply a scare tactic. The truth is, it highlights the fact that such an event is very rare, because with care, it is virtually avoidable. Healthy people are pretty sturdy and do not need food that is surgically sterile, just kitchen clean. If you are preparing food for the very young or the very old, special attention must be paid. It should not go without saying that if any guest is ill or has a compromised immune system, he or she might require a special meal.

10

M e n u s

One of the things that makes catering different from restaurant service is that the visual appearance of the meal must be created on the location. A customer can look at a restaurant and see if it is the right place for their party, but when you cater you must assure your client that everything will be not only delicious but presented in an organized and attractive way. Though they haven't the time or perhaps the skills to prepare and present food themselves, the public is informed about food through travel, television, and magazines. There is enthusiasm about American and regional specialties, and the cuisines of various countries have become mainstream. The menu is the way to show your clients you know what they like.

People turn to a professional because it is difficult for them to visualize a meal down to the smallest detail. They want maximum results, with a minimum of worry. The individuals or groups who come to you for catering services will be eager to read your menus and talk about food. No one is shy or indifferent about the subject, particularly when they are inviting guests. It is not enough that you know you can deliver, you must convince the public that you can. Catering means TLC.

Even if you and your cooking are known by reputation, your visual presentation is the selling tool that will attract them and hold their imagination. The menu is the page on which you create the events, from dream meals to calorie counters, that you are being paid for. It should excite and inspire confidence. Before you meet with clients, you should have an array of menus prepared. They are your portfolio and the key to successful merchandising.

From your point of view, the key to success is proper cost analysis. You need to know how much it will cost to deliver the various menus and be prepared to offer substitutes that are appropriate for the clients' budget. Be ready to present an item in a new way or to eliminate it entirely. You must have a breakdown of all the food items listed separately, for your eyes only, that tells you at a glance the comparative price of five pounds of chicken or veal, rice or potatoes. Remember, you are in business to make a profit and still be competitive. A fully analyzed menu puts complete cost control at your fingertips. As soon as you know the number of people you are expected to serve, you will need only a calculator to work from your price list.

Listen to your customer and make notes. If there is a lavish budget, each menu may be enhanced. Caviar, oysters, and Champagne can always be added, as well as hothouse fruits and vegetables out of season. Time-consuming, individually made hors d'oeuvres, miniature desserts, and other labor-intensive dishes can be included, too.

More often, however, you will find yourself trimming costs. A freshly tossed salad of inexpensive greens with the very best oil and vinegar is more memorable than endive poorly prepared. Make a large rectangular cake or tart and cut it into twenty-five portions rather than bake individual ones. Eliminate the appetizer and/or the soup. It is important to maintain a positive attitude about these alternatives and additions so that your client is assured he or she will have a beautifully presented spread. Steaming mugs of delicious soup, fresh salad, and savory sandwiches can be more fun than skimpy portions of expensive dishes.

Maintain an updated listing noting the availability of fresh foods in your area; fish, fruit, and vegetables vary with the seasons. It is vital to your reputation that you don't promise what you can't deliver. Pay attention to price changes. Large food companies list prices weekly, but most do it once a month. Dairy prices fluctuate regularly, as do specialty items. Always ask the purveyor or distributor the price of each item when you place your order. Never assume it is the same as it was the last time you looked. And remember, when you calculate costs you have to add rental items, special services, and nonfood items.

Menus change more frequently than recipes do. Fashions and trends are reflected in menus, but the largest number of dishes on them are still tried-and-true favorites, with some new accessories. This makes your job easier than it looks. Many of the recipes will already be in your files. Read the food pages of your local papers each week to keep up with food in the news. The Food Network and magazines will tell you a lot. Many of your patrons will get some of their ideas from those sources. Keep in mind that menu planning is essential not only for breakfast, lunch, and dinner, but for everything from cocktail parties to children's birthdays, receptions, barbecues, weddings, and holiday celebrations. You will receive requests that range from down-home to casual elegance, with a rare call for a traditionally formal affair.

The menu sets the mood. It also helps clients clarify exactly what they want and gives you an opportunity to make the notes that will serve as your outline for the specific job. It also opens the channels of communication in house and establishes the guidelines for your staff, schedule, shopping list, nonfood needs, preparation, and cleanup. Keep each used menu and mark it with the client's name, the date, how many people were served, and the location. Make a brief memo of the cost and fee paid. Take snapshots or Polaroids of the display. These will become part of your records so that your file will build and each successive job will be easier to estimate.

Before deciding on the menu, inquire about whether the service will be sit-down or buffet, or a combination. One possibility is hors d'oeuvres and appetizers as a buffet, or coffee and dessert from a buffet after a sit-down meal.

When you discuss menus with a customer, be prepared for individual preferences. A simple way to discuss alternatives is course by course. Are hors d'oeuvres and appetizers both required? Soup? (Remember it is not only the price of the soup that will be involved, but the extra prep time, setting pieces, and service.) Do you have to bake special bread, rolls, biscuits, and muffins, or will store-bought suffice? Crudités and salad? Will the entree(s) have to be prepared as individual portions, or will they be carved from a whole roast or served from a chafing dish? Do guests get a choice of entree? Will there be several relishes and accompaniments? Will vegetables be prepared simply or elaborately? Will there be fruit and cheese? Desserts have to be thought out carefully. Beverages must be planned in detail.

Your own recipe files will be a quick reference for you to calculate food prices on your job cost chart. If you price each menu out for 10, 25, and 50 people, you will be able to give your client a quick estimate. Some of the computer programs available for this are very helpful. While out-of-season strawberries are not in everybody's budget, apple tarts with a shiny raspberry glaze are a delicious alternative. Remember though, that while 10 individual tarts are not much more labor than 2 large ones, 50 individual ones will be more costly than fresh strawberries. Volume is as important as cost when figuring your fixed and variable expenses in order to arrive at your selling price. If you are ever on the spot, a rough rule of thumb is to offer a dish at five times the cost of the food itself.

If you envision each menu as a special occasion calling for certain kinds of foods, you will be able to provide your clients with a memorable meal. Go for the obvious unless begged not to. Traditional dishes with interesting variations and fresh interpretations are unbeatable. The quality of the preparation, special touches, and visual presentation are what make a meal an event.

Make sure the menus are clean and printed clearly. Many kinds of software will allow you to create your own logo and to format menus. Computer printers do a professional job, but if yours is not set up yet, the local copy shop can be used. If you have a logo, use it. If not, have your name printed boldly across the top, and make sure your address and phone number are printed somewhere on the menu as well.

Offer only four to six menus for any one meeting. Too many choices will only confuse your client. You must guide them and help them make a satisfactory decision. Early in the interview, you will ascertain how knowledgeable they are and how involved they want to be in the planning. It is your self-assurance and expert opinion that they are counting on, and most of the final choices are yours. The following menus cover many occasions that caterers are called on to provide for. These menus offer, for the most part, a fixed choice of main dishes. Use them as they are, or make them your own by adding or replacing your favorite dishes.

As a printing service for people who have various visual impairments, the Lighthouse Incorporated will duplicate any menu, invitation, or program in Braille or large-print text. The service generally takes a week to ten days. The average price is six dollars per page. Contact them at:

Lighthouse International
111 East 59 Street
New York, NY 10022-1202
Phone: 212-821-9200, 800-829-0500
Website: www.lighthouse.org

Sample Menus

New Year's Buffet

Easter Dinner

Passover Seder

Fourth of July Picnic

Thanksgiving Dinner

Christmas Day Dinner

Christmas Eve Supper

Wedding Reception

Graduation Party

Children's Birthday Party

Library Fund-Raiser

Executive Luncheon

Summer Garden Buffet

Summer Dinner

Autumn Lunch

Harvest Dinner

Winter Dinner

Spring Dinner

Chinese-Style Buffet

Indian Curry Buffet

French Dinner

Italian Dinner

Southern Hospitality

Santa Fe Supper

New Orleans Style

California Calorie Counter

American Tradition

New Year's Buffet

Madeira Consommé

Crinkled Chèvre Cups*

Assorted Small Muffins and Breads*

Flavored Butters

Sweet and Savory Confitures

Stuffed Hard-Cooked Eggs

Smoked Salmon Triangles*

Vegetable Slaw*

Mini Blini with Caviar*

Winter Fruit Compote

Raspberry Floating Island

Angel Food Cake*

Coffee, Tea, Mineral Water

Fresh-Squeezed Orange Juice

Mimosas, Bellinis

Champagne, Champagne Cocktails

Notes: [This space is for recommendations for visual presentation and service of each course, including substitutes and alternatives, and suggestions for buffet stations, table settings, dishes, flatware, glassware, linens, and decorations.]

Easter Dinner

Smoked Fish

Easter Eggs in Bread Nests

Asparagus and Sweet Red and Yellow Pepper Salad

Beet-Tangerine Salad*

Roast Lamb with Rosemary and Juniper

Squash Blossoms in Batter

Sweet and Sour Lentils

Pashka

Pascal Cake

Vanilla Fruit Salad

Coffee, Tea, Mineral Water

Assorted Juices, Wine

Notes:

Passover Seder

Traditional Seder Plate

Gefilte Fish with Horseradish Dressing

Chicken Soup with Matzoh Balls

Brisket of Beef

Sautéed Spinach

Tzimmes

Lemon-Walnut Soufflé Cake

Assorted Sorbets, Almond Macaroons

Coffee, Tea, Mineral Water

Passover Wine

Notes:

*Recipe given

Fourth of July Picnic

Hors d'Oeuvres*

Iced Cucumber and Shrimp Soup

Chicken Salad*

Pasta Salad with Leeks, Spinach, and Mint*

Broccoli Salad with Crespelle*

Tomato Salad with Fresh Basil

Assorted Breads, Breadsticks*

American-Flag Cake

Vanilla Mousse

Raspberry and Blueberry Sauce

Iced Coffee, Iced Tea

Mineral Water, Fruit Punch

Notes:

Thanksgiving Dinner

Quick Caviar Spirals*

Endive and Radicchio Leaves

Hummus*

Dipping Sauce* in a Hollow Pumpkin

Miniature Muffins (Pumpkin,* Cranberry, Double-Corn, Herb, Apple)

Flavored Butter and Fruit Butter

Roast Turkey with Mushroom-Giblet Gravy

Sausage, Chestnut, and Mushroom Stuffing

Cranberry-Beet Compote*

Tiny Onions and Raisins in Cassis

Baked Broccoli Puree

Maple Crisped Sweet Potatoes

Pecan Pie

Pumpkin-Mousse Pie

Coffee, Tea

Mineral Water, Cider

Fruit Wine

Notes:

*Recipe given

Christmas Day Dinner

Smoked Scallops and Shrimp

Red and Green Crudités

Roasted Eggplant Dip*

Saffron Buns

Naturally Cured Polish-Style Ham*

Maple-Glazed Apples, Pears, and Onions*

Sauteed Brussels Sprouts and Chestnuts*

Roasted Root Vegetables*

Cranberry Sauce with Kumquats and Dried Cherries

Pumpkin-Ginger Mousse*

Basket of Miniature Fruits

Walnut-Eggnog Cake*

Bûche de Noël

Coffee, Tea, Mineral Water

Eggnog, Wine, Assorted Liqueurs

Notes:

Christmas Eve Supper

Savory Puffs and Fritters

Seafood Bisque

Assorted Small Breads*

Tangy Halibut with Quick Tapenade*

Piquant Sweet Potatoes*

Scallops with Angel Hair Pasta in Lemon Cream Sauce*

Winter Green Salad with Sun-Dried Tomato–Hazelnut Dressing

Chestnut Trifle

Coffee, Tea

American Mineral Water

Fruit Wine

Notes:

Wedding Reception

Assorted Hot and Cold Hors d'Oeuvres*

Miniature Rolls

Whole Poached Salmon with Cucumber-Dill Dressing*

Fresh Fruit Salad on Bed of Mesclun

Crisp Duck à l'Orange*

Wild Rice and Mushrooms*

Asparagus Drizzled with Cream*

Strawberries and Whipped Cream

Wedding Cake with Edible Gold Leaf and Flowers

Chocolate-Champagne Truffles

Coffee, Tea, Mineral Water

Open Bar

Poured White and Red Wines

Champagne Toast

Notes:

Graduation Party

Roland Park Foolproof Pizza*

Caesar Salad*

Assorted Breads

Spaghetti with Rich Tomato-Mushroom Sauce*

Baked Ziti with Four Cheeses*

Fruit

Brownies, Chocolate-Chip Cookies

Popsicle Swirls

Mineral Water

Fresh Fruit Drinks

Iced Tea

Notes:

*Recipe given

Children's Birthday Party

Painted Cookie Place Cards

Carrot and Grapes Salad

Assorted Cut-Out Sandwiches

Salmon Burgers with Cranberry Ketchup*

Miniature Vegetables

Carousel Birthday Cake

Individually Molded Ice Cream

Flavored Skim Milk

Fresh Fruit Punch

Mineral Water

Notes:

Library Fund-Raiser

Emile Zola's Charcuterie

Tennyson's Dusky Loaves

Lewis Carroll's Soup of the Evening

Hemingway Lake Trout

John Hersey's Bluefish

Thomas Jefferson's Nouilly à Macaroni

Vegetables Alexandre Dumas

Veal Escalopes Colette

Mushroom Pudding Mrs. Joseph Conrad

Gertrude Stein's A Rose Is a Rose Sorbet and Lemon Ice Cream

Proust's Madeleines*

Coffee, Tea, Mineral Water

Champagne Cocktails

Wine

Notes:

Executive Luncheon

Wild Mushroom Soup

Mixed Green Salad

Assorted Small Biscuits*

Salmon Steaks*

Saffron Noodles*

Steamed Broccoli and Cauliflower

Individual Fruit Tarts

Fresh-Fruit Basket

Coffee, Tea, Mineral Water

Wine

Notes:

Summer Garden Buffet

Iced Fresh-Tomato Soup*

Deviled Eggs

Curried Charred Shrimp*

Assorted Biscuits*

Saffron Rice Seafood Salad*

Vegetables à la Grecque*

Skewered Chicken with Blueberry Dipping Sauce*

Roasted Potato Salad*

Corn and Barley Salad*

Berry Summer Pudding*

Melon Fruit Basket

Iced Coffee, Iced Tea

Mineral Water

Wine-Fruit Punch

Notes:

*Recipe given

Summer Dinner

Mixed Local Summer Field Salad

Pasta Salad Niçoise*

Small Crusty French Rolls

Regional Bouillabaisse*

Steamed Corn

Coleslaw*

White-Bean Salad*

Assorted Sorbets with Fresh Fruit

Pastel Petits Fours*

Coffee, Tea, Mineral Water

Regional Wine

Notes:

Autumn Lunch

Chicken Liver Salad*

Pumpkin Soup*

Zucchini Bread

Balsamic Roasted Pork with Prunes*

Sautéed Apples and Fennel

Polenta

Persimmon Pudding

Chocolate and Chocolate Cake*

Coffee, Tea, Mineral Water

Wine

Notes:

Harvest Dinner

Crab-Cake Bites with Maryland Crab Dipping Sauce*

Minestrone*

Assorted Grain Breads

Roasted Red Snapper*

Stuffed Small Squash

Andean Potatoes*

Bourbon-Pecan Bread Pudding*

Coffee, Tea, Mineral Water

Cider

Notes:

Winter Dinner

Alaska Shrimp Salad*

Deep-Green Split-Pea Soup*

Bread Basket*

Chicken Breasts Stuffed with Chèvre and Sun-Dried Tomatoes*

Polenta Squares*

Tomato Coulis*

Zucchini in Lemon-Mint Butter*

Winter Fruits

Chocolate Terrine in White-Chocolate Blizzard*

Coffee, Tea, Mineral Water

Wine

Notes:

*Recipe given

Spring Dinner

Endive, Watercress, and Citrus Salad

Wild Mushroom Soup

Assorted Small Breads

Tuna Medallions*

Cubed Potatoes*

Stir-Fried Broccoli*

Strawberry Shortcake

Coffee, Espresso, Tea

Mineral Water

Wine

Notes:

Chinese-Style Buffet

Assorted Steamed Dumplings

Skewered Pork and Papaya*

Plum Dipping Sauce*

Spiced Roasted Nuts*

Sweet and Sour Fish*

Szechuan Chicken Breasts*

Eggplants and Apricots*

Stir-Fried Snow Peas, Carrots, and Water Chestnuts*

Cold Sesame Noodles*

Rice with Black Mushrooms

Assorted Small Cakes

Citrus Salad

Tea, Mineral Water

Wine and Beer

Notes:

Indian Curry Buffet

Assorted Indian Breads (Paratha, Chapati, Puri)

Samosas (Filled Savory Pastries)

Pakoras (Vegetable Fritters)

Dosai (Stuffed Rice-Flour Pancakes)

Peas and Panir

Lentil Salad*

Beef Curry*

Shrimp and Cashew Curry

Peach Chutney*

Saffron Rice*

Seasoned Yogurt

Wild Rice and Carrot Cake*

Coffee, Tea, Mineral Water

Wine, Beer

Notes:

French Dinner

Hot Hors d'Oeuvres*

Duck Rillettes*

Crostini*

French Bread, Butter

Consommé à la Reine

Roast Beef Tenderloin with Madeira Sauce*

Braised Endive

Pommes Anna

Leaf Lettuce Salad

Individual Vacherins (Fruit Mousse in Meringue)

Coupe aux Marrons

Almond Tiles*

Coffee, Tea, Mineral Water

Wine

Notes:

*Recipe given

Italian Dinner

Antipasti Misti

Caponata*

Fennel with Shaved Parmesan*

Italian Bread, Bruschetta,* Breadsticks*

Chicken Scaloppine with Porcini Mushrooms

Spinach with Shallots, Pine Nuts, and Raisins*

Saffron Risotto*

Arugula Salad with Lemon-Walnut Dressing

Assorted Italian Cheeses

Semifreddo

Mixed Berries

Almond Biscotti*

Espresso, Cappuccino

Italian Mineral Water

Italian Wine Tasting

Notes:

Southern Hospitality

Tossed Salad with Edible Flowers

She-Crab Soup

Assorted Benne Rolls, Flavored Butters and Spreads

Southern-Fried Chicken in Biscuit Batter

Baked Yams

Sautéed Greens

Key Lime Sorbet

Peach Ice Cream

Pecan Pie

Coffee, Tea

Mineral Water

Virginia Wines

Notes:

Santa Fe Supper

Guacamole,* Salsa, Tortilla Chips

Corn-Bread Sticks,* Jalapeño Jam

Blue-Corn Muffins, Herbed Honey

Turkey Chili Mole*

Taco Salad*

Posole, New Mexican Style*

Fried Plantain Chips*

Chocolate and Chocolate Cake*

Piñon Ice Cream

Iced Chocolate, Cappuccino, Herb Teas

Mineral Water, Beer

Pitchers of Sangrita (mixture of tomato juice, grenadine,
orange juice, lime, and tequila)

Notes:

New Orleans Style

Crawfish Gratin

Sweet-Potato Bread

Blackened Catfish

Gumbo*

White Rice*

Pickled Vegetable Salad

Hush Puppies

Savory Sorbets

Mocha Cream Cake

Miniature Pralines

Coffee, Tea

Mineral Water

Wine

Notes:

*Recipe given

California Calorie Counter

Tangerine and Watercress Salad

Mushroom Consommé

Assorted Toasts

Baked Salmon Fillets on Roasted Tomatoes*

Steamed Baby Vegetables

Walnut Meringue Kisses

Raspberry Soufflé

Espresso, Tea

Mineral Water

Wine Spritzers

Notes:

An American Tradition

Mixed Green Salad

Assorted Biscuits and Muffins, Flavored Butters and Spreads

Clam Chowder*

Whole Maple-Roasted Chickens

Corn Bread and Pecan Stuffing

Boston Baked Beans*

Minted Carrots and Peas

Apple/Cherry Pies

Vanilla Ice Cream

Coffee, Tea

American Mineral Water

Regional American Wines

Notes:

*Recipe given

11

Recipe File

Mini Blini with Caviar

YIELD: 40 BLINI

1 envelope active dry yeast	2 eggs, separated
1 teaspoon sugar	1 teaspoon baking soda
½ cup warm (105° to 115°F) water	½ cup molasses
1 cup unbleached all-purpose flour	5 tablespoons unsalted butter, melted and cooled, plus butter for skillet
2 cups buckwheat flour	1 pint sour cream (optional)
1 cup buttermilk	8 ounces caviar or small red salmon roe
1 cup water	

1. In a large bowl, combine the yeast, sugar and warm water. Stir to dissolve the yeast. Let stand until foamy, about 10 minutes.

2. Stir in the flours, buttermilk, and water. Cover and let stand for 1 hour or refrigerate for 4 to 8 hours.

3. In a large bowl, beat the egg whites until stiff, glossy peaks form. In a small bowl, stir the baking soda into the molasses. Beat the egg yolks and melted butter into the batter, then fold in the molasses mixture.

4. Drop the batter by tablespoonfuls onto a lightly buttered griddle or large skillet. Cook until the edges bubble. Turn and cook about 30 seconds longer, or until firm.

5. Transfer to a warmed platter. Keep warm in a low oven. Repeat to cook the remaining batter.

6. To serve, top each blini with 1 teaspoon sour cream, if you like. Top with ½ teaspoon caviar and serve at once.

Jalapeño-Cheese Wafers

YIELD: 50 WAFERS

1¼ cups (5 ounces) shredded
Monterey Jack cheese with
jalapeño chiles

¾ cup all-purpose flour
5 tablespoons unsalted butter at
room temperature

1. In a medium bowl, combine all the ingredients and stir to blend.

2. Shape into a 1½-inch-thick log about 8 inches long. Roll in plastic wrap and refrigerate for 1 hour, or until firm.

3. Preheat the oven to 350°F. Line baking sheets with aluminum foil. Slice the dough to a ⅛-inch thickness. Place on the prepared baking sheets.

4. Bake for 12 minutes, or until the edges are slightly browned. Using a metal spatula, transfer to wire racks and cool slightly before serving. It may be necessary to peel the foil away.

Smoked Salmon Triangles

YIELD: 50 TRIANGLES

25 thin slices pumpernickel or rye bread, crusts trimmed

1½ cups (12 ounces) cream cheese at room temperature

3 tablespoons sour cream

2 tablespoons prepared red horseradish

2 lemons

8 ounces smoked salmon

50 capers, drained

Assorted olives for serving

Parsley springs and lemon slices for garnish

1. Cut each bread slice in half diagonally. In a small bowl, combine the cream cheese, sour cream, and horseradish. Stir to blend. Spread thinly on the bread.

2. Cut the lemons into paper-thin slices, then cut each slice into quarters. Cut salmon the slices into triangles and place a slice on each piece of bread. Top with a piece of lemon and a caper.

3. Accompany with olives and garnish with parsley and lemon slices.

Crinkled Chèvre Cups

YIELD: 48 CUPS

1 pound fresh or thawed frozen phyllo dough

1 cup (3 ounces) dry-packed sun-dried tomatoes, minced

2 fresh white goat cheese logs (9 ounces each)

1 cup (½ pound) unsalted butter, melted

1. Preheat the oven to 350°F. Butter a baking sheet.

2. Unroll the phyllo on a flat surface and cover with waxed paper, then a damp kitchen towel, to prevent it from drying out.

3. In a small bowl, combine the tomatoes and 1 cup hot water. Let stand until the tomatoes are softened, about 10 minutes.

4. Cut each cheese log in quarters lengthwise, and each quarter into 6 pieces. Drain the tomatoes and place on a flat dish.

5. Place a sheet of phyllo on a work surface and brush it with melted butter. Fold it in half and butter the surface. Press some tomato pieces around pieces of the cheese. Center the cheese on the folded phyllo and wrap the dough once tightly then again loosely around the cheese so that the outside resembles crumpled paper. Brush lightly with butter and place on the prepared baking sheet. Repeat with the remaining ingredients.

6. Bake for 15 minutes, or until golden brown. Carefully cut in half and serve cheese side up. The cups may be frozen before baking and baked just before serving.

Crab-Cake Bites with Maryland Crab Dipping Sauce

YIELD: 50 BITES

2 celery stalks

2 eggs, beaten

1/4 cup mayonnaise

1/4 cup dry white wine

1 teaspoon freshly ground black pepper

1/2 teaspoon coarse salt

1/4 teaspoon cayenne

1 1/2 pounds cooked crab meat, flaked

2 cups unsalted cracker crumbs

1 large onion, grated

1/4 cup minced fresh parsley

2 egg whites

3 tablespoons olive oil

3 tablespoons unsalted butter

Maryland Dipping Sauce (recipe follows)

1. Remove the strings from the celery and cut the celery into small dice. In a large bowl, combine the eggs, mayonnaise, wine, black pepper, salt, and cayenne. Stir to blend. Stir in the crab meat, cracker crumbs, onion, celery, and parsley.

2. In a medium bowl, beat the egg whites until soft peaks form, then fold into the crab mixture.

3. Melt the butter with the oil in large skillet over medium-high heat and drop tablespoonfuls of the crab mixture into the hot pan. Cook for 3 minutes, or until browned. Turn and cook for 2 or 3 minutes on the other side, or until browned. Using a slotted metal spatula, transfer to a baking sheet and keep warm in a low oven. Repeat to cook the remaining mixture.

4. Serve at once, with the dipping sauce.

Maryland Crab Dipping Sauce

YIELD: 3 CUPS

1 cup mayonnaise

½ cup mild mustard

¾ cup ketchup

½ cup drained pickle relish

¼ cup prepared white
horseradish

1 tablespoon Maryland crab
seasoning

¼ to ½ teaspoon hot pepper
sauce

In a medium bowl, combine all the ingredients and stir to blend. Cover
and refrigerate until ready to serve.

Duck Rillettes

YIELD: 2½ POUNDS

1 tablespoon coarse salt	One 5-pound duck with liver
¼ teaspoon each ground cloves, ground nutmeg, ground cinnamon, ground coriander, crumbled dried basil, dried thyme, and ground white pepper	1 cup dry red wine
	¼ cup Cognac
	6 shallots, minced
	Cornichons and warm crostini (recipe follows)

1. In a small bowl, combine the salt, cloves, nutmeg, cinnamon, coriander, basil, thyme, and white pepper. Stir to blend. Rub the duck inside and out with the salt mixture. Cover and refrigerate overnight.

2. Preheat the oven to 400°F. Quarter the duck and place with the liver on a rack in a roasting pan. Roast for 30 minutes. Drain the fat in small saucepan and reserve. Remove the liver and set aside. Continue roasting the duck for 1½ hours, or until very tender. Remove the duck to a platter.

3. Turn the oven off. Add the wine, Cognac, and shallots to the liquid in the roasting pan and stir. Return to the oven until ready to use.

4. Remove the skin from the duck and mince. Debone the meat and shred. Mince the duck liver. Stir the meat, liver, and skin into the liquid in the roasting pan. Transfer the mixture to a ceramic bowl or a 2-quart soufflé dish.

5. Cover and refrigerate for 3 hours, stirring every 30 minutes. If after 3 hours there is not enough fat on the surface to cover the duck mixture, cover with the reserved fat in saucepan.

6. Cover and refrigerate for up to one week. Just before serving, scrape the surface fat away. Serve with the cornichons and crostini.

Crostini

YIELD: 100 CROSTINI

6 baguettes, 12 ounces each   ½ teaspoon coarse salt
1 tablespoon herbes de Provence   ¾ cup olive oil

1. Preheat the oven to 350°F. Cut the bread into ¼-inch-thick slices. (If the baguettes are very narrow, cut on a diagonal.)

2. Mix the herbs and salt together. Arrange the bread slices in a single layer on baking sheets. Drizzle with olive oil and sprinkle with the herbed salt. Bake for 10 minutes, or until the edges are golden brown.

Skewered Chicken with Blueberry Dipping Sauce

YIELD: 50 SKEWERS

3 pounds boneless, skinless chicken breasts

Marinade:

1 tablespoon sesame oil	Pinch of cayenne (optional)
1 tablespoon olive oil	2 garlic cloves, minced
1 tablespoon curry powder	1½ cups orange juice
1 teaspoon ground cumin	½ cup reduced-sodium soy sauce

Blueberry Dipping Sauce (recipe follows)

1. Slice the chicken into thin strips and set aside.

2. To make the marinade, heat the oils in a small saucepan over medium-low heat. Stir in the curry powder, cumin, and cayenne. Add the garlic and cook for 1 minute; do not brown. Stir in the orange juice and soy sauce. Remove from heat.

3. Place the chicken and marinade in a shallow pan. Cover and refrigerate for 2 hours. Soak 50 wooden skewers in water for 30 minutes; drain.

4. Light a fire in a charcoal grill, preheat a gas grill to high, or preheat a broiler. Grill or broil for 3 minutes on each side, or until browned.

5. Serve warm, with the dipping sauce.

Blueberry Dipping Sauce

YIELD: 2 CUPS

3 cups blueberries

1 lemon, seeded and minced

1 cup packed brown sugar

½ cup granulated sugar

¾ cup raspberry or other berry vinegar

1 teaspoon ground allspice

1 teaspoon ground ginger

1. Combine all the ingredients in a nonreactive medium saucepan and bring to a boil. Reduce the heat to low and simmer for 30 minutes, stirring frequently.

2. Cover and refrigerate until chilled, at least 1 hour.

Curried Charred Shrimp

YIELD: ABOUT 50 SHRIMP

¼ cup olive oil

4 tablespoons unsalted butter

2 pounds shrimp (23 to 26/pound), peeled, with tails left on

3 tablespoons curry powder

1 teaspoon ground allspice

1 teaspoon paprika

Candied kumquats for garnish

1. Preheat the broiler.

2. Melt the butter with the oil in an ovenproof skillet over low heat. Stir in the curry powder, allspice, paprika, and shrimp and cook for 3 minutes. Place under the broiler about 4 inches from the heat source for 1 or 2 minutes, or until the shrimp are slightly charred.

3. Using a slotted spoon, transfer to paper towels to drain. Arrange on a platter and garnish with candied kumquats, if you wish.

Skewered Pork and Papaya

YIELD: 50 SKEWERS

For this recipe, use 6-inch wooden skewers that have been soaked in water for at least half an hour.

2½ pounds boneless pork

3 cups reduced-sodium soy sauce

1 cup honey

½ cup dry sherry

¼ cup minced peeled fresh ginger

2 large papayas, peeled, seeded, and cut into ¾-inch cubes

Plum Dipping Sauce for serving (recipe follows)

1. Trim excess fat from pork. Cut meat into ¾-inch cubes.

2. In a large bowl, combine the soy sauce, honey, sherry, and ginger; mix well. Add the pork and stir to coat. Marinate, covered, in the refrigerator for 3 hours.

3. Light a fire in a charcoal grill, preheat a gas grill to high, or preheat a broiler.

4. Alternately thread the pork and papaya on 50 small skewers. Broil or grill for 8 minutes, turning occasionally, or until the pork is fully cooked. Serve with the plum sauce alongside.

Plum Dipping Sauce

YIELD: 1 PINT

8 ounces purple plums, pitted and minced

1 cup ginger marmalade

1 cup reduced-sodium soy sauce

¼ cup Chinese-style mustard

Combine all the ingredients in a medium nonreactive saucepan. Bring to a slow boil, stirring occasionally. Remove from heat and serve warm or cold.

Guacamole

YIELD: 1 QUART

6 large ripe avocados, peeled and pitted (reserve 1 pit)

4 large ripe tomatoes, peeled, seeded, and diced

6 cloves garlic, minced

2 tablespoons chili powder

Juice of 2 limes, plus grated zest of 1 lime

½ cup minced fresh cilantro leaves

Tortilla chips for serving

1. In a nonreactive bowl, mash the avocados until creamy but still a little lumpy. Stir in the tomatoes. Add the garlic, chili powder, and lime juice and zest. Top with the cilantro.

2. If not serving immediately, insert the reserved avocado pit in the center of the guacamole, cover with plastic wrap pressed onto the surface, and refrigerate.

3. Serve at room temperature with tortilla chips.

Spiced Roasted Nuts

YIELD: 3 CUPS

3 cups whole almonds

½ cup packed brown sugar

2 tablespoons safflower oil

1 tablespoon crushed hot red pepper

1. Preheat the oven to 300°F. In a medium bowl, combine all the ingredients and stir. Spread on a nonstick baking sheet.

2. Bake for 10 minutes. Drain on paper towels. Serve warm.

Hot Honey Pecans

YIELD: 3 CUPS

3 tablespoons unsalted butter

2 tablespoons honey

½ teaspoon hot pepper sauce

3 cups pecan halves

1. Melt the butter in a large skillet over low heat. Add the honey and hot sauce. Stir in the pecans until evenly coated. Remove from heat and let cool.

2. Serve immediately or cool and store for up to 4 hours. Reheat in a low oven for 10 minutes to serve after storing.

Curried Walnuts

YIELD: 3 CUPS

2 tablespoons unsalted butter

2 tablespoons safflower oil

2 teaspoons curry powder

3 cups walnut halves

1. Preheat the oven to 350°F. Melt the butter with the oil in a small saucepan over low heat. Stir in the curry powder, then add the walnuts, stirring until well coated. Spread on a baking sheet.

2. Bake for 10 minutes. Spread on paper towels to drain.

Blue-Cheese Puffs

YIELD: 50 PUFFS

Pâte à Choux:

1 cup water

6 tablespoons unsalted butter

¼ teaspoon salt

1 cup instant flour (Wondra)

5 eggs

Blue-Cheese Filling:

8 ounces blue cheese, crumbled

3 ounces cream cheese at room temperature

½ cup milk or nonfat plain yogurt

½ cup chopped walnuts

Confectioners' sugar for dusting

1. Preheat the oven to 400°F. Butter foil-lined baking sheets and set aside.

2. To make the choux paste: In a large saucepan, combine the water, butter, and salt. Bring to a boil over medium heat. Remove from heat and add the flour all at once, beating vigorously until it forms a ball. Beat in the eggs one at a time.

3. Fill a pastry bag fitted with a ½-inch-diameter plain tip and drop ½-inch pieces 2 inches apart on the prepared baking sheets. Bake for 10 minutes. Reduce the oven temperature to 350°F and bake for 15 minutes longer, or until the sides are firm and golden brown.

4. Remove the pans from the oven and turn the oven off. Pierce each puff in the side with a small knife. Cut a cap from the top of each puff.

5. Replace the tops and return to the oven for 15 minutes. The puffs may be frozen before or after filling and warmed in oven or microwave before serving.

6. To make the filling: In a small bowl, blend the cheeses with the milk until smooth. Stir in the walnuts.

7. Fill each puff and set on baking sheets. Warm in a preheated 200°F oven for 10 minutes before serving. Place on a platter, dust lightly with confectioners' sugar, and serve at once.

Quick Caviar Spirals

YIELD: 50 SPIRALS

3 frozen 9-inch pie shells, thawed

8 ounces cream cheese at room temperature

¼ cup sour cream or milk

5 shallots, minced

6 ounces inexpensive black caviar, such as lumpfish

1. Preheat the oven to 325°F. Butter 2 baking sheets.

2. Gently press the pie shells flat. In a small bowl, mix the cream cheese, sour cream, and shallots together until smooth. Stir in the sour cream or milk. Divide the mixture among the 3 shells and spread evenly. Spoon the caviar in a 5-inch band across each shell.

3. Roll up each shell jelly-roll fashion. Trim the ends and cut the rolls into ½-inch-thick slices. Set, cut side down, on the prepared baking sheets.

4. Bake for 20 minutes. Serve warm, not hot.

Bruschetta

YIELD: 40 TOASTS

2 pounds Italian bread

1½ pounds mozzarella cheese, shredded (6 cups)

7 large red bell peppers, roasted, peeled, and cut into thin strips (see note)

1½ cups finely chopped fresh basil

1 cup extra-virgin olive oil

Coarse salt for sprinkling

1. Preheat the broiler. Cut the bread into ½-inch-thick slices and arrange on baking sheets.

2. Reduce the oven temperature to 350°F. Arrange the cheese, peppers, and basil on the bread slices. Toast for 5 minutes, or until edges are golden brown. Drizzle with olive oil and coarse salt before serving.

Variation: Substitute 3 pounds peeled, seeded, and chopped tomatoes for the peppers.

ROASTING PEPPERS: Preheat the broiler. Cut the peppers in half, seed, and derib. Place the peppers, cut side down, on a broiler pan and broil as close to the heat source as possible until the skins blacken and bubble. Place the peppers in a paper bag, twist shut, and steam for 3 minutes. Peel and slice into thin strips.

Caponata

YIELD: 20 SERVINGS

2 medium onions, sliced

¾ cup olive oil

1 can (28 ounces) tomato puree

½ cup dry red wine

½ cup sugar

2 eggplants, each about 9 inches long, cut into large dice

Coarse salt for sprinkling

¾ cup balsamic vinegar

1 head celery

1½ ounces salted capers, rinsed

½ cup coarsely chopped flat-leaf parsley

½ pound pitted large green olives, halved or quartered

1. In a large heavy saucepan over medium heat, cook the onions in ¼ cup of the olive oil until translucent. Stir in the tomato puree, wine, and sugar. Cook until bubbly. Reduce the heat and simmer for 30 minutes, or until the sauce becomes dark and thick.

2. Place the eggplant in a colander set over a large bowl or sink, sprinkle with salt, and let stand for 20 to 30 minutes, until moisture is extracted. Squeeze the moisture from the eggplant, using your hands or a square of cheesecloth. Heat the remaining olive oil in a large skillet. Sauté for 10 to 15 minutes, or until tender. Add more olive oil as needed.

3. Stir the vinegar into the tomato sauce, then add the eggplant. Cut the celery 5 inches from the root end and reserve the tops for another use. Separate into stalks and remove the strings. Cut into large dice and blanch in boiling water for 3 minutes. Drain and run under cold water to keep crisp. Add the capers, parsley, olives, and celery to the tomato sauce and stir over low heat for 5 minutes.

4. Remove from heat and let cool. Taste and adjust the seasoning. Cover and refrigerate for up to 3 days.

Hummus

YIELD: 6 CUPS

3 cups cooked chickpeas

1 cup tahini (Middle Eastern sesame paste)

1 cup water

½ cup olive oil

Juice of 2 lemons

3 tablespoons minced fresh flat-leaf parsley, plus sprigs for garnish

3 tablespoons minced fresh mint, plus sprigs for garnish

Crudités, pita bread, or crackers for serving

1. In a large bowl, mash the chickpeas with a potato masher. Set aside. In a medium bowl, blend the tahini, water, olive oil, lemon juice, and minced herbs until creamy. Add to the mashed chickpeas and blend.

2. Garnish with sprigs of parsley and mint and serve.

Roasted Eggplant Dip

YIELD: 6 CUPS

4 green bell peppers
4 large eggplants
8 garlic cloves
½ cup olive oil

1 teaspoon coarse salt
¼ teaspoon black pepper
Pomegranate seeds for garnish
Toasted pita-bread triangles for serving

1. Cook the eggplants over a direct flame or under a broiler close to the heat source for 20 minutes or until the eggplants are charred and runny, turning often to char skin. Alternatively, cut the eggplants in half lengthwise, rub all over with olive oil, and place cut-side down on a baking sheet; bake in a preheated 350°F oven for 45 minutes. Cut the eggplants in half and the scrape flesh from the skin into a large bowl. Discard the skin.

2. Char the green peppers like the eggplant, turning until the skin is blackened. Place a in paper bag, twist shut, and let cool to the touch. Remove and discard the skins and place the flesh in the bowl.

3. Chop the eggplant and green peppers until minced and mushy. Squeeze the garlic cloves through a press (discard the fibers that do not go through) into the olive oil and mix with the salt and pepper. Stir into the eggplant mixture. Cover and refrigerate until ready to serve.

4. Garnish with pomegranate seeds just before serving with toasted pita-bread triangles.

Vegetables à la Grecque

SERVES 50

2 cups dry white wine

1 cup olive oil

1 tablespoon dried thyme

6 bay leaves

4 sprigs fresh tarragon

4 garlic cloves stuck with several whole cloves

2 lemons, seeded and cut in half

3 pounds small white mushrooms

3 pounds baby green beans, trimmed

3 pounds mixed baby green and yellow zucchini

1 head cauliflower, separated into florets

2 pounds small white onions, peeled

1. In a large nonreactive saucepan, combine the wine, olive oil, thyme, bay leaves, tarragon, garlic, and 2 cups of water. Squeeze in the lemon juice and add the lemon halves. Simmer for 10 minutes; remove the lemon pieces. Add the mushrooms, bring to a boil, reduce the heat, and simmer for 15 minutes. Remove with a slotted spoon.

2. Add the green beans, simmer for 8 minutes, and remove. Add the zucchini and simmer for 6 minutes. Add the cauliflower and onions. Cook for 20 minutes. Drain, reserving the liquid.

3. Arrange all the vegetables on a rimmed platter, cover, and refrigerate at least 2 hours before serving.

4. Trim into bite-sized pieces. Serve on a bed of greens, drizzled with a little of the drained sauce.

Fennel with Shaved Parmesan

SERVES 20

6 large fennel bulbs, trimmed

½ cup extra-virgin olive oil

½ teaspoon coarse salt (optional)

10 ounces Parmesan cheese, shaved

Freshly ground pepper and freshly grated nutmeg to taste

1. Cut the fennel bulb into quarters and slice thinly with a food processor or by hand.

2. Arrange the fennel on a platter. Drizzle with olive oil and sprinkle with salt. Top with the shaved Parmesan. Grind pepper and grate nutmeg over all before serving.

Alaska Shrimp Salad

SERVES 20

1 cup mayonnaise

1 cup nonfat plain yogurt

1 cup marinated artichoke hearts, drained

⅓ cup pickle relish, drained

12 heads Belgian endive

1½ pounds cooked tiny pink shrimp (about 400 per pound)

1. In a medium bowl, blend the mayonnaise, yogurt, artichoke hearts, and relish.

2. Separate the endive leaves and arrange on plates or a platter. Top with the artichoke sauce. Arrange the shrimp over all.

Pasta Salad with Leeks, Spinach, and Mint

SERVES 20

3 pounds fresh papardelle, cut into 1½-inch lengths, or dried bow-tie pasta

5 leeks, white part only

⅔ cup olive oil

4 pounds spinach, stemmed, well washed, and shredded

½ cup chopped mint leaves

Salt and freshly ground pepper to taste

Freshly ground nutmeg to taste

1. Cook the pasta in a large pot of salted boiling water until tender, about 1 minute past al dente. Drain and place in a bowl of cold water until ready to use.

2. Cut the leeks in half lengthwise and cut into 1½-inch-thick slices. Heat the olive oil in a large skillet over medium-high heat. Add the leeks and sauté until lightly browned, 5 to 7 minutes. Turn off heat and stir in the spinach and mint.

3. Drain the pasta and toss to remove as much moisture as possible. In a large bowl, mix the pasta and vegetables together with salt and pepper and chill. Grind nutmeg over pasta before serving.

Pasta Salad Niçoise

SERVES 20

3 pounds multiflavored spiral pasta

¾ cup extra-virgin olive oil

⅓ cup white wine or other vinegar

2 pounds fresh tuna, diced

1 pound pitted ripe olives

1 pound diced boiled new potatoes

¼ cup drained capers

2 large red onions, diced

1 cup marinated or canned artichoke hearts, drained

½ cup marinated pimientos, diced and drained

Lettuce leaves

Sliced hard-cooked eggs and anchovies for garnish

1. In a large pot of salted boiling water, cook the pasta until al dente, about 10 minutes. Run under cold water and drain well. In a large bowl, toss with the oil and vinegar and chill.

2. Add the tuna, olives, potatoes, capers, onions, artichokes, and pimientos to the pasta.

3. Serve in a salad bowl for a buffet, or plate individually over lettuce leaves, arranging the ingredients in layers. Garnish with the sliced eggs and anchovies.

Saffron Rice and Seafood Salad

SERVES 50

1 cup olive oil

1 cup sherry vinegar

1 cup minced shallots

2 pounds cooked tiny shrimp

2 pounds cooked small squid

2 pounds cooked small scallops

1 quart mussels, steamed

3 quarts cold saffron rice (recipe follows)

Grated zest of 2 oranges

3 cups orange sections

1 large bunch Italian flat-leaf parsley, coarsely chopped

2 pounds green peas, shelled

1. In a large bowl, combine the oil, vinegar, and shallots. Whisk to blend. Add the seafood and toss to coat.

2. In another large bowl, combine the saffron rice, orange zest, and sections. Top with the seafood mixture. Mix the parsley and peas together. Place around the salad.

Saffron Rice

3 quarts water

1 pinch saffron threads (approximately 1/2 teaspoon)

Salt to taste

5 cups rice

1. Bring the water to a boil over high heat. Add the saffron and salt. Stir in the rice. Cover the pot. Lower heat to medium and cook 30 minutes or until each grain is tender.

2. Strain if necessary. Place in a large bowl and cool. Cover and refrigerate 3 hours or overnight.

Coleslaw

SERVES 50

2 cups raisins

2 cups apple juice

8 pounds cabbage

2 pounds carrots, scraped

2 cups mayonnaise

1 cup safflower oil

1 cup cider vinegar

3 tablespoons caraway seeds

2 tablespoons ground cumin

Salt and freshly ground pepper to taste

1. In a medium bowl, combine the raisins and apple juice. Let stand for about 20 minutes; drain.

2. Meanwhile, shred the cabbage and carrots.

3. In a very large bowl, combine the cabbage, carrots, and raisins. In a medium bowl, whisk together the mayonnaise, oil, vinegar, caraway, and cumin. Add the dressing to the slaw and toss to mix. Season with salt and pepper.

Chicken Salad

SERVES 50

Stalks from 1 head celery

2 pounds apples, peeled, cored, and cubed

2 pounds pears, peeled, cored, and cubed

Juice of ½ lemon

3 yellow bell peppers, roasted, peeled, and sliced

3 bunches watercress, trimmed

9 pounds cooked skinless, boneless chicken breast, cubed

2 cups walnut oil

1 cup sherry vinegar

¼ cup minced fresh tarragon

4 garlic cloves, minced

10 shallots, minced

Freshly ground pepper to taste

1 pound walnut pieces

Minced jalepeño chili to taste

Flat-leaf parsley or cilantro sprigs for garnish

1. Carefully remove the strings from the celery and slice the celery. Place the apples and pears in ice water with the lemon juice added. Drain the fruit.

2. In a large bowl, combine the celery, fruit, bell peppers, watercress, and chicken.

3. In a medium bowl, whisk the oil and vinegar together. Add half the tarragon, the garlic, shallots, and pepper. Blend. Toss the salad with the dressing and stir in the rest of the fresh tarragon and the walnuts. Garnish with parsley or cilantro.

Roasted Potato Salad

12 pounds potatoes, cut into
1-inch cubes

3 cups olive oil

Several sprigs fresh rosemary

2 cups white wine vinegar

8 bunches scallions, chopped

Salt and freshly ground pepper
to taste

1. Preheat the oven to 375°F. Place the potatoes in a shallow baking pan and coat with some of the oil. Place the rosemary sprigs over the potatoes. Roast for 20 minutes, or until tender when pierced with a skewer.

2. Combine the scallions with the remaining oil and the vinegar. Toss the scallion mixture with the potatoes. Add salt and pepper. Serve warm, at room temperature, or chilled.

Chicken Liver Salad

SERVES 20

5 heads garlic, tops cut off

½ cup olive oil

3 pounds chicken livers

1 cup Marsala

Grated zest and juice of 2
oranges

¼ cup raspberry vinegar

Leaves from 4 heads frisée,
torn into bite-sized pieces

8 ounces walnuts

½ cup minced parsley leaves

1. Preheat the oven to 350°F. Rub the garlic with some of the olive oil
and place on a baking sheet sprinkled with olive oil. Roast for 45 minutes, or until soft. Remove from the oven and let cool.

2. Clean the chicken livers and remove all membranes. Sauté in oil, add
the Marsala, and cook, stirring to scrape up the browned bits from the
bottom of the pan, until tender and cooked through. Using a slotted
spoon, transfer the livers to a plate and keep warm.

3. Add the orange zest and juice to the pan. Stir and remove from heat.
Add the remaining oil and the vinegar and whisk to blend.

4. On plates or a platter, place a bed of frisée, the chicken livers, walnuts, and individual garlic cloves, which have been squeezed from their
skins. Top with dressing and garnish with parsley.

Cooked Caesar-Salad Dressing

YIELD: 3 CUPS

6 egg yolks

½ cup wine vinegar

Juice of 2 lemons

1 teaspoon dry mustard

Dash of Worcestershire sauce

1 cup olive oil

½ cup safflower oil

1. In a small heavy saucepan, combine the egg yolks, vinegar, lemon juice, mustard, and Worcestershire. Cook over low heat, whisking constantly. Increase heat to medium and keep whisking until mixture thickens and starts to bubble. Remove from heat and let cool, stirring occasionally.

2. Whisk in the oils until well blended. Use now or refrigerate until needed. Shake or whisk before using.

Croutons

YIELD: 5 DOZEN

3 tablespoons olive oil

2 garlic cloves

4 slices white bread, crusts removed, each cut into 16 cubes

1. In a large skillet, heat the olive oil and garlic over medium heat until golden brown, about 5 minutes.

2. Add the bread cubes and brown on all sides in the oil. Using a slotted spoon, transfer to paper towels to drain.

White-Bean Salad

SERVES 20

5 cups cooked white beans

1 cup toasted walnut pieces (see note)

1 fennel bulb, trimmed and diced

¼ cup walnut oil

½ cup extra-virgin olive oil

¼ cup sherry vinegar

4 yellow peppers, roasted, peeled, seeded, and cut into strips

Italian flat-leaf parsley sprigs and lemon slices for garnish

1. Mix all the ingredients except the peppers and garnishes.

2. Place the pepper strips on top. Garnish with parsley and lemon slices.

TO TOAST WALNUTS: Preheat the oven to 350°F. Spread the nuts in a single layer on a baking sheet. Bake for 15 minutes.

Taco Salad

SERVES 20

Leaves from 3 large heads lettuce

2 bunches red radishes, trimmed

4 carrots, scraped

2 jalapeño chiles, seeded and minced

2 canned jalapeño chiles, or to taste, minced

2½ cups prepared green salsa

20 corn tortillas, crisped in the oven

12 large ripe tomatoes, sliced

4 large avocados, peeled, pitted, and sliced

2 pounds Monterey Jack cheese, cut into thin julienne strips

2½ pounds cooked chicken, cut into thin julienne strips

Sour cream for garnish

1. Shred the lettuce, radishes, and carrots.

2. In a small bowl, combine the chilies and salsa; stir to blend.

3. On individual plates or on platters, layer the tortillas, lettuce, carrots, radishes, and tomatoes. Place the chicken and cheese over the salad. Top with the avocados and chili mixture. Garnish with dollops of sour cream.

Beet-Tangerine Salad

SERVES 20

4 pounds medium beets, scrubbed

4 pounds unpeeled small onions

¾ cup ginger marmalade

½ cup cider vinegar

¼ cup olive oil

1 tablespoon Dijon mustard

Salt and freshly ground pepper to taste

10 tangerines, peeled and sectioned

1. Preheat the oven to 400°F. Trim the beets to ½ inch of stem end. Place the beets and onions on a baking sheet and bake for 45 minutes to 1 hour, or until tender when pierced with a knife. While still warm, peel and slice.

2. Place the beets, onions, and tangerine sections in a large bowl. In a small saucepan, combine the marmalade, vinegar, oil, mustard, salt, and pepper. Stir until blended. Heat over low heat until warm. In a large bowl, toss the beet, onions, and tangerines with the dressing. Pour over the salad and toss to coat. Cover and refrigerate until chilled, at least 2 hours.

Lentil Salad

SERVES 20

1½ pounds lentils

¼ cup olive oil

3 red onions, diced

2 cucumbers, peeled, seeded, and diced

Salt and freshly ground pepper to taste

2 tablespoons dried fines herbes

2 cups (10 ounces) fresh white goat cheese, crumbled

1 bunch Italian flat-leaf parsley, chopped

1. In a large saucepan, combine the lentils and 3½ cups water. Bring to a boil, reduce the heat to low, and simmer for 25 minutes or until tender but firm; drain. Let cool.

2. Stir in the oil, red onions, cucumbers, salt, pepper, and herbs. Top with crumbled cheese and parsley.

Shredded Vegetable Slaw

SERVES 20

3 pounds broccoli

6 carrots, scraped

4 turnips, peeled

1 small head red cabbage

1½ cups olive oil

1 cup safflower oil

¾ cup sherry vinegar

Juice of 1 lemon

3 tablespoons Dijon mustard

2 tablespoons sugar

Salt and pepper to taste

1. Using a food processor fitted with a shredding disc, shred the broccoli. Blanch in boiling water for 2 minutes; drain. Using the julienne disc, shred the other vegetables.

2. In a large bowl, combine all the vegetables.

3. In a medium bowl, whisk the olive oil, safflower oil, vinegar, lemon juice, mustard, and sugar. Add to the vegetables and toss to coat. Season with salt and pepper.

Broccoli Salad with Crespelle

SERVES 20

2½ pounds broccoli

6 red bell peppers

½ cup dry white wine

½ cup heavy cream

Crespelle:

6 eggs, separated

⅓ cup all-purpose flour

6 tablespoons grated Parmesan cheese

1 cup olive oil

2 garlic cloves

2 tablespoons prepared mustard

Freshly grated nutmeg to taste

¼ cup butter

¼ cup oil

1. Cut the broccoli into florets and the stems into slices. Blanch in boiling water for 2 to 3 minutes, or until crisp-tender. Drain and let cool.

2. Halve and seed the red peppers. Broil or place in 475°F oven for 10 minutes until skin blisters. Place in a paper bag, twist closed, and let stand for a few minutes. Rub skin off and slice into matchsticks.

3. In a blender, blend the wine, cream, oil, garlic, and mustard until smooth. Toss with the vegetables, adding the dressing slowly so that none pools on the bottom.

4. To make the crespelle: In a large bowl, whisk the egg yolks, flour, and Parmesan cheese together. In a large bowl, beat the egg whites until soft peaks form. Fold into the yolk mixture with the nutmeg.

5. In an 8-inch omelet or crepe pan, melt the butter with the oil as needed over medium heat. Add ¼ cup batter at a time, turning the pan to coat the bottom. Cook like omelets, pulling the batter back from the sides for the top to set. (You will have 4 or 5 pancakes.)

6. Roll each pancake and let cool. Slice the rolls on the diagonal and gently fold into the salad.

Corn and Barley Salad

SERVES 20

4 cups cooked barley

3 cups cooked corn kernels

3 tablespoons snipped fresh dill

1 tablespoon chopped fresh chives

1½ cups olive oil

½ cup fresh lemon juice

¼ teaspoon ground white pepper

1 quart cherry tomatoes for garnish

1. In a large bowl, mix the barley, corn, dill, and chives.

2. In a small bowl, whisk the olive oil, lemon juice, and pepper together. Pour over the salad and toss. Serve surrounded by the cherry tomatoes.

Saffron Buns

YIELD: 36 BUNS

1 cup milk

½ cup (¼ pound) unsalted butter, melted

1 teaspoon saffron threads, crumbled

1 envelope active dry yeast dissolved in ¼ cup warm (105° to 115°F) water

2 tablespoons sugar

2 eggs, beaten

4 cups unbleached all-purpose flour

½ teaspoon salt

½ cup chopped candied orange peel

½ cup dried currants

½ cup chopped citron

1. In a small saucepan, scald the milk over low heat until bubbles form around the sides of the pan. Remove from heat and add the butter and saffron, stirring to dissolve. Pour into a large bowl and let cool to lukewarm.

2. In a small bowl, combine the yeast, water, and sugar. Stir to dissolve the yeast. Let stand for 10 minutes, or until foamy.

3. Add the yeast mixture to the saffron mixture. Gradually whisk in the eggs, flour, and salt, switching to a spoon when necessary. Gradually add the orange peel, currants, and citron.

4. Turn the dough out onto a lightly floured board and knead for 5 minutes, or until smooth and elastic. Place the dough in a greased bowl, turn to coat, and cover with plastic wrap or a damp towel. Let rise for 1 hour, or until doubled in bulk. Reserve ½ cup dough.

5. Butter 2 baking sheets. Divide the remaining dough into 36 pieces. Shape each into a round bun. Place on the prepared pan. Pinch the reserved dough into 36 pieces. Shape each into a ball. Top each bun with a ball of dough. Cover with a towel and let rise for 1 hour, or until double in bulk.

6. Preheat the oven to 350°F. Bake the buns for 25 minutes, or until golden. Let cool on wire racks.

Miniature Pumpkin Muffins

YIELD: 20 MINIATURE MUFFINS

2½ cups all-purpose flour

1½ cups sugar

Pinch of salt

1 tablespoon baking powder

1 teaspoon ground allspice

2 eggs, beaten

4 tablespoons unsalted butter, melted

¼ cup safflower oil

1 cup milk

1 can (16 ounces) solid-pack pumpkin puree

¾ cup chopped walnuts

1. Preheat the oven to 400°F. Lightly grease and flour twenty ⅓-cup size muffin cups.

2. Combine the flour, sugar, salt, baking powder, and allspice in a large bowl. Stir to blend. In a medium bowl, stir the eggs, butter, oil, and milk together. Stir the egg mixture into the flour mixture. Add the pumpkin and nuts and stir until smooth. Fill each muffin cup with ¼ cup batter. Put some water in any empty muffin wells.

3. Bake for 20 minutes, or until a tester inserted in the center of a muffin comes out clean.

Miniature Scones

YIELD: 20 MINIATURE SCONES

4 cups all-purpose flour

6 tablespoons sugar

1 tablespoon cream of tartar

2 teaspoons baking powder

4 tablespoons cold unsalted butter, diced

1½ cups milk

1 cup dried cherries or currants

1. Preheat the oven to 425°F. Butter a baking sheet.

2. In a large bowl, combine the flour, sugar, cream of tartar, and baking powder. Stir to blend. Using a pastry cutter or 2 dinner knives, cut the butter into the flour mixture until it resembles cornmeal. Stir in the milk until the mixture forms a soft dough. Stir in the dried cherries or currants.

3. On a lightly floured board, roll or pat the dough to a ½-inch thickness. Cut with a 1½-inch round cutter. Place on the prepared baking sheet. Bake for 10 minutes, or until a tester inserted in the center of a scone comes out clean. Serve warm.

Savory Cheese Biscuits

YIELD: 30 SMALL BISCUITS

1 envelope active dry yeast
1 tablespoon sugar
Large pinch of salt
½ cup warm water
3½ cups all-purpose flour
2 teaspoons baking powder

1½ cups milk
½ cup (1 stick) unsalted butter, melted
6 ounces shredded Monterey Jack cheese with jalapeños

1. Preheat the oven to 425°F. Lightly butter and flour baking sheets.

2. In a small bowl, combine the yeast, sugar, salt, and warm water. Stir to dissolve the yeast. Let stand for 10 minutes, or until foamy.

3. In a large bowl, mix stir the flour and baking powder together. In a small bowl, mix the milk and melted butter together. Add the yeast mixture and stir. Beat into the flour with an electric mixer on medium speed. Stir in the shredded cheese.

4. On a floured surface, knead lightly and roll out to a ½-inch thickness. Cut out biscuits with a 1½-inch cutter and cover with a damp kitchen towel. Let rise for 1 hour, or until doubled. Place on the prepared baking sheets.

5. Bake for 20 minutes. Serve warm or reheat.

Parmesan-Herb Breadsticks

YIELD: 72 BREADSTICKS

1 envelope active dry yeast

2 teaspoons sugar

½ teaspoon salt

1 cup warm water

3 cups all-purpose flour

½ cup olive oil

3 ounces Parmesan cheese, grated

1 tablespoon mixed dried herbs

1. In a small bowl, combine the yeast, sugar, salt, and warm water. Stir to dissolve the yeast. Let stand for 10 minutes, or until foamy.

2. Put the flour in a large bowl and mix in the oil and the yeast mixture until blended. Add the cheese and herbs, mixing until the batter is smooth and elastic. Cover with plastic wrap or a damp towel and let rise for about 1 hour, or until doubled. (The dough will have a film of oil). Divide the dough in half.

3. Preheat the oven to 400°F. Lightly oil and flour baking sheets.

4. Roll 1 dough half out on a floured surface into a 12-by-16-inch rectangle ⅛ inch thick. Cut into strips a little under 1 inch wide and 6 inches long. Lift each strip. Fold in half and pull and twist till the braid is 6 inches long again. Place on the prepared baking sheets. Repeat with the second half.

5. Bake for 8 to 10 minutes, or until golden brown. Turn the oven off and let the bread sticks sit in the oven for 1 hour.

Corn-Bread Sticks

YIELD: 20 BREAD STICKS

½ cup diced dry-packed sun-dried tomatoes

2 cups cornmeal

1½ cups all-purpose flour

½ teaspoon salt

1 tablespoon baking powder

4 eggs, beaten

2 cups buttermilk

5 tablespoons unsalted butter, melted

2 cups corn kernels

1. Preheat the oven to 425°F. Grease corn-stick pans, place in the oven, and let heat while the oven preheats.

2. In a small bowl, pour boiling water over the dried tomatoes. In a large bowl, mix all dry ingredients together. In a medium bowl, beat the eggs, milk, and butter together until blended. Drain the tomatoes.

3. Stir the egg mixture into the cornmeal mixture just until blended. Fold in the tomatoes and corn. Fill the prepared pans two-thirds full.

4. Bake for 20 minutes or until a tester inserted in the center of a bread stick comes out clean. Let cool slightly and unmold. Serve warm.

Minestrone

SERVES 24

6 quarts beef or vegetable stock

12 ounces sun-dried tomato paste

2 cups diced tomatoes

Pieces of Parmesan cheese rind (optional)

½ lemon, seeded and studded with cloves

1 onion, plus 2 cups diced onions

3 sprigs fresh rosemary

Up to 1 cup olive oil

2 cups diced leeks

2 cups green peas

2 cups diced peeled potatoes

2 cups diced zucchini

2 cups diced celery

Salt and freshly ground pepper to taste

2 cups cooked white beans

2 cups cooked chickpeas

3 cups tubetti or small elbow macaroni

2 cups (8 ounces) grated Parmesan cheese, plus more for serving

½ cup minced fresh flat-leaf parsley

1. In a large soup pot, combine the stock, tomato paste, tomatoes, optional cheese rind, lemon, whole onion, and rosemary. Bring to a boil, then reduce heat to a simmer.

2. Heat the olive oil in a large skillet and sauté the diced onions and leeks until translucent, about 5 minutes. Add the potatoes, zucchini, and celery and sauté for 5 minutes. Add to the soup. Add the salt and pepper, white beans, and chickpeas. Simmer for 45 minutes.

3. Add the pasta and peas and cook for 15 minutes. Remove the cheese rinds and stir in the Parmesan cheese and parsley. Serve with garlic bread and additional grated Parmesan.

Clam Chowder

SERVES 20

¾ cup unsalted butter
1½ cups diced onions
1½ cups diced celery
1 cup all-purpose flour
3 quarts clam broth
1 tablespoon dried fines herbes

1½ quarts chopped clams
6 cups boiled cubed potatoes
1 quart milk
1 quart heavy cream
Salt and pepper to taste
Paprika for garnish

1. Melt the butter in a stockpot over medium heat. Add the onions and celery and sauté until the onions are translucent, about 5 minutes. Stir in the flour until well blended. Add the clam broth and herbs and simmer for 20 minutes. Add the clams and potatoes.

2. Reduce heat to a simmer and cook for 5 minutes. Stir in the milk, cream, salt, and pepper. Heat until the chowder is quite hot, stirring so that it doesn't scorch. Serve sprinkled with paprika.

Iced Fresh-Tomato Soup

SERVES 20

20 tomatoes, peeled, seeded, and coarsely chopped

3 cucumbers, peeled and seeded

5 quarts beef or vegetable stock

4 garlic cloves

One 4-inch piece fresh ginger

2 cups toasted bread cubes

Salt and freshly ground pepper to taste

4 cups nonfat plain yogurt

Curry powder to taste

1 pound cooked tiny pink shrimp and ½ cup toasted sunflower seeds for garnish (see note)

1. In a food processor, puree batches of tomatoes, cucumbers, and 4 quarts of the stock. Empty into a large bowl. Process the garlic, ginger, and bread cubes with the remaining 1 quart stock and add to the tomato puree. Add salt and pepper and refrigerate until ready to serve.

2. In a medium bowl, mix the yogurt with curry powder to taste. Ladle into a tureen for a buffet or individual soup bowls. Top with the curried yogurt. Garnish with shrimp and sunflower seeds.

TOASTING SEEDS: In a dry skillet over medium-low heat, stir the seeds until they are fragrant and lightly toasted, 2 or 3 minutes.

Pumpkin Soup

4 tablespoons unsalted butter

¼ cup safflower oil

4 leeks (white part only), washed and sliced

4 cloves garlic

2 pounds white mushrooms, stemmed

4 pounds pumpkin puree or canned solid-pack pumpkin

4 cinnamon sticks

2 teaspoons ground cumin

Salt and freshly ground pepper to taste

5 quarts chicken or vegetable stock

2 cups dry sherry (optional)

3 cups heavy cream, plus more for garnish

Salsa for garnish

1. Melt the butter with the oil in a large skillet. Sauté the leeks, garlic, and mushroom stems for 5 to 7 minutes, or until browned. Using a slotted spoon, transfer the vegetables to a bowl. In the same pan, sauté the mushroom caps until browned. Set aside.

2. In a stockpot, combine the pumpkin, leek mixture, cinnamon sticks, cumin, salt, pepper and stock. Bring to a boil, reduce heat, and simmer until quite tender, about 1 hour. Remove the cinnamon sticks, let cool slightly, and puree in a food processor in batches. Return to the pot with the sliced mushrooms and sherry.

3. Heat to serve, or refrigerate for up to 3 days and heat when needed. Serve garnished with swirls of heavy cream and a touch of salsa.

Deep-Green Split Pea Soup

SERVES 20

1 pound green split peas

1 ham bone (optional)

1 onion, stuck with 10 whole cloves

6 quarts water or stock

1 bunch parsley, stemmed and minced

3 pounds spinach, stemmed, washed, and chopped

6 carrots, scraped and diced

6 stalks celery, strings removed, diced

2 large onions, diced

Several sprigs fresh thyme, or 2 teaspoons dried thyme

2 jalapeño chiles, seeded and diced (optional)

Salt and pepper to taste

Fresh Croutons (page 201) for garnish

1. Rinse the split peas and pick them over.

2. Place the water, onion with cloves, and ham bone in a stockpot. Bring to a boil. Add the split peas, vegetables, herbs, and chiles. Bring to a boil again, stirring frequently. Reduce heat to a simmer, continue stirring, and cook until the peas are tender, about 1½ hours. If the soup gets too thick at any point, add some water or stock. Add salt and pepper. Garnish with croutons to serve.

Cold Sesame Noodles

SERVES 20

1 pound short flat Chinese
noodles

¼ cup Asian sesame oil

Sauce:

½ cup Chinese sesame seed
paste, plus liquid from sesame
seed paste jar

1½ cups reduced-sodium soy
sauce

¾ cup honey

⅓ cup Asian sesame oil

Hot chili oil to taste

Optional Toppings—one or all may be used:

1 large cucumber, peeled, seeded,
and cubed

1 cup roasted peanuts, chopped

½ cup sesame seeds, toasted

½ pound preserved tofu, cubed

½ cup minced fresh cilantro

½ cup finely chopped scallions,
including tender green parts

1. In a large pot of boiling water, cook the noodles according to the
package directions. Drain and run under cold water, drain again, and
coat with the ¼ cup sesame oil. Cover and refrigerate.

2. To make the sauce: Combine all the ingredients using an immersion
blender or mixer on slow. Cover and refrigerate for up to 1 week. Stir
before using and add 1 to 2 tablespoons boiling water if needed.

3. Toss the sauce with the noodles. Add one or more toppings just
before serving.

Baked Beans

SERVES 20

2 pounds small white or brown beans

6 quarts water

2 cups chopped onion

1 cup honey

1 cup molasses

½ cup bourbon

½ cup packed brown sugar

1 cup cider vinegar

2 tablespoons dry mustard

1 pound salt pork, cubed (optional)

1. Rinse and pick over the beans. Soak the beans overnight in water to cover by 2 inches. Drain. In a large pot, combine the beans with water to cover by 2 inches. Bring to a boil, reduce heat to a simmer, and cook for 1 hour, or until tender. Drain.

2. Preheat the oven to 300°F. Combine the beans and all the remaining ingredients in a deep baking dish or bean crock. Cover and bake for 2 hours, or until tender, stirring occasionally. Remove the cover and bake another 30 minutes.

Spaghetti with Rich Tomato-Mushroom Sauce

SERVES 20

½ cup olive oil

6 pork chops, bone in

3 onions, diced

4 celery stalks, diced

4 carrots, scraped and diced

3 pounds white mushrooms

8 pounds tomatoes, crushed, peeled, and seeded; or four 30-ounce cans crushed tomatoes

1¼ cups (10 ounces) tomato paste

2 heads garlic

2 cups basil leaves

1 cup minced fresh flat-leaf parsley

2 cups dry red wine

1 lemon, cut into quarters and seeded

½ cup sugar

2 tablespoons dried oregano, crumbled

4 pounds spaghetti

Freshly grated Parmesan cheese

1. Brown the pork chops in a large heavy Dutch oven.

2. Add the onions, celery, and carrots and sauté until slightly browned. Stir in the mushrooms. Add the remaining olive oil. Add all the remaining ingredients except the spaghetti and cheese. Reduce heat to low and cook, uncovered, for 3 hours, stirring occasionally. The sauce will be thick. Add wine or water splashed with balsamic vinegar (up to two cups) if necessary. Remove the pork chops, debone, and cut into bite-size pieces. Return the pork to the sauce.

3. In a large pot of salted boiling water, cook the pasta until al dente, about 10 minutes. Drain.

4. Toss the pasta with the sauce and serve at once with Parmesan cheese alongside.

Saffron Risotto

4 cups dried mushrooms (weight varies)

3 quarts turkey or chicken stock, preferably unsalted

3 cups dry white wine

¼ cup olive oil

4 onions, chopped

6 cups Arborio rice

1 teaspoon saffron threads, crumbled, dissolved in ¼ cup hot water

4 ounces (1 cup) grated Parmesan cheese

5 tablespoons unsalted butter

Freshly ground pepper to taste

1. Pour boiling water over the dried mushrooms just to cover. Set aside.

2. In a stockpot, bring the stock to a boil, add the wine, and reduce heat to a simmer.

3. Heat the oil in a large, heavy-bottomed saucepan over medium heat and sauté the onions until translucent, about 5 minutes. Add the rice and stir until the grains are coated, about 4 minutes. Do not brown the onions or rice.

4. Add 2 cups of the simmering broth to the risotto and stir constantly until almost all the liquid is absorbed. Repeat. After 15 minutes, start adding the undrained mushrooms.

5. Add half of the saffron mixture and continue adding stock. After 25 minutes, taste a grain and see if it is tender but firm. Add the remaining saffron. All the liquid may not be needed, but if more is needed, add water.

6. Remove from heat and stir in the Parmesan and pepper. Serve immediately.

Saffron Noodles

SERVES 20

1 teaspoon saffron threads, crumbled

4 pounds flat egg noodles

Salt and freshly ground pepper to taste

2 cups (1 pound) unsalted butter, melted

1. Stir the saffron into ¼ cup hot water and let stand for 15 minutes. Melt the butter and incorporate the saffron liquid and the salt and pepper.

2. In a large pot of salted boiling water, cook the noodles until just past al dente, about 10 minutes, or follow package directions.

3. Stir the saffron mixture and toss with the noodles.

NOTE: The addition of chicken livers and roasted red peppers sautéed with chives and wine turns this into a main dish for lunch or buffets.

Baked Ziti with Four Cheeses

SERVES 20

4 pounds ziti pasta

⅓ cup olive oil

2 cups dry white wine

3 pounds fresh ricotta cheese

1 pound mozzarella cheese, shredded (4 cups), plus 1 pound mozzarella cheese, thinly sliced

1 pound fontina cheese, shredded

8 ounces Parmesan cheese, grated (2 cups)

4 cups milk

½ cup chopped fresh basil leaves

Salt and freshly ground pepper to taste

1 tablespoon freshly grated nutmeg

1. Preheat the oven to 350°F.

2. In a large pot of salted boiling water, cook the ziti until al dente, about 10 minutes; drain. Return to the pot and toss with the olive oil and wine.

3. Reserve 1 cup of the Parmesan for topping. Stir the ricotta, shredded mozzarella, fontina, remaining 1 cup Parmesan, the milk, basil, salt, pepper, and nutmeg into the pasta until blended.

4. Turn into a 10-quart roasting pan or two smaller pans. Top with the sliced mozzarella and the reserved Parmesan.

5. Bake for 30 minutes, or until lightly browned and bubbly.

NOTE: Oil-packed sun-dried tomatoes or minced pancetta or prosciutto ends may be added to the mixture before baking.

Roland Park Foolproof Pizza

SERVES 20

1 envelope active dry yeast	Cornmeal for pan
¼ cup warm water	½ cup tomato paste
1 teaspoon sugar	½ teaspoon dried oregano
2½ cups plus ½ cup all-purpose flour	¾ cup thinly sliced mushrooms (about 4 ounces)
½ teaspoon salt	2½ cups (10 ounces) shredded mozzarella cheese
½ cup cold water	
¼ cup plus 2 tablespoons olive oil	

1. In a medium bowl, combine the yeast, water, and sugar. Stir to dissolve the yeast. Let stand until foamy, about 10 minutes.

2. Whisk in 2½ cups of the flour, the salt, cold water, and the ¼ cup olive oil. Stir thoroughly. Turn out onto a floured board and knead for 4 minutes, adding up to ½ cup of the remaining flour 1 tablespoon at a time to keep from sticking, until the dough is smooth and elastic.

3. Place the dough in an oiled large bowl. Turn to coat. Cover with plastic wrap or a damp cloth. Let rise in a warm, draft-free place for 45 minutes to 1½ hours. When the dough has approximately doubled in size it is ready to roll out for baking. Once it rises it will be a little sticky, which is what makes it crisp in a home oven.

4. Preheat the oven to 450°F. Place a baking stone in the oven if you are using one.

5. On a flour-dusted surface using a floured rolling pin, roll the pizza to a 16-by-20-inch rectangle, curling up a ¾-inch border.

6. Sprinkle medium-ground cornmeal on a lightly oiled baking sheet before laying on the dough or place dough directly on the stone.

7. Bake for 7 minutes. Remove from the oven, spread with the tomato paste, and drizzle with the 2 tablespoons olive oil. Sprinkle with the oregano and mushrooms. Top with the mozzarella.

8. Return to the hot oven and bake 8 to 10 minutes longer. Using a pizza cutter or chef's knife, cut into 4-inch squares, leaving gaps to allow moisture to escape. Serve with crushed red pepper.

Posole, New Mexican Style, with Fried Plantain Chips

SERVES 20

2½ pounds posole (see note)

Up to 1 cup Spanish olive oil

5 pounds boneless chicken thighs, each cut into 3 pieces

2 large Spanish onions (1 pound)

8 dried chile pepper pods

Cloves from 2 heads garlic, peeled

2 pounds sweet potatoes, peeled and diced

2 pounds carrots, scraped and cut into thin julienne strips

6 twigs epazote

1 tablespoon dried oregano

2 teaspoons ground cinnamon

5 cinnamon sticks

½ teaspoon ground mace

6 tablespoons tomato paste

1 quart beer

Salt and pepper to taste

3 large ripe avocados, diced

2 large ripe papayas, peeled, seeded, and diced

Sour cream, lime slices, and chopped fresh cilantro for garnish

Fried Plantain Chips (recipe follows)

1. After the posole has been soaked, rinse it and set to boil in a large covered stockpot. Lower heat and simmer for 3 hours, or until the kernels pop and open. Check every 30 minutes or so and add water only if needed. Taste a grain of the posole to make sure the texture is soft and chewy.

2. Heat ¼ cup of the oil in a Dutch oven or comparable pot over medium heat. Add the chicken pieces and cook until they start to sizzle. Add the onions, peppers, garlic cloves, sweet potatoes, carrots, herbs, and spices. Stir well, reduce heat to low, and cook for about 20 minutes, adding olive oil as needed to keep from sticking.

3. Add the chicken and vegetables to the posole and stir in the tomato paste, beer, salt, and pepper. Cook for another 30 minutes. Remove the peppers and cinnamon sticks. Cover the pot and let stand for up to 30 minutes.

4. Serve topped with diced avocados and papayas and garnished with sour cream, slices of lime, and chopped cilantro. Accompany with fried plantain chips.

NOTE: Posole is blue or yellow dried hominy with the parchment skin in place. Uncooked posole must be soaked in 3 quarts of water for 12 to 15 hours. Do not substitute traditional hominy.

Fried Plantain Chips

YIELD: 6 CUPS

4 green plantains, peeled	1 tablespoon brown sugar
Vegetable oil for deep frying	$\frac{1}{2}$ teaspoon cayenne
$\frac{1}{2}$ teaspoon coarse salt	$\frac{1}{2}$ teaspoon ground cinnamon

1. Using a food processor fitted with a slicing disk, cut the plantains into $\frac{1}{16}$-inch-thick slices.

2. In a large saucepan or deep fryer, heat 3 inches of oil to 375°F. Fry the plantain slices, in batches if necessary, until crisp and lightly browned. Transfer to paper towels to drain.

3. Mix together the salt, sugar, cayenne, and cinnamon and sprinkle over the plantains.

Poached Whole Salmon with Cucumber-Dill Dressing

SERVES 20

One 10-pound whole salmon, cleaned and scaled

2 quarts water

2 cups dry white wine

2 strips lemon zest

3 sprigs fresh parsley

¼ cup chopped celery

1 onion stuck with several cloves

2 bay leaves

Sauce Mousseline (recipe follows), optional

Cucumber-Dill Dressing (recipe follows)

Cucumber slices and cooked green beans for garnish

1. Cut a piece of cheesecloth large enough to wrap the fish in twice. Dampen the cheesecloth and wring it out. Wrap the salmon in at least 2 turns of the cheesecloth in such a way that it will be easy to remove. It will probably be necessary to remove the head of the fish so that it comfortably fits in the poacher.

2. Remove the rack from a fish poacher and place the water, wine, zest, parsley, celery, onion, and bay leaves in the poacher. Bring to a boil over two burners on top of the stove. Reduce the heat and simmer for 15 minutes. Set the salmon on the poaching rack.

3. Carefully lower the fish into the simmering water, which should cover the fish. Cover the poacher, and gently return to a simmer. Simmer for about 10 minutes per inch of greatest thickness, about 45 minutes.

4. Lift out the fish on its rack and place on a tray that has been covered with foil-covered cardboard. Remove the cheesecloth using a sharp knife or scissors to cut the cloth where it sticks and gently slide it out from under the fish.

5. Usually, salmon is served flat, with only the top skin discarded. Remove the fins and any small bones with your fingers or a pair of tweezers. Scrape the brown flesh where visible to show only a pink surface. Cover with plastic wrap and refrigerate for at least several hours or overnight.

6. If using the sauce mousseline, spread a thin layer on the salmon 1 hour before serving. Return the platter to the refrigerator for 1 hour to set the sauce. Gently slide the fish off the foil-lined cardboard onto a serving platter.

Sauce Mousseline

YIELD: 4 CUPS

6 egg yolks	1 cup (½ pound) cold unsalted
Pinch each of salt, pepper, and	butter, cut into thin slices
grated nutmeg	1 cup heavy cream

1. In the top of a double boiler set over simmering water, whisk the egg yolks with the salt, pepper, and nutmeg until warm. Gradually whisk in the butter to make an emulsified sauce. Remove from the heat and let cool completely.

2. In a deep bowl, beat the cream until stiff peaks form. Fold in the egg yolk mixture. Shortly before serving, add another layer of mousseline and return to the refrigerator. Decorate the fish with cucumber slices to resemble fish scales and use strips of green beans placed in half-circles to outline the scales.

Cucumber-Dill Dressing

YIELD: 4 CUPS

4 cucumbers, peeled	½ cup minced fresh dill
Salt	½ cup cider vinegar
2 cups nonfat plain yogurt	½ cup sugar
1 cup prepared white horseradish	Salt and freshly ground pepper to taste

1. Cut the cucumbers in half lengthwise, seed, and cut into ¼-inch-thick crosswise slices. Place in a colander, sprinkle liberally with salt, and let drain for 30 minutes. Rinse the cucumber and drain well.

2. In a bowl, mix together the yogurt, horseradish, dill, vinegar, and sugar. Stir to dissolve the sugar. Add the cucumber and blend well. Cover and refrigerate until serving time. If desired, salt and pepper to taste.

Salmon Burgers with Cranberry Ketchup

SERVES 20

5 pounds cooked salmon

5 egg whites

1 cup grated red onion

1½ cups salsa

3 tablespoons minced drained capers

3 cups fresh cornbread crumbs

Juice of 2 lemons

Freshly ground pepper to taste

Safflower oil

Cranberry Ketchup (recipe follows)

1. Flake the salmon. In a large bowl, beat the egg whites until opaque and foamy but not stiff. Add the salmon and all the remaining ingredients except the oil and shape into 20 patties, each about ¾ inch thick.

2. Brush a griddle or a large skillet heavily with safflower oil and heat over medium-high heat. Cook the patties until lightly golden, about 3 minutes on each side.

3. Serve hot, with cranberry ketchup alongside.

Cranberry Ketchup

YIELD: 1 PINT

4 cups (1 pound) fresh or frozen cranberries

⅓ cup distilled white vinegar

¾ cup sugar

2 cinnamon sticks

2 teaspoons ground allspice

Salt and freshly ground pepper to taste

Crushed hot red pepper to taste

1. In a medium saucepan, combine the cranberries with water to cover. Bring to a boil, remove from heat, and let cool. Drain.

2. In a food processor, puree the berries until smooth. Return to the saucepan, add all the remaining ingredients, bring to a simmer over low heat, and cook for 20 minutes.

Baked Salmon Fillets on Roasted Tomatoes

SERVES 20

5 pounds firm tomatoes, peeled and seeded

Cloves from 1 head garlic, peeled

½ cup plus ¾ cup olive oil

2 cups dry white wine

1 tablespoon dried thyme

1 teaspoon ground cumin

Freshly ground pepper to taste

20 salmon fillets, 6 to 7 ounces each

Saffron Noodles (page 223) for serving

1. Preheat the oven to 500°F. Place the tomatoes and garlic in a single layer in roasting pans and drizzle with the ½ cup olive oil. Roast for 10 minutes.

2. In a small bowl, combine the wine, thyme, cumin, and pepper. Pour into the pans. Lay the fillets in a single layer over the tomatoes and drizzle the ¾ cup olive oil over the fish. Reduce the oven temperature to 400°F.

3. Bake for 15 minutes, or until fish is opaque on the outside and slightly translucent in the center. Serve with saffron noodles.

Sweet and Sour Fish

SERVES 20

1½ cups instant flour (Wondra)

1½ cups chestnut flour or cornstarch

5 pounds scrod or pollock fillets, cut into 1-inch cubes

¼ cup saffflower oil

1 large or 2 medium pineapples, peeled, cored, and cut into ¾-inch dice

8 large firm tomatoes, each cut into 8 wedges

¼ cup sugar

¾ cup cider vinegar

½ cup dry sherry

½ cup reduced-sodium soy sauce

1 cup ginger preserves

1½ cups water

1. Lightly dredge the fish in a mixture of flour and chestnut flour or comstarch. Heat the oil in a large skillet over medium-high heat. Sauté the fish in batches for 4 or 5 minutes. Transfer to a warmed platter.

2. Drain the oil from the skillet and add the pineapples and tomatoes. Sauté over medium-high heat for 5 minutes. Stir in the remaining ingredients and cook for 10 minutes, or until heated through. Pour over the fish. Accompany with rice.

Scallops with Angel Hair Pasta in Lemon Cream Sauce

SERVES 20

2 cups finely ground bread crumbs

1 cup all-purpose flour

4 pounds bay scallops

1 stick (4 ounces) unsalted butter

½ cup olive oil

Grated zest and juice of 4 lemons

2 cups minced shallots

2 tablespoons sugar

4 cups dry white wine

1 quart skim milk

1 quart heavy cream

3½ pounds spinach fettuccine

1 cup chopped fresh parsley leaves

Grated lemon zest, freshly grated nutmeg, and freshly ground pepper for serving

1. Slice the scallops, if large. Combine the bread crumbs and flour and stir to blend. Dredge the scallops in the bread crumb mixture. Reserve the remaining mixture. Heat the butter and oil in a nonreactive pan and sauté the scallops and lemon zest over low heat. Remove and keep warm.

2. Add the shallots to the pan and sauté for about 3 minutes, or until translucent. Stir in the lemon juice, sugar, and reserved flour mixture. Whisk in the wine and milk and cook for 15 minutes, stirring occasionally. Whisk in the cream and cook 5 minutes longer. Add the scallops.

3. Meanwhile, cook the pasta in a large pot of salted boiling water until al dente; drain. Return to the pot. Add the sauce and toss to coat.

4. Serve on warmed platters, topped with parsley and accompanied with lemon zest, nutmeg, and pepper.

Tuna Medallions

SERVES 20

¾ cup olive oil

⅓ cup Dijon mustard

⅓ cup fresh lemon juice

1 teaspoon cracked black pepper

Twenty 6-ounce tuna steaks, each 2 inches thick

Cubed Potatoes (recipe follows) for serving

Steamed green and yellow zucchini for serving

1. Preheat the broiler. In a small bowl, combine the oil, mustard, lemon juice, and pepper. Stir to blend.

2. Brush both sides of the tuna steaks with the oil mixture. Broil under flame or on a stovetop broiler, 4 minutes on each side.

3. Serve with cubed potatoes and steamed zucchini.

Cubed Potatoes

SERVES 20

10 baking potatoes, peeled and cut into ½-inch dice

Paprika

40 whole cloves

40 small shallots

½ cup olive oil

4 or 5 sprigs fresh rosemary

Coarse salt

1. Drop the diced potatoes into ice water, drain, and dry. Sprinkle potatoes with paprika. Peel the shallots and insert a clove in each shallot.

2. In a very large skillet, combine the oil and rosemary sprigs. Add the shallots and potatoes and sauté, stirring, until brown and tender. Using a slotted spoon, transfer to paper towels to drain. Serve sprinkled with coarse salt.

Pan-Roasted Red Snapper

SERVES 20

1 cup olive oil

6½ pounds red snapper fillets

2 cups chopped red onion

2 cups chopped yellow bell pepper

1 teaspoon ground cumin

1 teaspoon red pepper flakes

2½ cups chopped fresh cilantro or flat-leaf parsley

1½ cups pimiento-stuffed Spanish olives

1 cup orange juice

½ cup lemon juice

½ cup lime juice

Olives and chopped parsley for garnish

Andean Potatoes (recipe follows) for serving

1. Preheat the oven to 400°F. Coat a roasting pan with ¼ cup of the olive oil. Place the fish in the pan.

2. Heat the remaining olive oil in a large skillet over medium-high heat. Add the onion, cumin, and pepper flakes and sauté until wilted, about 5 minutes. Roast for 10 minutes. Add the cilantro and olives.

3. Add the juices to the oil mixture in the skillet and pour over the fish. Roast 10 minutes longer, or until the fish flakes easily. Garnish with olives and chopped parsley. Serve with Andean potatoes.

Andean Potatoes

SERVES 20

4 pounds potatoes, peeled, boiled, and mashed

6 ounces white Cheddar cheese, shredded (1½ cups)

1 teaspoon chili powder

1 cup heavy cream

1 cup plain yogurt

½ cup lemon juice

1. Place the potatoes in a large warm serving bowl.

2. Stir in the cheese, chili powder, and cream, then the yogurt and lemon juice. Serve warm.

Bouillabaisse

Salt and freshly ground pepper to taste

1 head fennel, trimmed

1 head celery, trimmed 6 inches from root

1 large white onion

4 leeks, white part only

¼ cup minced fresh basil

8 tomatoes, peeled and seeded

20 small red potatoes, quartered

6 tablespoons tomato paste

2 teaspoons crushed saffron threads

Grated zest of 1 orange

3 small bluefish

6 whitings

1 weakfish

2 pounds clams

2 pounds mussels

½ cup Pernod or other anise-flavored liqueur

½ cup minced fresh flat-leaf parsley

Garlic bread for serving

1. Bring 1½ gallons of water to a boil with a little salt and pepper in a nonreactive saucepan. Dice the fennel, celery, onions, leeks, basil, and tomatoes. Add the diced vegetables to the pot. Cook for 30 minutes.

2. Add the potatoes, tomato paste, saffron, and orange zest. Cook for 15 minutes.

3. Discard the skin and bones from the fish. Shell the shellfish. Reduce heat so the stock is simmering and add the fish. Cook for 8 minutes and add the shellfish. Cook for 4 minutes and remove from heat. Stir in the Pernod and parsley. Serve with garlic bread.

Gumbo

4 tablespoons unsalted butter

¾ cup all-purpose flour

5 slices bacon, diced (optional)

½ cup olive oil

1 cup each diced onion, celery, carrot, and green bell pepper

4 quarts fish stock, or 3 quarts water

2 pints clam juice

2 tablespoons tomato paste

1 teaspoon dried oregano

1 teaspoon dried thyme

5 bay leaves

¼ teaspoon white pepper

¼ teaspoon black pepper

¼ teaspoon cayenne or to taste

2 pounds andouille sausage, sliced

2 pounds small okra, rinsed, dried, and halved lengthwise

2 pounds shrimp, shelled and deveined

3 pounds crabmeat

3 pounds peeled diced fresh tomatoes

White Rice (recipe follows) for serving

1. Melt the butter in a Dutch oven over medium heat. Stir in ¼ cup of the flour. Add the diced bacon and stir until brown but not crisp. Stir in ¼ cup of the oil, then another ¼ cup of flour, blending well. Stir in the remaining ¼ cup oil and the remaining flour.

2. Add 2 cups of the liquid and stir until the mixture thickens. Add liquid pint by pint, stirring continuously. Bring to a boil. Add the diced vegetables, tomato paste, herbs, and seasonings.

3. Add the sausage and okra. Cook for 20 minutes, or until the okra is crisp-tender. Add the shrimp and stir for 3 or 4 minutes, or until pink.

4. Add the crabmeat and cook for 5 minutes. Remove from heat and stir in the tomatoes. Serve with plain white rice.

White Rice

SERVES 20

4½ cups (2 pounds) southern
white rice

3 quarts water

1 lemon, quartered and seeded

6 fish bouillon cubes (optional)

1. In a large pot, bring the water to a boil. Stir in the rice, lemon, and bouillon cubes, if using. Cover, reduce heat to a simmer, and cook for 20 minutes.

2. Remove from heat. Lift the lid, place a towel over the pot, and replace the lid. Let stand for 5 minutes. Stir with a slotted spoon and serve.

Salmon Steaks with Onion Jam

SERVES 20 AS A MAIN DISH OR 40 AS AN APPETIZER

For a main dish, serve 1 fish steak per person; for an appetizer or buffet, cut in half and remove the bone.

20 salmon steaks, 6 or 8 ounces each

Safflower oil for brushing

Juice of 4 lemons

Onion Jam (recipe follows) for serving

1. Preheat the broiler.

2. Brush the steaks with oil and sprinkle with lemon juice. Broil for 5 minutes on each side, or until opaque on the outside and barely translucent at the bone. Serve with onion jam.

Onion Jam

SERVES 20

1 cup (4 ounces) dried cherries

20 onions

4 tablespoons unsalted butter

¼ cup olive oil

¼ cup sugar

2 cups dry red or white wine

1 cup crème de cassis

1. Pour ¾ cup boiling water over the cherries and let stand for 15 minutes. Peel and slice the onions, separating the rings.

2. Melt the butter with the oil in a large sauté pan, add the onions, and sauté over medium heat until translucent. Stir in the sugar. Reduce heat to low and stir in the wine and crème de cassis.

3. Add the cherries to the pan, stirring until all the liquid has been absorbed.

Tangy Halibut with Quick Tapenade

SERVES 20

1 cup unsalted butter

1 cup olive oil

Twenty 8-ounce halibut steaks

3 lemons, sliced paper thin

Quick Tapenade (recipe follows)

Piquant Sweet Potatoes (recipe follows)

1. Preheat the oven to 400°F. Melt the butter and mix with the olive oil. Using the butter mixture, brush enough roasting pans to hold the fish in one layer.

2. Put the fish flat in pans and drizzle the remaining butter and oil over the fish, then lay the lemon slices on top.

3. Place in the oven and roast for 15 minutes, or until the fish is no longer transparent. Using a slotted spatula, transfer to warm plates.

4. Serve with tapenade and sweet potatoes.

Quick Tapenade

YIELD: 2½ CUPS

½ cup olive oil

5 garlic cloves, sliced

2 cans flat anchovy fillets, drained

2 tablespoons salted capers, well rinsed

1 jar (7 ounces) black olive paste, or chopped olives

Juice of 1 lemon

¼ cup Cognac

Heat the olive oil in a medium saucepan and add the garlic. Cook for 1 or 2 minutes, or until the garlic slices are glossy. Add the anchovies and capers, stirring until the anchovies are almost dissolved. Stir in the olive paste, lemon juice, and Cognac. Cook until heated through and plate with halibut.

Piquant Sweet Potatoes

SERVES 20

1 cup (8 ounces) unsalted butter

1 cup packed brown sugar

8 pounds cooked sweet potatoes, peeled and cut into 2-inch cubes

2 pounds tomatoes, peeled, seeded, and diced

½ cup peeled, chopped shallots

3 tablespoons drained, chopped preserved serrano chile

1. Preheat the oven to 350°F. Heat the butter and brown sugar in a roasting pan until the butter is melted. Stir in the remaining ingredients.

2. Bake for 25 minutes, or until fork tender and browned.

Sichuan Chicken Breasts

SERVES 20

4 bunches scallions, including tender green parts

½ cup peanut oil

1 tablespoon aniseed

1 tablespoon ground ginger

½ cup packed brown sugar

2 tablespoons ground Sichuan peppercorns

5 pounds boneless, skinless chicken breasts

3 large green bell peppers

1¼ pounds white button mushrooms

2 cups raw unsalted peanuts or cashews

3 cups chicken broth

2 cups reduced-sodium soy sauce

1 cup dry sherry

1. Cut the chicken into strips. Seed and julienne the peppers. Thickly slice the mushrooms. Trim the scallions of roots and tough green parts. Cut the scallions lengthwise into quarters.

2. It is probably necessary to do this divided in two batches. Heat the peanut oil in two large woks or skillets over high heat and add half the aniseed, ginger, sugar, and ground peppercorns to each. Add half the chicken, bell peppers, mushrooms, scallions, and nuts to each. Cook, stirring, for 7 minutes, or until the chicken is opaque throughout and firm. Reduce heat and add half the broth, soy sauce, and sherry to each. Simmer for 10 minutes.

Chicken Breasts Stuffed with Chèvre and Sun-Dried Tomatoes

SERVES 20

2 pounds crumbly chèvre

5 ounces olive paste

1 cup diced sun-dried tomatoes in oil

20 boneless chicken breast halves, with skin on

Olive oil

Paprika

Tomato Coulis (recipe follows)

Polenta Squares (recipe follows)

1. Preheat the oven to 450°F. Set out roasting pans large enough to hold the chicken in a single layer.

2. In a bowl, mix the cheese, olive paste, and sun-dried tomatoes together. Gently lift the skin on each breast and spread 2 tablespoons of filling between chicken and skin. Smooth the skin to cover the filling.

3. Oil the roasting pans and place the chicken in the pans in one layer. Drizzle oil over the chicken and sprinkle with paprika.

4. Bake for 15 to 20 minutes, or until thoroughly cooked. Plate each chicken breast on tomato coulis, with 2 polenta squares alongside.

Tomato Coulis

YIELD: 5 CUPS

3 tablespoons olive oil

2 red onions, diced

6 garlic cloves

1 can (24 ounces) tomato puree

2 ounces tomato paste

½ cup balsamic vinegar

2 tablespoons sugar

Coarse salt and freshly ground pepper to taste

2 pounds ripe tomatoes

Basil leaves for garnish

½ cup grated Parmesan cheese

1. In a food processor, combine all the ingredients except the fresh tomatoes, basil leaves, and Parmesan cheese. Pulse until smooth. Pour into a bowl. If the coulis seems too thin, thicken with Parmesan cheese.

2. In a medium nonreactive saucepan, heat the coulis until barely simmering. Keep on low heat.

3. Peel, seed, and dice the tomatoes and mix into the sauce. Garnish with basil.

Polenta Squares

YIELD: 36 SQUARES

3 quarts water

2 teaspoons coarse salt

4 cups polenta

1 cup (8 ounces) unsalted butter, cut into small pieces

Olive oil

1. In a large pot, bring the water to a boil. Add the salt. Pour in the polenta slowly, stirring continuously. When the polenta has been added and blended, simmer for 20 minutes, stirring frequently, until cooked to taste.

2. Remove from heat and stir in the butter. Pour into two 18-by-12-by-3-inch pans and let set. Cut into 3-inch squares.

3. Lightly brush the top of each square with olive oil and broil for 2 to 3 minutes, or until the top is crisp and lightly browned.

Crisp Duck à l'Orange

SERVES 20

5 whole ducks with necks and giblets	1 teaspoon ground mace
12 seedless oranges	1 teaspoon dried thyme
5 sprigs fresh thyme	2 cups chopped shallots
1 onion	2 tablespoons unsalted butter
10 whole cloves	2 tablespoons olive oil
6 bay leaves	1 cup Triple Sec or other orange liqueur

1. Preheat the oven to 400°F. Clean and dry ducks and remove and reserve the necks and giblets. Cut up 5 of the oranges and place one in the cavity of each duck with a sprig of thyme. Pierce the skin in several places and place the ducks on racks in roasting pans and roast for 30 minutes, until a good deal of fat has dripped into the pans.

2. While the ducks are roasting, bring 2 quarts of water to a boil with a little salt and pepper. Peel the onion and insert the cloves, then place in the water with bay leaves, mace, thyme, and necks and giblets except for livers. Simmer the necks and giblets for 20 minutes.

3. Grate the zest of 5 of the oranges, reserving the oranges. Place in a small saucepan, cover with water, and bring to a boil. Reduce heat and continue to simmer.

4. Melt the butter with the oil in a small sauté pan and sauté the duck livers and shallots in butter and olive oil. When the liver is cooked, remove from heat and dice. Remove the necks and giblets from the simmering water and dice. Continue simmering the water to reduce.

5. In a blender or food processor, combine the orange zest and its cooking water, livers, shallots, and necks and giblets and pulse until smooth. Pour into a medium saucepan. Add the Triple Sec and 4 cups of the giblet stock. Taste and adjust the seasoning. Set aside and keep warm.

6. Discard all fat from the roasting pans and put the racks back in the pans with the ducks on them. Squeeze the juice of 1 orange over each duck and place thinly sliced oranges over all. Reduce the oven temperature to 325°F and roast for another hour, or until a drumstick moves easily and the meat pulls from the bone; or test for doneness with a meat thermometer.

7. Present on a platter garnished with orange slices and pass the sauce alongside. Or, serve on plates with a few slices of meat and an occasional drumstick. Discard the wing tips.

Turkey Chili Mole

SERVES 20

Safflower oil

3 large onions, diced

Cloves from 1 large head garlic, minced

5 assorted dried chiles (ancho, cascabel, etc.), minced

¼ cup best-quality chili powder

7 pounds ground turkey

Two 28-ounce cans crushed tomatoes

1 can (12 ounces) tomato paste

1 tablespoon ground cinnamon

½ teaspoon ground cloves

2 teaspoons ground cumin

1½ teaspoons black pepper

8 ounces bittersweet chocolate, broken up

Up to 1 quart water or stock, as needed

1. Heat the oil in a large stew pot and wilt the onions for about 5 minutes, or until translucent. Add the garlic and cook for 1 minute. Stir in the chiles and chili powder. Gradually stir in the ground turkey and crushed tomatoes, then the tomato paste, cinnamon, cloves, cumin, and pepper. Stir frequently as the chili starts to simmer. Stir in the chocolate.

2. Cook for 1½ hours, stirring often, until the chili is dark and thick. Add water or stock only if it starts sticking.

3. Serve with yellow rice mixed with pine nuts, raisins, and sliced pimiento-stuffed Spanish olives, if you wish.

Beef Curry

SERVES 20

1 quart nonfat plain yogurt

¼ cup best quality curry powder

1 tablespoon ground cumin

1 tablespoon ground cardamom

2 teaspoons crushed hot red pepper, or to taste

One 4-inch piece peeled fresh ginger

8 pounds boneless sirloin, cut into 2-inch cubes

All-purpose flour

2 cups ghee or half butter and half vegetable oil

4 large onions, sliced

5 large apples, sliced

2 pounds button mushrooms, sliced

Up to 1 quart apple juice, as needed

White rice for serving

Chopped fresh cilantro for garnish

Peach Chutney (recipe follows) for serving

1. In a food processor, combine the yogurt, curry powder, cumin, cardamom, red pepper, and ginger. Puree until blended. Dredge the beef in flour to coat.

2. Melt the ghee in a large skillet and brown the beef and onions in a single layer. Repeat, adding more ghee or butter mixture as needed.

3. Transfer the beef and onions to a stew pot. Sauté the apple slices in the same skillet. Add to the pot. Set the pot over medium heat. Stir in the yogurt-spice blend and the mushrooms.

4. Cook over medium heat for 1 hour. If the mixture gets dry, add up to 1 quart apple juice, 1 cup at a time. Transfer to a warm covered serving casserole.

5. Place the rice in a lightly oiled bowl, pack with a spoon, and gently unmold on a platter. Garnish with chopped cilantro. Serve with peach chutney alongside.

Peach Chutney

YIELD: 8 CUPS

10 pounds peaches, halved and pitted

1⅓ cups (8 ounces) raisins, finely chopped

3 large Spanish onions, diced

5 lemons, seeded and diced, peel and all

2 tablespoons crushed red pepper (this will be quite hot, use to taste)

1 tablespoon dry mustard

2 cups granulated sugar

2 cups packed brown sugar

4 to 6 short cinnamon sticks

Cider vinegar to cover

1. Cut each peach half into 8 pieces. Place in a nonreactive stockpot set over medium heat. Add the remaining ingredients and stir until the mixture starts to boil. Reduce the heat and simmer, stirring frequently, for 2 hours.

2. If the chutney will be used within a few weeks, wash hinged preserving jars with rubber gasket in hot soapy water, rinse thoroughly, dry-fill, and refrigerate.

Roast Beef Tenderloin with Madeira Sauce

SERVES 20

Two 6-pound filet mignon roasts
¾ cup prepared mustard
Freshly ground black pepper to taste

Madeira Sauce (recipe follows)

1. Rub the trimmed roasts with the mustard and a touch of pepper. Set on a rack in a roasting pan.

2. Preheat the the oven to 425°F. No more than 45 minutes before serving, place the roasts in the hot oven for 15 minutes, then reduce the oven temperature to 400°F and roast for 20 minutes, or until a meat thermometer registers 140°F (medium rare).

3. Cut parallel to the grain and serve with Madeira sauce. Asparagus and potatoes are good accompaniments.

Madeira Sauce

YIELD: 4 CUPS

2 pounds small whole white button mushrooms, thickly sliced
¾ cup minced shallots
1 cup (8 ounces) plus 4 tablespoons butter
¾ cup red currant jelly

½ cup instant flour (Wondra)
3 cups beef stock
1 cup Madeira wine
⅓ cup minced parsley leaves
Salt and pepper to taste

1. In a sauté pan over medium heat, brown the mushrooms and shallots in the 1 cup butter. Stir in the jelly until dissolved. Set aside and keep warm.

2. Melt the 4 tablespoons butter in a medium saucepan over low heat. When the butter starts to color, whisk in the flour. Gradually add the beef stock and Madeira. Reduce slightly. Add the mushrooms and parsley and stir.

Naturally Cured Polish-Style Ham

SERVES 20

One 16- to 17-pound naturally cured Polish-style ham

2 cups Peach Chutney (page 250), plus more for garnish

½ cup prepared mustard

About 25 whole cloves

Cinnamon sticks for garnish (optional)

Wild Rice and Mushrooms (recipe follows)

1. Preheat the oven to 375°F. Remove the rind from the ham and trim fat to a ⅛-inch layer. Score a checkerboard pattern into the fat. Puree the chutney and mustard and coat the ham. Insert a clove in the center of each square. Bake for 30 minutes. Reduce the oven temperature to 300°F and continue baking for 1 hour.

2. Transfer to a platter and garnish with chutney and cinnamon sticks. Serve with Wild Rice and Mushrooms.

Wild Rice and Mushrooms

SERVES 20

4 quarts water

2 ounces dried mushrooms, crumbled into chunky pieces

4½ cups wild rice

1 cup minced shallots

Salt and pepper to taste

1. Bring the water to a boil in a stockpot. Pour 2 cups of the boiling water over the mushrooms in a small bowl and set aside until ready to use.

2. Add the rice to the boiling water in the stockpot. Reduce heat to medium. Add the shallots and a touch of salt and pepper. Cover and cook for 30 minutes.

3. Stir in the mushrooms and cook, uncovered, 10 minutes longer, or until the liquid is absorbed and the rice is tender.

Balsamic Roasted Pork with Prunes

SERVES 20

One 7-pound trimmed boneless pork loin

3 cups sliced onions

6 garlic cloves, minced

2 tablespoons dried herbes de Provence

1 teaspoon freshly ground black pepper

½ teaspoon ground allspice

½ cup balsamic vinegar

¼ cup olive oil

1 pound pitted prunes

1 cup dry red wine

1. In a large bowl, marinate the pork loin in all ingredients except prunes and wine for 2 to 6 hours in the refrigerator. Turn the meat over 2 or 3 times to marinate evenly.

2. Preheat the oven to 375°F. Place the pork and marinade in a shallow uncovered roaster and baste. Roast for 30 minutes. Reduce the oven temperature to 325°F. Roast 45 minutes longer, basting occasionally. Add the prunes and wine and roast for about 1 hour longer, or until internal temperature registers 160°F on a meat thermometer. Remove pork and prunes to a warm platter.

3. Place the roasting pan on the stovetop over medium-low heat. Cook to reduce the sauce. Taste and adjust the seasoning. Slice the pork before serving and plate with the prunes and sauce.

Pumpkin-Ginger Mousse

SERVES 20

⅓ cup brandy

2 teaspoons unflavored gelatin

½ cup chopped candied ginger

4 eggs, separated

1 teaspoon cream of tartar

⅔ cup sugar

4 cups pumpkin puree, or one can (29 ounces) solid-pack pumpkin can be substituted

1 teaspoon ground cinnamon

½ teaspoon ground ginger

¼ teaspoon ground cloves

Grated zest and juice of 1 orange

1 pint vanilla ice cream, softened

1 cup heavy cream, whipped

½ cup chopped, toasted almonds

1. Oil a 6-inch-wide strip of parchment paper and tie a collar around a 3-quart soufflé dish so that paper stands up 2 inches from the rim.

2. Warm the brandy in a small saucepan. Remove from heat and stir in gelatin until dissolved. Add the chopped ginger. Set aside.

3. In a small bowl, beat the egg whites and cream of tartar with an electric mixer on high speed until stiff, glossy peaks form. Set aside.

4. In a large bowl, beat the egg yolks and sugar with an electric mixer for 3 minutes. Stir in the pumpkin, cinnamon, ginger, cloves, and orange zest and juice. Stir in the brandy mixture and the softened ice cream until well blended.

5. Alternately add whipped cream and beaten egg whites to the pumpkin mixture. Spoon into the soufflé dish and cover with the almonds. Freeze for 30 minutes or refrigerate for 6 hours, or until firm and well chilled.

Cranberry-Beet Compote

SERVES 20

2 pounds cranberries

⅔ cup sugar

⅔ cup water

2 pounds beets, cooked, peeled, and diced

1 cup red currant jelly

½ cup Campari (optional)

1. In a large heavy saucepan, combine the cranberries, sugar, and water. Bring to a boil over high heat and cook until the berries start to pop. Reduce heat to medium. Stir in the beets and cook for about 10 minutes. Add the red currant jelly, stirring until dissolved.

2. Pour into a serving dish. Cover and refrigerate until ready to serve.

Maple-Glazed Apples, Pears, and Onions

SERVES 20

5 Granny Smith apples

5 Bosc pears

2 Spanish onions, sliced

3 red onions, sliced

2 tablespoons unsalted butter

2 tablespoons safflower oil

1 cup maple syrup

1. Core the apples and pears. Slice vertically, but do not peel.

2. Melt the butter with the oil in a large, heavy skillet over medium heat. Sauté the onions for about 12 minutes, or until golden. Add the apples and pears and sauté for another 5 minutes, or until tender. Reduce heat to low and stir in the maple syrup. Serve hot.

Sautéed Brussels Sprouts and Chestnuts

SERVES 20

12 ounces freshly peeled, cooked
chestnuts

2 quarts Brussels sprouts

2 tablespoons unsalted butter

2 tablespoons safflower oil

Salt and freshly ground pepper
to taste

1. Trim the Brussels sprouts.

2. In a large pot of salted boiling water, cook the Brussels sprouts for 5
minutes. Drain.

3. Melt the butter with the oil in large, heavy skillet over medium-low
heat. Add the Brussels sprouts and cook, stirring occasionally, for 15
minutes. Add the chestnuts and sauté another 10 minutes. Season with
salt and pepper. Serve hot.

Roasted Root Vegetables

3 pounds white potatoes

3 pounds carrots

3 pounds parsnips

Stalks from 1 large head celery

Cloves from 3 heads garlic, peeled

½ cup olive oil

Salt to taste

3 tablespoons herbes de Provence

½ cup minced fresh flat-leaf parsley

1. Preheat the oven to 400°F. Bring water to boil in a medium pot.

2. Peel the potatoes, carrots, and parsnips. Cut into 2-inch pieces. Separate the celery stalks and destring them. Cut into 2-inch slices.

3. Oil a roasting pan and spread the vegetables and garlic cloves in the pan. Drizzle with the remaining oil. Sprinkle with salt and herbes de Provence. Roast for 45 minutes, or until tender.

4. Arrange the vegetables on a platter and top with parsley to serve.

Eggplants and Apricots

SERVES 20

15 thin Chinese eggplants

8 ounces dried apricots, diced

¼ cup safflower oil

2 tablespoons minced peeled fresh ginger

6 scallions, minced

2 tablespoons Chinese chili paste

½ cup reduced-sodium soy sauce

1 teaspoon sugar dissolved in 1 tablespoon vinegar

1 cup water or chicken broth

1 tablespoon sesame oil

1. Discard the bases and tips of the eggplants. Cut the eggplants into lengthwise quarters and then crosswise into ½-inch chunks.

2. Pour boiling water over the apricots. Let stand for 15 minutes; drain.

3. In a wok or large skillet, heat the oil and add the ginger and eggplant, stirring until lightly browned. Add the scallions and apricots and stir for a few minutes more.

4. Mix all the remaining ingredients and pour into the pan. Cook for about 10 minutes, or until the eggplant is tender but still firm.

Stir-Fried Snow Peas, Carrots, and Water Chestnuts

SERVES 20

3 pounds snow peas

5 carrots

1 pound fresh water chestnuts

¼ cup peanut oil

2 tablespoons minced peeled fresh ginger

½ cup soy sauce

1 tablespoon Sichuan peppercorns, pounded

1. Trim ends and strings, if any, from peas. Scrape carrots and cut into julienne. Scrub, peel, and slice water chestnuts just before cooking.

2. Heat the oil in a wok or large skillet over high heat. Add the snow peas, carrots, and water chestnuts, stirring continuously. Add 1 cup of hot water if necessary to keep the vegetables from burning.

3. Add the ginger, soy sauce, and peppercorns. Cook, stirring, about 5 minutes, or until tender-crisp.

Spinach with Shallots, Pine Nuts, and Raisins

SERVES 20

6 tablespoons unsalted butter

6 pounds fresh spinach

¾ cup minced shallots

⅓ cup pine nuts

⅓ cup raisins

Grated zest and juice of 1 lemon

Freshly grated nutmeg to taste

Coarse salt and freshly ground pepper to taste

1. Trim spinach, rinse, and drain, but do not dry.

2. Melt the butter in a large skillet. Sauté the shallots, pine nuts, and raisins in the butter.

3. Add the spinach, with the water still clinging to the leaves, stirring as it wilts. Cook for 10 minutes or until cooked through.

4. Remove from heat and stir in the lemon zest and juice. Season with nutmeg, salt, and pepper. Serve hot.

Asparagus Drizzled with Cream

SERVES 20

5 pounds asparagus

3 cups heavy cream

Three 1-inch pieces fresh ginger, peeled and minced

Grated zest of 2 lemons

1. Break off tough ends of the asparagus and trim only if necessary. Bring a large pot of salted water to a boil, add asparagus, reduce heat, and simmer for 5 minutes, or until firm-tender. Drain and place on a warm platter.

2. In a small, heavy saucepan, heat the cream over medium heat. Press the ginger in a garlic press or twist in cheesecloth to extract the liquid into the cream. Add the ginger pieces and lemon zest. Cook, stirring, until the cream is reduced to about 2½ cups. Remove the ginger pieces and pour the cream over the asparagus.

Stir-Fried Broccoli

SERVES 20

12 broccoli stalks

¼ cup safflower oil

½ cup sesame oil

2 bunches watercress

½ cup reduced-sodium soy sauce or oyster sauce

12 garlic cloves, crushed

¼ cup toasted sesame seeds

1. Separate the broccoli florets and slice the stems on the diagonal.

2. Bring a large pot of water to a boil and parboil the broccoli for 4 minutes. Drain.

3. Heat the oils in a wok or large skillet. Add the broccoli, watercress, and garlic and cook, stirring, for 6 minutes, or until the broccoli is crisp-tender. Stir in the sesame seeds. Serve hot or cold.

Zucchini in Lemon-Mint Butter

12 young (not mini) yellow zucchini	1 red and 1 yellow bell pepper, skinned, seeded, and diced
20 young green zucchini	⅔ cup minced fresh mint leaves
¾ cup (8 ounces) unsalted butter	Juice of 3 lemons

1. Scrub zucchini and trim stem and flower ends. Cut in half crosswise and lengthwise.

2. In a large pot of salted boiling water, cook the zucchini for 8 to 10 minutes, or until crisp-tender. Drain.

3. In a skillet, melt the butter and stir in the peppers and mint. When the peppers are wilted, not browned, remove from heat and stir in the lemon juice. Stir in the zucchini. Serve warm.

Desserts and Sweets

Professional bakers and students use the "bakers percent" system, which is recommended by the American Institute of Baking. The Institute is a good resource for both educational advice and information. Membership allows you hotline information calls to answer specific questions. Eventually foodservice professionals need to bake and scale up by using weight measures.

Beginning caterers, who do not yet have professional ovens and equipment, usually cannot do really large-scale baking. The 18-by-26-inch sheet pans or the many layers needed for volume presentation will not be accommodated by domestic ovens. They can, however, use a 13-by-18-inch half sheet, which will serve 24 and can be made in multiples.

The following cakes and tidbits can be made in a variety of ovens, including portable convection ones. Though many start-up caterers use the services of professional bakers, a simple cake baked from the best ingredients and decorated with candied flowers mixed with edible ones and tied with a foil mesh ribbon, or plated with fresh berries and a dollop of whipped cream, will satisfy your guests and please your accountant.

The cakes in this chapter can be mixed and matched for attractive buffet service. Several of them freeze well, and unused portions can be used for trifles or toasted for tea. They are not fancy and are quite forgiving. If there is any difficulty in transporting even a small cake, the final assembly and trimming can be done on location.

Almond Biscotti

YIELD: 40 BISCOTTI

1 pound slivered almonds

½ cup granulated sugar

2 cups all-purpose flour

1½ cups packed light brown sugar

1½ teaspoons ground cinnamon

1 teaspoon baking powder

¼ cup (2 ounces) unsalted butter

3 eggs, lightly beaten

1. Preheat the oven to 350°F. Lightly grease and flour a baking sheet.

2. Toast the almonds in a single layer on a baking sheet for 10 minutes. Leave the oven on and remove the almonds. Cool. Place 1 cup of the almonds and the granulated sugar in a food processor and pulse until almonds are the consistency of medium-fine bread crumbs.

3. In a large mixing bowl, stir the flour, brown sugar, cinnamon, baking powder, and almond mixture. Put the remaining almonds in processor with the butter and process for 3 or 4 seconds, or until chunky. Add to the flour mixture and blend in the eggs. Knead until all the ingredients are incorporated.

4. Divide the dough in half and form into ropes about 1 inch in diameter. Place side by side on the prepared baking sheet. Flatten gently.

5. Bake for 20 minutes, or until lightly browned.

6. Cut the ropes into ¾-inch slices, leaving them on the baking sheet. Turn the oven off and let the slices stand in oven for 20 minutes. Let cool on wire racks. Store in an airtight container.

Curled Almond Tiles

YIELD: 36 TILES

2 egg whites
1 egg yolk
½ cup sugar
½ teaspoon vanilla extract
3 tablespoons unsalted butter, melted and cooled

3 tablespoons all-purpose flour
2 tablespoons ground almonds
½ cup sliced almonds

1. Preheat the oven to 400°F. Grease and lightly flour baking sheets.

2. In a medium bowl, beat the egg whites, yolk, sugar, and vanilla with an electric mixer for 3 minutes, or until the mixture is syrupy. Incorporate the butter, flour, and ground almonds.

3. Drop by teaspoons onto the prepared pans and spread gently into 2-inch circles. Sprinkle with the almond slices. Leave 3 inches between cookies. Make 12 at a time unless you have an assistant to speed the curling process.

4. Bake for 4 minutes. Immediately lift the warm cookies, one by one, with a metal spatula and curl over a cannoli mold or a rolling pin. Flat cookies can be returned to the warm oven to soften if they harden while you are preparing the curls.

5. Let the tiles cool completely. Store in an airtight container for up to one week.

Angel Food Cake

12 egg whites

2 teaspoons cream of tartar

1 tablespoon lemon juice

1¼ cups granulated sugar

1½ teaspoons vanilla extract

1½ cups cake flour

2¾ cups confectioners' sugar, sifted

1. Preheat the oven to 350°F.

2. In a large bowl, beat the egg whites with an electric mixer and, as they start to stiffen, slowly add the cream of tartar and lemon juice. As they stiffen more, gradually beat in the granulated sugar and vanilla until soft peaks form.

3. In a separate bowl, mix the flour and confectioners' sugar. Gently fold into the egg whites.

4. Turn into a dry 10-inch tube pan and bake for 30 minutes, or until the cake springs back when lightly touched. Let cool in the inverted pan. If the pan does not have "legs," invert over a funnel or bottle.

Berry Summer Pudding

SERVES 20

1 pound strawberries, hulled

1 pound blueberries

1 pound raspberries

1 pound blackberries or pitted cherries

2 cups sugar

1 large loaf of sliced white sandwich bread

1 cup whipped unsalted butter at room temperature

Frozen yogurt or crème fraîche for serving

1. Place all the berries in a bowl of water to drain of any grit. Drain in colander until dry. In a large bowl, combine the berries and sugar. Stir gently to blend.

2. Trim the crusts from the bread and butter the bread slices. Line a pudding bowl or charlotte mold with the bread slices, buttered side out. Place one-third of the berries in the mold, and press the berries up the sides with a large spoon. Repeat twice, topping with bread slices, buttered side down.

3. Place a plate or removable tart tin bottom on top to press the mixture down. Put a weight on top and refrigerate for several hours, or up to a day.

4. Unmold and serve with a scoop of frozen yogurt or a dollop of crème fraîche.

Bourbon-Pecan Bread Pudding

SERVES 20

2 cups pecan halves

12 jumbo eggs

1½ cups sugar

1½ quarts nonfat milk

1 cup bourbon

1 tablespoon vanilla extract

3 large loaves Italian bread, cut into 80 slices

2 cups plumped raisins

¼ cup (4 ounces) butter, softened for pan

1 teaspoon freshly grated nutmeg

Whipped cream for garnish

1. Preheat the oven to 350°F. Butter a 12-by-18-inch, deep baking pan. Spread the pecans in a single layer on a baking sheet and toast for 5 minutes, or until fragrant. Set aside.

2. In bowl large enough to hold all ingredients, beat the eggs and 1¼ cups of the sugar with an electric mixer until thick. Stir in the milk, bourbon, and vanilla. Soak the bread in the egg mixture until soaked through. Fold the raisins and nuts into the bread batter.

3. Place the bread, layer by layer, in the prepared pan. Pour any remaining batter over all. Bake now, or refrigerate for up to 3 hours before baking.

4. Place the pudding dish in a larger pan and add hot water to a depth of 1 inch to the larger pan. Bake for 30 to 45 minutes, or until a knife inserted in the center comes out clean.

5. Sprinkle with nutmeg before serving. Accompany with cream whipped with maple sugar.

Wild Rice and Carrot Cake

YIELD: ONE 13-BY-18-INCH CAKE

6 eggs, separated

1 cup granulated sugar

2 cups packed brown sugar

2 cups safflower oil

3 cups grated carrots

3 cups nonfat milk

1 tablespoon vanilla extract

4 cups all-purpose flour

1 tablespoon baking powder

2 teaspoons baking soda

1 tablespoon ground cinnamon

1 tablespoon ground nutmeg

4 cups cooked wild rice

1 cup flaked coconut

1 can (8 ounces) crushed pineapple in pineapple juice, drained

Cream Cheese Topping:

20 ounces light cream cheese at room temperature

6 cups confectioners' sugar

Sour cream, as needed to make it spreadable

1. Preheat the oven to 375°F. Lightly grease and flour a 13-by-18-by-3-inch pan.

2. In a bowl large enough to hold all ingredients, beat the eggs and sugars together until pale and thickened. Add the oil and carrots. Stir in the milk and vanilla.

3. In a medium bowl, combine the flour, baking powder, baking soda, cinnamon, and nutmeg. Stir to blend. In another bowl, combine the wild rice, coconut, and pineapple. Stir to blend. Alternately add the flour and rice mixtures to the liquid in the bowl. Pour into the prepared pan.

4. Bake for 50 minutes to 1 hour, or until a tester inserted in the center of the cake comes out clean. Transfer the pan to a wire rack and let cool completely.

5. To make the topping: In a medium bowl, combine the cream cheese and sugar. Stir in the sour cream as needed to reach spreading consistency.

6. Spread the topping evenly over the cake. Miniature marzipan carrots are an attractive decoration.

Chocolate Terrine in White-Chocolate Blizzard

YIELD: ONE 9-BY-5-INCH LOAF; SERVES 20

4 tablespoons butter, melted, plus 1 cup (8 ounces) unsalted butter, cut into chunks

½ cup brewed espresso

2 tablespoons coffee liqueur

⅓ teaspoon ground cinnamon

2 cups sugar

2 ounces unsweetened chocolate, chopped

6 ounces bittersweet chocolate, chopped

5 eggs

White-Chocolate Blizzard Frosting:

¾ cup heavy cream

6 ounces white chocolate

4 tablespoons unsalted butter

2 tablespoons framboise or other berry eau de vie

Meringue mushrooms and/or candied roses and violets (optional)

1. Preheat the oven to 325°F. Butter a 9-by-5-by-3-inch loaf pan. Line with aluminum foil and brush thoroughly with the melted butter.

2. In a small saucepan, combine the coffee, coffee liqueur, cinnamon, and 1 tablespoon of the sugar. Stir until the sugar is dissolved. Remove from heat.

3. In a double boiler over barely simmering water, melt the 1 cup butter and the chocolate. Set aside to cool.

4. In a large bowl, beat the eggs and the remaining sugar with an electric mixer for 5 minutes, or until the mixture forms a ribbon when dropped from a beater. Stir in the cooled coffee mixture, then the chocolate mixture.

5. Pour into the prepared pan. Cover securely with aluminum foil and place in a larger pan. Add hot water to come halfway up the sides of the loaf pan. Bake for 1½ hours, or until firm. Let cool thoroughly on a wire rack. Unmold.

6. To make the frosting: In a heavy saucepan, heat the cream over medium heat until the surface starts to roll. Reduce heat and, without letting it boil, stir to thicken. Stir in the chocolate and butter until smooth. Pour into a bowl, add the framboise, and stir until lukewarm.

7. Spread the frosting over the top and sides of the terrine. Scrape with a decorating comb or fork to form swirls and ridges. If desired, decorate with meringue mushrooms and/or candied roses and violets. Refrigerate until ready to serve. May be frozen after frosting. Serve at room temperature.

Chocolate and Chocolate Cake

YIELD: ONE 10-INCH TUBE CAKE

½ cup (4 ounces) unsalted butter at room temperature

2½ cups packed light brown sugar

1 cup sour cream

3 large eggs

1 tablespoon vanilla extract

4 ounces unsweetened chocolate, melted

2 cups all-purpose flour

2 teaspoons baking powder

1 teaspoon baking soda

½ teaspoon salt

2 cups chocolate chips

Chocolate Cream (recipe follows)

1. Preheat the oven to 350°F. Grease and lightly flour a 10-inch tube pan with a removable bottom.

2. In a large bowl, cream the butter with an electric mixer until fluffy. Beat in the sugar, then the sour cream, eggs, vanilla, and melted chocolate.

3. In a medium bowl, stir together the flour, baking powder, baking soda, and salt. Stir into the chocolate batter. Mix until well blended. Fold in the chocolate chips. Pour the batter into the prepared pan.

4. Bake for 45 to 55 minutes, or until a tester inserted in the center of the cake comes out clean. Let cool on a wire rack for 30 minutes, then remove from the pan. Serve with chocolate cream.

Chocolate Cream

YIELD: 4 CUPS

6 ounces sweet chocolate, chopped

2 cups heavy cream

2 teaspoons vanilla extract

1. In a double boiler over simmering water, melt the chocolate in a small saucepan, adding up to ¼ cup water to make a smooth syrup.

2. In a deep bowl, whip the cream with the vanilla until thick. Fold in the chocolate mixture. Seasonal berries are a nice accompaniment.

Madeleines

YIELD: 40 MADELEINES

2 eggs

1 cup sugar

1 cup all-purpose flour

¾ cup (6 ounces) unsalted butter, melted and cooled

Grated zest of 1 lemon

Confectioners' sugar for dusting

1. Preheat the oven to 350°F. Grease and lightly flour 40 madeleine wells.

2. In a double boiler over simmering water, beat the eggs and sugar together for 2 minutes, or until warm and blended.

3. Place the top of the double boiler in bowl of ice water and continue beating for 5 minutes. Remove from the ice water and alternately blend in the flour and the cooled melted butter and lemon zest. Stir only until blended.

4. Use one tablespoon of batter for each madeleine or follow pan manufacturer's directions. Bake for 12 minutes. Let cool for 1 minute in pan. Unmold and let cool on wire racks. Dust with confectioners' sugar to serve.

Pastel Petits Fours

YIELD: 24 PETITS FOURS

7 eggs, separated

2 teaspoons lemon juice

9 tablespoons sugar

½ teaspoon vanilla extract

½ teaspoon almond extract

½ cup cold water

¾ teaspoon cream of tartar

1½ cups cake flour

¼ teaspoon salt

Icing:

1 egg white

2 cups sifted confectioners' sugar

⅓ to ½ cup water, as needed

Candied violets, roses, and silver dragées for decoration

1. Preheat the oven to 350°F. In a large bowl, beat the egg yolks until pale and thick, about 5 minutes. Set aside.

2. In a medium bowl, combine the lemon juice, sugar, vanilla, almond extract, and cold water. Stir until the sugar is dissolved.

3. In a large bowl, beat the egg whites with the cream of tartar until stiff, glossy peaks are formed. In a small bowl, combine the flour and salt. Stir to blend. Mix the lemon mixture into the beaten egg yolks, then fold in the egg whites. Gently fold in the flour mixture.

4. Bake in 2 ungreased 9-inch square cake pans for 30 minutes, or until the cakes spring back when touched. Let cool completely on wire racks. Cut each cake into 12 diamonds, squares, or triangles.

5. To make the icing: In a medium bowl, stir the egg white into the sugar. Gradually stir in water to make a spreadable paste. Quickly divide among 4 small containers and tint each batch lightly with food coloring. Frost the petits fours. Decorate with candied violets, roses, and silver dragées.

Mocha Cream Cake

YIELD: ONE 9-INCH LAYER CAKE

Vanilla Sponge Layers:

6 eggs

1⅓ cups sugar

2 teaspoons vanilla extract

1½ cups all-purpose flour

3 tablespoons comstarch

¼ cup (4 ounces) butter, melted

Mocha Buttercream (recipe follows)

Chocolate curls, chocolate-covered coffee beans, or crushed toasted nuts for garnish

1. To make the sponge layers: Preheat the oven to 350°F. Butter and flour two 9-inch layer cake pans.

2. In a small nonreactive saucepan, beat the eggs, gradually incorporating the sugar. Continue beating and set over low heat until the egg mixture is quite warm. Remove from heat, transfer to a bowl, and continue beating until cool. Add the vanilla.

3. In a small bowl, mix the flour and cornstarch. Stir into the egg mixture until blended. Pour into the prepared pans.

4. Bake for 20 to 25 minutes, or until a tester inserted in the center of the cake comes out clean. Cool for 10 minutes, then remove from the pans and let cool on a wire rack.

5. Fill and frost immediately, or freeze for for up to 1 month. Fill and top with mocha buttercream, or fill with mocha and cover with chocolate. Garnish with chocolate curls, chocolate-covered coffee beans, or crushed toasted nuts.

Mocha Buttercream

YIELD: 2 CUPS

3 egg yolks

½ cup sugar

½ cup brewed espresso

1 cup (8 ounces) unsalted butter, cut into small dice

2 tablespoons coffee liqueur

1. In a small bowl, beat the egg yolks with an electric mixer on medium until pale and thick.

2. In a small, heavy saucepan, bring the sugar and espresso to a boil, reduce heat, and simmer for 2 to 3 minutes.

3. Pour the coffee mixture in a thin stream into the egg yolks and keep beating. Return mixture to saucepan and beat over very low heat for 5 or 6 minutes, or until thick enough to coat a wooden spoon.

4. Quickly beat in the butter and coffee liqueur. Remove from heat, stirring until fluffy. The mixture will thicken as it stands.

Chocolate Buttercream Cake

YIELD: ONE 9-INCH LAYER CAKE

2 vanilla sponge layers (page 276)

½ cup heavy cream

½ cup (4 ounces) unsalted butter, sliced

4 ounces bittersweet chocolate, coarsely chopped

2 ounces milk chocolate, coarsely chopped

1. Prepare the vanilla sponge layers.

2. To make the chocolate buttercream: In a small saucepan, heat the cream just until the surface ripples. Reduce heat and cook, stirring constantly, for 3 or 4 minutes. Stir in the butter and chocolates and mix until smooth. Remove from heat and stir until fluffy.

3. Fill and top the sponge layers with the buttercream.

Walnut Eggnog Cake

YIELD: ONE 10-INCH TUBE CAKE

1½ cups (12 ounces) unsalted butter at room temperature

2 cups sugar

6 eggs, separated

⅔ cup milk

½ cup Cognac or brandy

1 teaspoon vanilla extract

2 cups unbleached flour

2 cups whole-wheat flour

1 teaspoon cream of tartar

2 cups (8 ounces) broken walnut pieces

Confectioners' sugar for dusting

1. Preheat the oven to 275°F. Grease and lightly flour a 10-inch tube pan.

2. In a large bowl, cream the butter and sugar with an electric mixer until thoroughly combined. Beat in the egg yolks. In a small bowl, combine the milk, Cognac, and vanilla. In another bowl, stir the flours together. Stir into the butter mixture alternately with the liquid.

3. In a deep bowl, beat the egg whites with the cream of tartar until almost stiff. Add the walnuts to the batter, then fold in the beaten egg whites. Pour into the prepared pan.

4. Bake for 2¼ hours. Let cool upright for 30 minutes, then invert and let cool 1 hour longer. Dust with confectioners' sugar.

12

Beverages

After all the food selections have been made, the caterer has to determine what beverages are to be served. Does the client want to provide bottled water, and if so, what kind? Basic, good-tasting non-carbonated water, either tap or bottled, must be available at all events. Whether to supply carbonated mineral water, mixers, and flavored soft drinks depends on the nature of the event and the client's preferences. Iced tea is a very popular drink and easy to have on hand. Urns of varying sizes for coffee, decaf, and assorted teas are usually required. Espresso machines, which are available for purchase and rental, are being called for more frequently, not only for demitasse but cappuccinos, lattes, and other specialty drinks as well. These days it is in your best interest to know about smoothies and chai as well. They seem here to stay.

Wine and Spirits

As for alcohol, most events include wine and sometimes beer and a variety of water and soft drinks. Often, a limited offering of premier-quality vodka, gin, bourbon, and Scotch is offered; either on the rocks or with a simple mixer, these drinks don't require a bartender or two. A full bar, however, must always be staffed.

281

Once you have a license to do business as a caterer, you may apply for a liquor license. Applications and requirements vary widely from state to state. Contact your state alcohol commission for information. Your lawyer will provide guidelines on your responsibilities when catering a party for which you are ordering and serving liquor. He or she will also help you decide whether you want a liquor license. A liquor license can sometimes be obtained on a per-event basis, generally for things like cash bars at fund-raisers. Your lawyer and state alcohol commission are the sources for specific information. It is an important issue and must be considered from many viewpoints that leave the caterer hospitable and accountable. It is necessary both to be generous and to control alcohol consumption.

Most distributors have information about reasonable amounts required to stock a full bar. For wine, the Sommelier Society is most helpful in offering not only certification courses, but also less formal meetings, tastings, and general advice. Even a few classes are likely to be extremely helpful. The Educational Foundation of the National Restaurant Association offers many courses, and graduates receive a manager or server certificate. The International Sommelier Guild has an accreditation program that is considered a benchmark in training. They also have facilitated tastings and tutored wine and food pairings.

The Wine Spectator School offers professional classes in understanding professional wine sales and service. You can even take a sample course if you go to their website. There is also the Pacific Rim Wine Education Center, which has excellent instructors.

Tasting and reading are important. One of the best continuing-education tools for people in the food industry is *Santé,* a monthly magazine that reviews an enormous number of wines from all over the world that are available at regional distributors. Rob Costantino, wine editor of *Santé,* told me they can review so many varieties because they have developed a network of restaurant professionals whom they trust. These selections are not rated, just described, and the cost listed.

Eric Lilavois, who has various international wine certifications, publishes a newsletter called the *Lila Vine.* Each month, he tastes a dozen or so midprice wines and writes as though he were talking to you about them. It is a little like having a personal consultant. You can read about his selections, then taste the wines that appeal to you or that you think will appeal to your client. There is information that will let you contact the wine source directly.

As for selecting wines, reading is helpful, but it really is the liquid in the bottle that is the ultimate learning experience. There is a lot to know, as people are interested today in a more sophisticated way than in the past, when simply a red and a white would suffice.

The aroma or bouquet is usually your first introduction to the wine in the glass. Savor the fragrance and then taste the wine. You don't want too small a sip; you need enough to feel it on your tongue and the back of your mouth. You can determine the body by the apparent weight in your mouth: light, medium, heavy. Is the taste floral, fruity, grapey? What word comes to mind to describe it? If you really like a wine, *elegant* is always a safe word. If you don't like what you are tasting, move on. Have some water or bread and taste the next. You will gradually learn the appellations, viticultural regions, barreling, and the rest. At the end of the day, taste is still what decides for people.

A few phone calls will start you networking, and you will soon discover what the area prizewinners are. If you are starting out on a small scale, it is good to establish a relationship with a well-stocked liquor store in your neighborhood, so that suggestions will be knowledgeable, prices good, and returns accepted for unused bottles. As usual, however, be sure you have qualified bar help with whom you can consult. Often clients will order the liquor directly to their taste or on your recommendation of selections and quantity. If there are no specific requests, the needs of most contemporary diners are usually met with a good-quality Bordeaux and Chardonnay—the Chardonnay served well chilled, and the red *à chambre,* or about 60°F. With a very young red wine, letting it breathe smooths out the mouth feel. As with food, choose the best quality you can comfortably afford, as a smaller measure will then satisfy the palate.

A cool Beaujolais Nouveau can be served from its presentation in the fall until May 1. In the summer, chilled Tavel is an extremely pleasant rosé, and there are several Italian *frizzante* wines, like prosecco, with a light tingle, that are refreshing. From the various regions of Italy and Spain to Australia and Chile come flavorful and discrete wines. There are also more and more viticultural designations in this country that are producing excellent wines. Regional wines you grow to know will become good choices, though they can be a little expensive.

Fortified wines like sherry or port are often served when there is a full bar or, of course, if they are specifically requested for dessert. Brandies, Cognacs, liqueurs, grappas, ice wines or other dessert wines, and eau-de-vie occasionally accompany coffee and tea. For special service, you can rent a liqueur cart.

When wines and liquors are stocked for cooking, the appropriate portions are factored into the cost of the dish, not with the beverages. Sweet and savory sauces, marinades, and deglazing can be enhanced with specially chosen aromatic spirits. Crepes, cakes, and mousses are often made with liqueurs. In most states no license is needed for this use.

Often, Champagne or other sparkling wines are offered for their versatility and the celebratory mood they set. They are equally good with hors d'oeuvres, desserts, or after-dinner dancing. Jeroboams, which contain the equivalent of four bottles, are sometimes used for Champagne toasts. The giant-sized Nebuchadnezzar, which holds the equivalent of eighteen bottles, is used on rare showy events.

The very best Champagne is best drunk well chilled, and in small amounts for small groups. Often moderately priced sparkling wines are delicious, and discovering them is a challenge to the skill and taste of the purchaser. Classic Champagne drinks like Champagne cocktails, mimosas, and Bellinis are served not only for brunches, but for summer parties as well. Fresh peach or orange juice and bitters can be kept at the bar. The addition of framboise or crème de cassis creates the popular Kir Royale.

A Kir is white wine and crème de cassis, served over ice or not. Made with red wine, it is called a Cardinale. Framboise is another good Champagne or white wine mixer. Spritzers are a way to serve something festive with reduced alcohol and calories. Punches are again coming into favor as people are becoming more adventurous, and contemporary versions are made with style and a light hand. They are served warm and mulled in the winter and icy cold in the summer, with citrus fruit and spices or aromatic herbs.

Unless your client has no preference, don't order a case or more of wine that you yourself have not tasted and approved, preferably with a second opinion. Your wine purveyor will be helpful, as will your network of friends and acquaintances. Don't be shy about asking until you build up a repertoire of wines for various meals and events. A caterer does not have to build a wine cellar as many restaurants do. There is nothing wrong in repeatedly serving labels and vintages you know and trust as you expand your palate.

Another item to check is whether locations allow alcohol—some public spaces do not—or require a special license or permit for liquor to be served on a single-function basis. The obligations of the caterer, the host, and the bar server must be defined.

No minor is to be served alcohol, no intoxicated person can be served, and pregnant women must be notified of the potential dangers of alcohol. Any guest who is deemed under the influence must not be permitted to drive from the event. It is necessary to talk with your lawyer about who is responsible for what. Logic dictates the host must be discreetly informed that a guest needs transportation home. The staff never drinks.

Most wine is bottled in 75-centiliter bottles that equal twenty-four ounces. A standard bottle will provide six 4-ounce glasses each; sparkling wines and Champagne pour 7 glasses to a bottle. With meals the following are average portions: lunch 1½ glasses a person; an evening party, 2 glasses; and for a full dinner, 2 to 3 glasses each. If there are two kinds of wine, it might come out to 2 glasses of each wine per guest. For a lengthy affair, it is a good idea to stock an extra case of whatever is being served.

If the client requests it, good-label bottles of bourbon, gin, Scotch, and vodka are easily stocked along with tonic, seltzer, cranberry, grape-fruit, orange, and tomato juices. Lemon and lime sections and Worcestershire and Tabasco sauces should be on hand at the bar also.

Sometimes a specific pitcher of cocktails is requested. Whether it is margaritas, daiquiris, piña coladas, martinis, or Bloody Marys, follow your favorite recipe or that of your client, setting the portion of alcohol at about 2 ounces a drink.

There is some equipment, like good-quality corkscrews, bottle and can openers, paring knives, and zesters that you will want to own. Companies such as Metrokane are good suppliers. Skewers, stirrers, straws, swizzle sticks, small doilies, and cocktail napkins can be bought inexpensively in bulk. Bar shakers and strainers, buckets, and stands can be rented. Containers for ice will vary with the service style. It may be useful to have a few conventionally sized ones for small bar setups and large ones for locations that do not have icemakers or adequate freezer storage.

Consider buying a supply of stemmed red and white wine glasses as well as water and iced-tea glasses. You will use them enough to warrant the purchase. If the client wants something special, it can be rented.

Always have water available for guests when you serve wine or any alcohol so that they do not quench their thirst with liquor. Wine is generally a more moderate drink than hard liquor because it is usually sipped and accompanied with food, either hors d'oeuvres, dinner, or dessert.

Coffee

Good coffee always brings smiles, but no one forgives a bad cup. People are very passionate about coffee. Aromatic or artificially flavored coffees have no place on a food menu. There are so many coffees from all over the world and so many ways of roasting, grinding, and preparing them, that the chemical addition of other flavors overpowers the bouquet of a really good cup of coffee or espresso. The artificial aromatic blends have a bit too much perfume and are not the best complement for a meal. You are better off simply sticking to the highest and freshest grade of a standard house blend for standard cups of coffee and decaf. Espresso is increasingly popular, along with cappuccinos and lattes.

For standard coffee, the proportion is 1 coffee measure (2 level tablespoons) to ¾ cup water. Keep everything very clean, as oil residue builds up, breeds germs, and attracts dirt. For this reason, it is not a good idea to use a brewer larger than 25 servings. Only 80 percent of your guests will want coffee after dinner these days, and one-third of those will probably want decaf.

Jan Anderson at FrancisFrancis! sells aesthetically pleasing heavy-duty espresso machines that make a style statement as well as a very functional one. For recurring large events, the FrancisFrancis! X2 espresso machine is unbeatable for catering. At about twice the size of a conventional home espresso machine, the the 5-liter reservoir will produce 100 cups of espresso in a very short time at 1,100 watts. The easy-to-read gauges will let you know when everything is ready. It even has a clock. The water tanks can be easily refilled from the top, and the tank does not have to be removed. The handles have inserts so that they can take the Illy easy-serving individual serving pods as well as loose coffee. The pods, of course, make for a neater station under heavy use.

Myra Fiori at Illy Caffè stresses the importance of organization in coffee service. They rent espresso/cappuccino machines and either train someone to use them or supply a server. The Pasquini Livia 90 has a 1-gallon reservoir and can generate espresso and steam milk at the same time. The company has received the ISO 9001 certification, which is the top European standard for quality control. Illy guarantees their coffee and the production process.

Contrary to popular opinion, all espresso has less caffeine per ounce than American-style coffee. It is, as Dr. Illy says, an almost guilt-free indulgence. He recommends not storing espresso in the freezer and never serving it with lemon peel, which was originally used to cover a bitter taste. Store in airtight containers at room temperature for 1-day use and refrigerate for longer storage.

More than a passing nod should be given to selecting and serving coffee, as it has become an easy way to extend social time for people looking for low-calorie and nonalcoholic pleasures.

Tea

Green, black, and oolong teas have been the subject of much study showing these teas to be beneficial for you. As a result, they have become more and more popular and acceptable in a culture that primarily drinks coffee. As with all other ingredients, the best-possible-quality tea prepared with attention to detail will give the most pleasure. There are numerous tea websites on the Internet, both general ones and sites for teas associated with specific companies such as Bigelow, Celestial Seasonings, Fortnum & Mason, Tazo, and Twinings. Porto Rico Coffee has a tremendous selection of teas and tea equipment available for tea brewing needs.

One pound of tea equals 200 teaspoons or 200 tea bags, which will make 200 cups of tea. It follows that ½ pound of tea will make one hundred 5- to 6-ounce cups of hot tea, certainly a beverage bargain.

Most caterers serve tea by placing a quality tea bag on a saucer beside a cup or in a small teapot of hot water brought to the table. For buffet serving, an assortment of tea bags—regular, decaf, and herbal— are placed on each table or at the coffee and tea station, next to an urn of near-boiling water. For a large crowd, this seems the best system, especially for herbals.

A more elegant way to serve a single kind of tea is to make it from concentrate: Pour 4 cups of boiling water over ⅔ cup of tea leaves, cover, and steep for 5 minutes. Strain into a pitcher, cover, and keep at room temperature for no more than 3 or 4 hours. Add 3 quarts of hot water for 25 cups of hot tea. Serve in a large teapot on a tray set with a pot of hot water and the option of lemon slices, milk, or cream.

For small groups, you can pour freshly boiling water over the leaves and steep for 3 to 5 minutes. Or, with some of the press-style tea infusers, it would be possible to set one at each table and replace them as needed.

Iced tea is a very popular beverage and an easy one to supply. For fresh iced tea, place 12 tea bags or ⅓ cup loose tea in a large pitcher and add 4 cups of water that has just been brought to a boil. Sweeten or spice to taste, steep for 5 minutes, and add 4 cups cold water. Add orange slices, lemon slices, whole cloves, cinnamon sticks, or fresh ginger slices for your personal blends.

When working with limited range space, a microwave oven can be used to make iced teas. For 8 cups, place 12 tea bags and 3 cups water in a 4-cup Pyrex measuring cup, run the microwave on high for 2 minutes, remove, and let stand for 3 minutes. Remove the tea bags, sweeten to taste if desired, then add 5 cups cold water.

Smoothies, Chai, Juices, Water

Smoothies have grown in popularity, and your guests, especially the health-conscious ones, may require them. With a couple of machines like a Vita-Mix, you can make enough for a crowd and keep them coming. As with all professional equipment, a juicer or blender should never be left unattended. A large supply of ice, fruit, berries, and a variety of liquids such as water, yogurt, low-fat milk, and soy milk will give guests the options they enjoy. A basic smoothie can be made from a ripe banana, 1 cup of blueberries, 2 cups of vanilla low-fat yogurt, and 1 cup of ice cubes. Blend all the ingredients on high for 10 to 15 seconds for a refreshing drink.

Chai has increased in almost surprising popularity. Traditionally it is black tea mixed with spices and sugar or honey, brewed in skim or soy milk. Sometimes nondairy creamers are used. There are many commercial dispensers available for both concentrates and mixes. Oregon Chai offers a great variety, including single-serve packages that are excellent if you want to test your audience. Their original chai is made of black tea, honey, vanilla, and spices. It has the same caffeine content as a lightly brewed cup of tea. It is good to remember that chais average 150 calories a cup hot and about 200 in the iced tea format. People seem to like the sweet spicy tea, hot or cold. It is also available in decaf or with a green tea base. Pacific Tea and Tazo Tea offer top-of-the-line chais, but you can develop your own recipe. Feel free to experiment, but not on the job.

Fruit drinks—pure, blended fresh, or pasteurized—are another consumer favorite. Fresh juice should be fresh, either made on site or the night before and kept under refrigeration. Aerating it will revive it before serving. There are also many fruit drinks and nectars that you might offer on request.

Water must be available at all events. The decision of which to serve and in what style has to be reviewed with your client.

Though beverages are an accent at a meal, people are becoming more and more aware of the quality of what they imbibe. It is the caterer's task to make certain that the beverage service adds to the aura of hospitality clients rely on.

How to Find All the Help You Need: Resource Directories for the Professional Caterer

The directories that follow are a starting point, a Resources 101, if you will. There is an abundance of virtually instant gratification in response to queries of culinary interest with a a click of the mouse to the Internet, an 800-telephone number, and a magazine subscription. By and large there is more information than a goal-oriented person can process. Journals such as *Catering*, *Culinary Art Trends*, *Food Arts*, and *Hospitality*, along with the gazillions of organizations, growers, and producers that print newsletters all offer a wealth of information, recipes, and products.

The following lists will give you access to what you need most of the time.

Please note: In some listings there is only a name and an 800-telephone number and/or a website addres, with no mailing address. If you contact these resources they will supply you with their mailing address, if necessary.

BEVERAGE DIRECTORY

Aabree Coffee Company
tel: 888-280-8584
website: www.aabree.com

Bigelow Tea
tel: 8000 244 3569
website: www.bigelowtea.com

Celestial Seasonings
Consumer Services
4600 Sleepytime Drive
Boulder, Colorado 80301
tel: 800-351-8175
website: www.celestialseasoning.com

Coca-Cola
Consumer Affairs
tel: 800-995-2653
website: www.cokecce.com

Evian Water
website: www.evianwater.com

FrancisFrancis!
Jan Anderson
Route 2, Box 133
Garrison, New York 10524
tel: 845-424-3016
fax: 845-424-4564
website: www.francisfrancis.com

Illy Caffè
Myra Fiori
200 Clearbrook Road
Elmsford, New York 10523
tel: 914-784-0500
fax: 914-784-0580
website: www.illy.com

International Sommelier Guild
P.O. Box 610
Montchanin, Delaware 19710
website:
www.internationalsommelier.com

Metrokane
tel: 212-759-6262
website: metrokane.com
Rabbit corkscrews and accessories.

National Coffee Association
of the U.S.A.
110 Wall Street
New York, New York 10005
tel: 212-344-5596
fax: 212-425-7059
website: www.ncausa.org

Odwalla
120 Stone Pine Road
Half Moon Bay, California 94019
tel: 650-726-1888/800-ODWALLA
(638-4635)
website: www.odwalla.com

Oregon Chai
1745 NW Marshall
Portland, Oregon 97209
tel: 888-874-CHAI
website: www.sellchai.com

Pacific Chai
12263 Deerhill Road
Midlothian, Virginia 23112
tel: 888-882-4248
website: www.pacificchai.com

Pacific Rim Wine Education Center
website: www.pacrimwine.org

Perrier/Group San Pellegrino
777 West Putnam Avenue
Greenwich, Connecticut 06836
tel: 203-868-0200/800-937-2002
websites: www.perrier.com;
www.sanpellegrino.com

Poland Spring Water
website: www.polandspringwater.com

Porto Rico Importing Company
201 Bleecker Street
New York, New York 10012
tel: 212-477-5421/800-453-5908
fax: 212-979-2303
website: www.portorico.com

The Republic of Tea
8 Digital Drive, Suite 100
Novato, California 94949
website: www.republicoftea.com

Snapple
website: www.snapple.com

Starbucks Coffee Company
Specialty Sales Department
2203 Airport Way South
Seattle, Washington 98124
tel: 800-344-1575
website: www.starbucks.com/
    business/foodservice

State Liquor Authority of New York
250 Broadway
New York, New York 10013
tel: 212-417-4002
website: www.abc.state.ny.us

Sommelier Society of America
P.O. Box 20080, West Village Station
New York, New York 10014
tel: 212-679-4190
fax: 212-255-8959
website:
www.sommeliersocietyofAmerica.org

Tazo Tea and Chai
website: www.tazo.com

Vita-Mix Corporation
Food Service Division
8615 Usher Road
Cleveland, Ohio 44138
website:
www.vitamix.xom/foodservice

Web Bartender
website: www.webtender.com

Wine-Searcher
website: www.wine-searcher.com

Wine Spectator
387 Park Avenue South
New York, New York 10016
tel: 212-684-4224
fax: 212-684-5424
website:
www.winespectatorschool.com

Tea Association of the United States
230 Park Avenue
New York, New York 10169
tel: 212-986-9415
website: www.teausa.com

Local listings in the Yellow Pages and
Internet: bottled water distributors
and soft drink distributors; discount
wine and liquor vendors; professional
culinary and sommelier schools;
restaurant supply houses; state liquor
licensing organization; local wine and
liquor distributors

LOCATION DIRECTORY

Barns of Wolf Trap
1635 Trap Road
Vienna, Virginia
tel: 703-938-8463
website: www.wolftrap.org

Belmont Mansion
Fairmont Park
Philadelphia, Pennsylvania 19131
tel: 215-878-8844
website: www.philaparks.org/ewaabm

Biltmore Estate
One Biltmore Plaza
Asheville, North Carolina 28803
tel: 704-274-1776
website: www.biltmore.com

Brooklyn Botanical Garden
1000 Washington Street
Brooklyn, New York 11225
tel: 718-622-4433
website: www.bbg.org

Cathedral of St. John the Divine
1047 Amsterdam Avenue
New York, New York 10025
tel: 212-316-7469
website: www.stjohndivine.org

The Daybreak Star Indian Cultural
Center
Discovery Park
Seattle, Washington 98199
tel: 206-285-4425
website: www.unitedindians.com

Drayton Hall
3380 Ashley River Road
Charleston, South Carolina 29414
tel: 843-769-2600
fax: 843-766-0878
website: www.draytonhall.org

Frederick C. Robie House
5757 South Woodlawn Avenue
Chicago, Illinois 60637
tel: 773-834-1847
fax: 773-834-1538
website: www.robiehouse.org

Ladew Topiary Gardens
3535 Jarrettsville Pike
Monkton, Maryland 21111
tel: 410-557-9570
website: www.ladewgardens.com

Lincoln Park Zoo
2200 North Canon Drive
Cafe Brauer
Chicago, Illinois 60614
tel: 312-280-2767
website: www.lpzoo.com
Indoor and outdoor available.

Los Angeles County Arboretum
301 North Baldwin Avenue
Arcadia, California 91006
tel: 818-821-3211
website: www.arboretum.org

Milwaukee Art Museum
700 North Art Museum Drive
Milwaukee, Wisconsin
tel: 414-224-3200
website: www.mam.org

National Museum of Women in the
Arts
1250 New York Avenue, NW
Washington, D.C. 20005
tel: 202-783-5000
website: www.nmwa.org

The Nature Conservancy
tel: 800-628-6860
website: www.nature.org
Will provide information about sites
from pine barrens, prairies, bird preserves, and riverbanks to waterfalls,
savannahs, and seashores that permit
and have the capacity to accommodate special events.

Old Town Hall
3999 University
Fairfax, Virginia 22030
tel: 703-385-7976
website: www.ci.fairfax.va.us/
    parksrec/oldtowninformation

Point Defiance Zoo and Aquarium
5400 North Pearl Street
Tacoma, Washington
tel: 206-305-1000
website: www.pdza.org

Touro Synagogue
85 Touro Street
Newport, Rhode Island 02840
tel: 401-847-4794
fax: 401-845-6790
website: www.tourosynagogue.org

Union Station
The Columbus Club
50 Massachusetts Avenue NE
Washington, D.C. 20002
tel: 202-289-8300
website: www.unionstationdc.com

Local phone books and online listings
offer these generic locations in many
cities and towns: arboretums; botanic
gardens; chambers of commerce; convention and visitors centers; cultural
councils; landmark commissions;
museums; national historic sites;
parks departments; yacht clubs and
marinas.

Note: Check your local directory for
valet parking services and try
Mapquest.com to find a route to locations that you are scouting.

BUSINESS DIRECTORY

Blumberg Legal Forms
62 White Street
New York, New York 10013
tel: 212-431-5000
website: www.blumberg.com

College of Insurance
101 Murray Street
New York, New York 10007
tel: 212-962-4116
website: www.tci.edu

General corporation start-up
information website:
www.mycorporation.com

Insurance Information Institute
110 William Street
New York, New York 10038
tel: 212-669-9200
website: www.iii.org

Internal Revenue Service
website: www.irs.gov

Kornreich Insurance Services
919 Third Avenue
New York, New York 10022
tel: 212-688-9700/800-321-2122
Fax: 212-319-7509
website: www.niagroup.com

Triple S
Insurance Administration for the
Food Processing Industry
1401 New York Avenue NW,
Suite 400
Washington, D.C. 20005
tel: 202-628-4435
website: www.nfpa-food.org/
  insurance

United States Department of Labor
Office of the Assistant Secretary for
Policy
200 Constitution Avenue NW
Washington, D.C. 20210
tel: 202-219-6197
website: www.dol.gov/elaws
Small business handbook, laws, regulations, and technical assistance service.

U.S. Small Business Administration
House of Representatives
2361 Raybum House Office Building
Washington, D.C. 20515
tel: 800-U-ASK-SBA Answer Desk
website: www.sba.gov

The Wall Street Journal
website: www.wsj.com

CaterPro Software
1174 Stone Pine Lane
Lincoln, California 95648
tel: 916-645-848/800-606-1597
website: www.caterprosoftware.com

Caterware
CaterPlus Software
1601 West Fifth Avenue, Suite 211
Columbus, Ohio 43212
tel: 614-481-7699/800-853-1017
website: www.caterware.com

Cost Guard
CostGuard Software
450 Bronxville Road
Bronxville, New York 10708
tel: 914-337-9030/888-FC-LOWER
fax: 914-337-9031
website: www.costguard.com

EATEC Corporation
1350 Ocean Avenue
Emeryville, California 94608
tel: 510-594-9011
fax 510-594-9091
website: www.eatec.com

ESHA Research
P.O. Box 13028
Salem, Oregon 97309
tel: 503-585-6242
fax: 503-585-5543
website: www.esha.com

Horizon Business Services
Caterease Software
1020 Goodlette Road North
Naples, Florida 34102
tel: 941-261-5828/800-863-1616
fax: 941-261-0067
website: www.caterease.com

Lotus Development Corporation
55 Cambridge Parkway
Cambridge, Massachusetts 02142
website: www.lotus.com

Dine Systems
DineHealthy4 Software
586 French Road, Suite 2
Amherst, New York 14228
tel: 716-688-2492
fax: 716-688-2505
website: www.dinesystems.com

CATERING INFORMATION DIRECTORY

International Association of Culinary
Professionals
304 West Liberty Street, Suite 201
Louisville, Kentucky 40202
tel: 502-581-9786
website: www.iacp.com

International Association of Women
Chefs and Restaurateurs
401 East 80th Street, Suite 4K
New York, New York 10021
tel: 212-879-2709
fax: 212-861-1367
website: www.chefnet.com./wcr

International Special Events Society
401 North Michigan Avenue
Chicago, Illinois 60611
tel: 312-321-6853/800-688-4737
website: www.ises.com
Local chapters in cities throughout
the country.

National Association of Catering
Executives
304 West Liberty Street, Suite 201
Louisville, Kentucky 40202
tel: 502-583-3783
fax: 502-589-3602
website: www.nace.net

Women's Foodservice Forum
401 North Michigan Avenue
Chicago, Illinois 60611
tel: 312-245-1047
fax: 312-673-6994
website:
www.womensfoodserviceforum.com

Small Business Administration
Answer Desk
tel: 800-U-ASK-SBA
website: www.sba.gov

United States Government
Printing Office
Superintendent of Documents
710 Capitol Street NW
Washington, D.C. 20401
tel: 202-783-3238
fax: 202-512-2250
website: www.access.gpo.gov

CULINARY SCHOOL DIRECTORY

American Institute of Baking
1213 Bakers Way
Manhattan, Kansas 66502
tel: 913-537-4750/800-633-5137
fax: 913-537-1493
website: www.aibonline.org

The Art Institute of New York
(formerly New York Restaurant
School)
75 Varick Street
New York, New York 10013
tel: 212-226-5500/800-654-2433
website: www.ainyc.artinstitutes.edu

Baltimore International College
17 Commerce Street
Baltimore, Maryland 21202
tel: 410-752-4710/800-624-9926
fax: 410-752-3730
website: www.bic.edu

Bellingham Technical College
3028 Lindberg Avenue
Bellingham, Washington 98225
tel: 206-676-6490
website: www.beltc.ctc.edu

California Culinary Academy
625 Polk Street
San Francisco, California 94102
tel: 415-771-3536/800-229-2433
website: www.baychef.com

Cambridge School of Culinary Arts
2020 Massachusetts Avenue
Cambridge, Massachusetts 01240
tel: 617-354-3836
fax: 617-576-1963
website: cambridgeculinary.com

School of Confectionery
34 West 22nd Street
New York, New York 10011
tel: 212-675-2253
website: www.bakingshop.com

Cornell University
School of Hotel Administration
Statler Hall
Ithaca, New York 14853
tel: 607-256-5106
website: www.hotelschool.cornell.edu

Culinary Arts Division
New School for Social Research
100 Greenwich Avenue
New York, New York 10011
tel: 212-255-4141
website: www.nsu.newschool.edu

Culinary Institute of America
433 Albany Post Road
Hyde Park, New York 12538
tel: 800-283-2433
website: www.ciachef.edu

French Culinary Institute
Jacques Pépin, Dean of Special
Projects
Alain Sailhac, Dean of Culinary Arts
462 Broadway
New York, New York 10013
tel: 212-219-8890/888-FCI-CHEF
website: www.frenchculinary.com

IACP International Directory
of Cooking Schools
304 West Liberty Street, Suite 201
Louisville, Kentucky 40202
tel: 502-581-9786
fax: 502-589-3602
website: www.iacp.com

The Institute of Culinary Education
(formerly Peter Kump's School of
Culinary Arts)
50 West 23rd Street
New York, New York 10010
tel: 212-847-0700
website: www.iceculinary.com

Johnson and Wales University
8 Abbott Park Place
Providence, Rhode Island 02903
(also South Carolina, Virginia,
Florida, and Colorado)
tel: 800-342-5598
fax: 401-598-2948
website: www.jwu.edu

L'Académie de Cuisine
François Dionot, President
16006 Industrial Drive
Gaithersburg, Maryland 20877
tel: 301-670-8670/800-664-CHEF
fax: 301-670-0450
website: www.lacademie.com

Le Cordon Bleu Schools USA
website:
www.lecordonbleuschoolsusa.com

National Restaurant Association
The Educational Foundation
250 South Wacker Drive, Suite 1400
Chicago, Illinois 60606
tel: 800-765-2122
website: www.nraef.org

Natural Gourmet Cookery School
48 West 21st Street, 2nd Floor
New York, New York 10011
tel: 212-645-5170
website:
www.naturalgourmetschool.com

New York University
Dept. of Nutrition and Food Studies
The Steinhardt School of Education
35 West Fourth Street
New York, New York 10012
tel: 212-998-5580/800-771-4NYU
fax: 212-995-4194
website: www.nyu.edu

Radcliffe College
The Arthur and Elizabeth Schlesinger
Library
3 James Street
Cambridge, Massachusetts 02138
tel: 617-495-8647
website: www.libdex.com

The Restaurant School at Walnut Hill
College
4207 Walnut Street
Philadelphia, Pennsylvania 19104
tel: 215-222-4200
website:
www.therestaurantschool.com

Santa Fe School of Cooking
116 West San Francisco Street
Santa Fe, New Mexico 87501
tel: 505-983-4511
fax: 505-983-7540
website:
www.santafeschoolofcooking.com

School of Natural Cookery
P.O. Box 19466
Boulder, Colorado 80308
tel: 303-444-8068
website: www.naturalcookery.com

Texas Culinary Academy
(formerly Le Chef College of
Hospitality Careers)
6020 Dillard Circle
Austin, Texas 78752
tel: 512-323-2511
fax: 512-323-2126
website: www.lechef.org

University of Iowa
Chef Louis Szathmary Collection of
Culinary Arts
Iowa City, Iowa 52242
tel: 319-335-5921
website: www.uiowa.edu

EQUIPMENT DIRECTORY

Ace Mart Restaurant Supplies
website: www.acemart.com/merchant

AGA Stoves
17 Towne Farm Road
Stowe, Vermont 05672
tel: 802-253-9727
website: www.aga-ranges.com

Artex International Linens
P.O. Box 309
Highland, Ilinois 62249
tel: 618-654-2113; 800-851-8671
fax: 618-654-7672
website: www.artex-int.com

Blaze Products
P.O. Box 339
Shelbyville, Kentucky 40066
tel: 800-456-1017
fax: 502-633-0685
website: www.blazeproducts.com

Blodgett Corporation
website: www.blodgett.com
Grills and ranges.

Bragard Uniforms
215 Park Avenue South, Suite 705
New York, New York 10003
tel: 212-982-8031
fax: 212-353-0318
website: www.bragard.com

Bridge Company
214 East 52nd Street
New York, New York 10022
tel: 212-838-6746
website: www.bridgekitchenware.com

Catering Equipment World
2413 Forsyth Road
Orlando, Florida 32807
tel: 800-821-9153
website: www.cateringworld.com

Chef's Choice
EdgeCraft Corporation
825 Southwood Road
Avondale, Pennsylvania 19311
tel: 800-342-3255
website: www.edgecraft.com

Chefwear
3111 North Knox
Chicago, Illinois 60641
tel: 800-568-2433
website: www.chefwear.com

Chicago Cutlery
441 East Bonner Road
Wauconda, Illinois 60084
tel: 708-526-2144
website: www.chicagocutlery.com

CresCor Metal Products
12711 Taft Avenue
Cleveland, Ohio 44108
tel: 216-851-6800
website: www.crescor.com
Insulated cabinets and dollies.

Culinary Classic Apparel
1628 South Prairie Avenue
Chicago, Illinois 60616
tel: 800-373-2963
website: www.culinaryclassics.com

Custom Linen Service
14332 Wadkins Avenue
Gardena, California 90249
tel: 310-324-2465
website:
www.customlinenservice.com

Delivery Concepts
58356 CR 3 South
Elkhart, Indiana 46517
tel: 219-294-4050/800-654-1857
website: www.deliveryconcepts.com
Hot and cold trucks and vans.

EdgeCraft
825 Southwood Road
Avondale, Pennsylvania 19311
tel: 610-268-0500
website: www.edgecraft.com

Europaeus
8 John Walsh Boulevard
Peekskill, New York 10566
tel: 914-739-1900
fax: 914-739-5229
website: www.europaeus.com
Imported tableware.

FrancisFrancis! USA
Route 2, Box 133
Garrison, New York 10524
tel: 845-424-3016
fax: 845-424-4564
website: www.francisfrancis.com

Frette Linens
200 West 57th Street
New York, New York 10019
tel: 212-262-2740/800-72-FRETTE
fax: 212-262-2740
website: www.frette.com

Garland Ranges
111 West Chicago Avenue
Hinsdale, Illinois 60521
tel: 708-323-1011
website: www.garland-group.com

Gourmet Gear Culinary Apparel
233 Market Street, Suite C
Venice, California 90291
tel: 310-450-6698/800-682-4635
fax: 310-392-4657
website: www.gourmetgear.com

Hilden Halifax Table Linens
P.O. Box 1098
South Boston, Virgina 24592
tel: 800-431-2514
fax: 804-572-4781
website: www.hildenAmerica.com

Hobart Mixers
Troy, Ohio 45374
tel: 513-332-3000
website: www.hobartcorp.com

Homer Laughlin China
Sixth Street and Harrison
Newell, West Virginia 26050
tel: 304-387-1300/800-452-4462
fax: 304-387-0593/800-533-8918
website: www.hlchina.com

Hubert
9555 Dry Fork Road
Harrison, Ohio 45030
tel: 800-543-7374
website: www.hubert.com

Igloo Products
website: www.igloocommercial.com

iSi
30 Chapin Road
P.O. Box 616
Pine Brook, New Jersey 07058
tel: 201-227-2426
fax: 201-227-9140
website: www.isi-store.com
Siphons and cream whippers.

KitchenAid
St. Joseph, Michigan 49085
tel: 800-422-1230
website: www.kitchenaid.com
Portable appliances.

Lenox Hotelware China
100 Lenox Drive
Lawrenceville, New Jersey 08648
tel: 609-896-2800
website: www.lenox.com

Libbey Glass
P.O. Box 919
Toledo, Ohio 43693
tel: 419-247-5000/800-824-1667
fax: 419-727-2433
website: www.corporatedepot.com

Lodge Cast Iron
P.O. Box 380
South Pittsburgh, Tennessee 37380
tel: 423-837-7181
website: www.lodgemfg.com

Sweet Celebrations
(formerly Maid of Scandinavia)
3244 Raleigh Avenue
Minneapolis, Minnesota 55416
tel: 800-328-6722
website:
www.maidofscandinavia.com
Cake and decorating supplies and
ingredients; also packaging equipment.

Metrokane
tel: 212-759-6262
website: www.metrokane.com
Rabbit corkscrews and accessories.

Milliken Linens
920 Milliken Road
Spartanburg, South Carolina 29303
tel: 864-503-1761/800-322-TEAM
fax: 864-503-1716
website: www.millikentablelinen.com

Nordic Ware
website: www.nordicware.com

Oneida Silversmiths, Foodservice
Division
Oneida, New York 13421
tel: 800-258-1220
fax: 315-361-3290
website: www.oneida.com

Polder
8 Slater Street
Port Chester, New York 10573
tel: 914-937-8200/800-431-2133
fax: 914-937-8297
website: www.polderinc.com
Thermometers.

Robot Coupe USA
P.O. Box 16625
Jackson, Mississippi 39236
tel: 800-824-1646
fax: 601-898-9134
website: www.robotcoupeusa.com

Shoes for Crews
website: www.shoesforcrews.com

Special event site
website: www.specialeventsite.com
Resource to the event industry.

Sub-Zero Refrigeration
P.O. Box 4130
Madison, Wisconsin 53711
tel: 608-271-2233
website: www.subzero.com

Syracuse China Corporation
P.O. Box 4820
2900 Court Street
Syracuse, New York 13221
tel: 800-448-5711
fax: 315-455-6763
website: www.syracusecentral.com

Tentsite
website: www.tentsite.com
Directory of tent providers.

Unic Espresso Machines
Silver Spoon Ltd.
12114 Nebel Street
Rockville, Maryland 20852
tel: 301-984-0970
fax: 301-984-0973

Viking Stoves
111 Front Street
Greenwood, Mississippi 38930
tel: 601-455-1200
website: www.vikingrange.com

Villeroy & Boch
41 Madison Avenue
New York, New York 10010
tel: 212-683-1747/800-223-1762
fax: 212-481-0283
website: www.villeroy-boch.com

Vita-Mix Corporation
8615 Usher Road
Cleveland, Ohio 44138
tel: 440-235-4840
fax: 440-235-3726
website: www.vitamix.com

Volrath Kitchen Supplies
P.O. Box 611
Sheboygan, Wisconsin 53082
tel: 414-457-4851
fax: 414-459-6570
website: www.volrathco.com
An extensive catalog, including catering specialties.

Vulcan-Hart Stoves
P.O. Box 696
Louisville, Kentucky 40201
tel: 502-778-2791/800-333-8021
fax: 800-333-1808
website: www.vulcanhart.com

WAG Industries
627 North Albany Avenue
Chicago, Illinois 60612
tel: 773-638-7007/800-621-3305
website: www.cateringtrucks.com
Specialty food trucks.

Wilton Enterprises
2240 West 75th Street
Woodridge, Illinois 60517
tel: 718-963-7100
website: www.wilton.com
Cake and decorating supplies and ingredients. They also offer regional classes.

Wüsthof Trident Cutlery
1 Westchester Plaza
Elmsford, New York 10523
tel: 914-347-2185
website: www.wusthof.com

Alaska Seafood Marketing Institute
526 Main Street
Juneau, Alaska 99801
tel: 907-586-2902
website: www.alaskaseafood.org/
    flavor/recipes

Bazzini Company
200 Food Center Drive
Bronx, New York 10474
tel: 718-842-8644/800-288-0172
website: www.bazzininuts.com

Bell & Evans Chicken
P.O. Box 39
Fredericksburg, Pennsylvania 17026
tel: 717-865-6626
website: www.bellandevans.com

Cabot Dairy
website: www.cabotcheese.com

California Specialty Farms
2420 Modoc
Los Angeles, California 90021
tel: 800-HERBS02
website:
www.californiaspecialtyitems.com
Vegetables, herbs, and edible flowers.

Caprilands Herb Farm
534 Silver Street
Coventry, Connecticut 06238
tel: 203-742-7244
website: www.caprilands.com

Barry Callebaut USA
Pureland Industrial Park
400 Eagle Court
Swedesboro, New Jersey 08085
tel: 856-467-0099
website: www.callebaut.be
Chocolate.

Ghirardelli Chocolate Company
1111 139th Avenue
San Leandro, California 94578-2631
tel: 800-877-0338/510-438-6970
website: www.ghirardelli.com

Lindt & Sprüngli (USA)
One Fine Chocolate Place
Stratham, New Hampshire 03885
tel: 800-338-0839/603-778-8100
website: www.lindt.com

Valrhona
website: www.valrhona.com

Ciao Bella Gelato
website: www.ciaobellagelato.com
Ice cream, sorbet, frozen yogurt.

D'Artagnan
399-419 St. Paul Avenue
Jersey City, New Jersey 07306
tel: 800-DARTAGNAN
fax: 201-792-0588
website: www.dartagnan.com
Foie gras, charcuterie, game.

De Choix Specialty Foods
58-25 52nd Avenue
Woodside, New York 11377
tel: 718-507-8080/800-332-4649
website: www.dechoix.com

Ethnic specialties
website: www.ethnicgrocer.com

Fish and seafoodwebsite:
www.freshfishonline.com

Franklin Mushroom Farms
P.O. Box 18
North Franklin, Connecticut 06254
tel: 203-642-7551
fax: 203-642-6407
website: www.franklinfarms.com

H & H Bagels
tel: 800-581-7599
website: www.hhbagels.com

Hillman Oyster Company
tel: 800-582-4416
website: www.hillmanscallops.com

Homestead Healthy Foods
1313 West Live Oak Street
Fredricksburg, Texas 78624
tel: 888-861-5670
fax: 830-997-5932
website:
www.homesteadhealthyfoods.com

Horizon Organic Dairy
website: www.horizonorganic.com

Keller's Hotel Bar Foods
650 New Country Road
Secaucus, New Jersey 07094
tel: 201-865-3000
fax: 201-865-8261
Plugra clairfied butter and other
butters.

Kosher Food
website: www.mykoshermarket.com

La Preferida, Inc.
3400 West 35th Street
Chicago, Illinois 60632
tel: 312-254-7200
fax: 312-254-8546
website: www.lapref.com
Foods from Mexico, South America,
and the West Indies.

Lobel's Fine Meat and Poultry
1095 Madison Avenue
New York, New York 10028
tel: 877-738-4512
website: www.lobels.com

Lobster
website: www.lobsterexpress.com
website: www.lobstertogo.com

Los Chileros de Nuevo Mexico
P.O. Box 6215
Santa Fe, New Mexico 87502
tel: 505-471-6967
website: www.hotchilepepper.com
Gourmet New Mexican foods.

Maple Leaf Farms Duck
website: www.mapleleaffarms.com

McIlhenny Company
Dept. 12-A
Avery Island, Louisiana 70513
tel: 800-634-9599
website: www.tabasco.com

Morgan Mills
201 Morgan Mill Road
Brevard, North Carolina 28712
tel: 828-862-4084
Fresh-ground flour, grits, and meals.

National Association for the Specialty
Food Trade website:
www.specialtyfoodmarket.com

Oregon Spice Company
1630 SE Rhine Street
Portland, Oregon 97202
tel: 503-238-0664/800-565-1599
website:
www.oregonspicecompany.com

Paprikas Weiss
1546 Second Avenue
New York, New York 10028
tel: 212-288-6117

Phillips Mushroom Farms
P.O. Box 190, Kennet Square
Kennet, Pennsylvania 19348
tel: 800-722-8818
fax: 215-444-4751
website:
www.phillipsmushroomfarms.com

Pike Place Fish
86 Pike Place
Seattle, Washington 98101
tel: 206-682-7181
website: www.pikeplacefish.com

Raffetto's Fresh Pasta
156 Leroy Street
New York, New York 10014
tel: 212-727-8222
fax 212-727-0047

Robison State Herb Garden
Cornell University Campus Plantation
One Plantation Road
Ithaca, New York 14850
tel: 607-255-3020
website: www.plantations.cornell.edu

S. Wallace Edwards & Sons
P.O. Box 25
Surry, Virginia 23883
tel: 804-294-3121/800-222-4267
website: www.edwardsham.com
Hams and smoked meats.

Sahadi Importing Company
187 Atlantic Avenue
Brooklyn, New York 11201
tel: 718-624-4550
fax: 718-643-4415
website: www.sahadi.com
Middle Eastern foods.

Sitka Sound Seafood
329-333 Katlian Street
Sitka, Alaska 99835
tel: 907-747-6867
website: www.ssssitka.com

Uwajimaya
P.O. Box 3003
Seattle, Washington 98114
tel: 206 624-6248
website: www.uwajimaya.com

Yonah Schimmel
137 East Houston Street
New York, New York 10002
website: www.yonahschimmel.com
Knishes and specialty foods.

Nature's Wild Rice Company
P.O. Box 1593
Bemidji, Minnesota 56619
tel: 800-223-5085
website: www.naturesrice.com

Zingerman's Bread
website: www.zingerman.com

**FOOD SAFETY AND HANDLING
DIRECTORY**

American Council on Science
and Health
website: www.acsh.org/food

American Frozen Food Institute
website: www.afi.com

American Institute of Baking Online
Sanitation Course Certification
website: www.aibonline.org/
   education/diplomacourses/
   bstdiary/week4.PDF

Association of Food and Drug
Officials
website: www.afdo.org/
   seafoodhaccp.asp
Seafood Alliance HACCP training for
fish and seafood handling safety.

Dean O. Cliver Ph.D.
website:
www.faculty.vetmed.ucdavis.edu/
   faculty/docliver

FDA Miscellaneous
website: www.cfsan.fda.gov/~dms/
   fs-toc.html

Food and Nutrition Information
Center
National Agricultural Library
10301 Baltimore, Maryland 20705
website: www.nal.usda.gov/fnic

Food Research Institute at the
University of Wisconsin
website:
www.wisc.edu/fri/whoare.htm

Food Safety and Inspection Service,
USDA
website: www.foodsafety.com

Food Safety Training and Education
Alliance
website: www.fstea.org

International Association of Food
Protection
website: www.foodprotection.org/

International Food Service Executives
Association
website:www.ifsea.com/
   Foodsafety.htm
Food-safety certification.

Interstate Shellfish Sanitation
Conference
website: www.issc.org

Local Contacts (in telephone
directory or online)

Culinary schools

State Department of Education

State Department of Health, Field
Services

National Restaurant Association
website: www.restaurant.org/
   government/issues/foodcode

Ohio State University Consumer
Sciences
website:
www.ohioline.osu.edu/lines/food.html

United States Department of
Agriculture
website: www.usda.gov

United States Department of Health
and Human Services
website: vm.cfsan.fda.gov

U.S. Food and Drug Administration,
Hazard Analysis and Critical Control
Points website:
vm.cfsan.fda.gov/~lrd/haccp.html

HUMAN RESOURCES DIRECTORY

Small Business Administration
website: www.sba.gov

Department of Labor
website: www.dol.gov

Equal Employment Opportunity
Commission
website: www.eeoc.gov/facts

Occupational Safety and Health
Administration
website: www.osha.gov

Social Security Employer Forms
website: www.ssa.gov/employer

Workers Compensation Board
website: www.dol.gov/esa

United States Government
Department of Treasury
Internal Revenue Services
website: www.irs.gov

QUANTITY RECIPE DIRECTORY

Alaska Seafood Marketing Institute
1111 West Eighth Street, Suite 100
Juneau, Alaska 99801
tel: 907-586-2902
website: www.alaskaseafood.org/
    flavor/recipes

Alaskan Harvest
320 Seward Street
Sitka, Alaska 99835
tel: 800-824-6389
website: www.alaskanharvest.com

American Cancer Society
Cooking Smart
3340 Peachtree Road NE
Atlanta, Georgia 30026
tel: 800-227-2345
website: www.cancer.org/docroot

American Heart Association
National Center
7320 Greenville Avenue
Dallas, Texas 75231
tel: 214-373-6300
website: www.deliciousdecisions.org

American Egg Board
website: www.aeb.org/recipes

American Institute of Baking
1213 Bakers Way
Manhattan, Kansas 66502
tel: 800-633-5137
fax: 913-537-1493
website: www.aibonline.com

American Lamb Council
6911 South Yosemite Street, Suite
200
Englewood, Colorado 80112
tel: 303-771-3500
fax: 303-771-8200
website: www.lambchef.com

Athens Food
Apollo Filo Dough
13600 Snow Road, Dept. 19
Cleveland, Ohio 44142
tel: 800-837-5683
website: www.Athens.com

Bell and Evans
P.O. Box 39
Fredericksburg, Pennsylvania 17026
tel: 717-865-6626
website: www.bellandevans.com

Bertolli Olive Oil
website: www.bertolli.com/usa

Bread Bakers Guild of America
tel: 412-823-2080
www.bbga.org

California Dry Bean Advisory Board
P.O. Box 943
Dinuba, California 93618
tel: 209 591-4866
website: www.calbeans.com

Cheese recipes online
website: www.cheesenet.com

Citrus fruit
website: www.sunkist.com

Dairy Council of Wisconsin
website: www.dcw.net.org

Fleischmann's Yeast Expert
tel: 800-227-6202
website: www.breadworld.com

Florida Tomato Committee
P.O. Box 140635
Orlando, Florida 32814
tel: 407-894-3071
website: www.floridatomatoes.com

Food Channel
website: www.foodtv.com

Hershey's Chocolate
website:
www.hersheys.com/foodservice

Internet miscellaneous recipes
website: www.epicurious.com

Jacques Torres Chocolate
website: www.jacquestorres.com

Kansas Wheat Commission
2630 Claflin Road
Manhattan, Kansas 66502
tel: 913-539-0255
website: www.kswheat.com

Louisiana Seafood Promotion &
Marketing Board
P.O. Box 70648
New Orleans, Louisiana 70172
tel: 800-222-4017
website: www.louisianaseafood.com

Maine Potato Board
744 Main Street
Presque Isle, Maine 04709
tel: 207-769-5061
website:
www.mainepotatoes.com/recipes

McIlhenny Company
Dept. 12-A
Avery Island, Louisiana 70513
tel: 800-HOT-DASH
website:
www.tabascofoodservice.com

Mushrooms
website: www.mushroom.com
website: www.gmushrooms.com

National Pork Board
website: www.otherwhitemeat.com

Oaklyn Plantation
1312 Oaklyn Road
Darlington, South Carolina 29532
tel: 843-395-0793
fax: 843-395-0794
website: www.freerangechicken.com

The Sugar Association
1101 15th Street NW, Suite 600
Washington, D.C. 20005
tel: 202-785-1122
fax: 202-785-5019
website: www.sugar.org

United States Department of
Agriculture
Human Nutrition Information Service
6505 Belcrest Road
Hyattsville, Maryland 20782
tel: 301-436-8498
website: www.usda.gov/recipes

Vegetarian recipes
website: www.vegweb.com

Washington State Apple Commission
Tacoma, Washington 98801
tel: 509-663-9600
website: www.bestappples.com/recipes

Wisconsin Beef Council
6806 Grand Canyon Drive
Madison, Wisconsin 53719
tel: 608-833-7177
fax: 608-833-4725
website: www.beeftips.com

DIRECTORY OF PROFESSIONALS

Annemarie Colbin
The Natural Gourmet Cookery School
48 West 21st Street, 2nd Floor
New York, New York 10010
tel: 212-645-5170
fax: 212-989-1493
website:
www.naturalgourmetschool.com

Bob Kinkead
Kinkead's
2000 Pennsylvania Avenue NW
Washington, D.C. 20006
tel: 202-296-7700
website: www.kinkead.com

Kinkead's Colvin Run Tavern
8045 Leesburg Pike
Vienna, Virginia 22182
tel: 703-356-9500
fax: 703-356-1008

Eric Lilavois and Henry Meer
City Hall
131 Duane Street
New York, New York 10013
tel: 212-227-7777
fax: 212-577-6287
website: cityhallnewyork.com
e-mail: dine@cityhallnyc.com

Eric Lilavois
254 West 25th Street, Suite 5A
New York, New York 10001

François Dionot
L'Académie de Cuisine
16006 Industrial Drive
Gaithersburg, Maryland 20877-1414
tel: 301-670-8670/800-664-CHEF
fax: 301-670-0450
website: www.lacademie.com
e-mail: info@lacademie.com

Jacques Pépin and Alain Saihac
French Culinary Institute
462 Broadway
New York, New York 10013
tel: 212-219-8890/888-FCI-CHEF
website: www.frenchculinary.com

Jason Scholz, Executive Chef
High Cotton
Maverick Southern Kitchens
199 East Bay Street
Charleston, South Carolina 29401
website: www.high-cotton.net
website:
www.mavericksouthernkitchens.com

Jim McMullen and Stephen Rowan
Annie and Jim McMullen Catering
1381 Third Avenue #300
New York, New York 10021
tel: 212-988-7676

Joe McDonnal and Virginia Wyman
The Ruins
570 Roy Street
Seattle, Washington 98109
tel: 206-285-RUIN (7846)
fax: 206-285-0675
website: www.theruins.net
Private dining club/on and off-
premises catering.

Linwood Dame
Linwood's/Due
25 Crossroads Drive
Owings Mills, Maryland 21117
tel: 410-356-3030
catering: 410-581-4920
website: www.linwoods.com

Liz Neumark
Great Performances
287 Spring Street
New York, New York 10013
tel: 212-727-2424
fax: 212-727-2820
website: www.greatperformances.com
email: info@greatperformances.com

Peter Dent and Allen Smith
Adobo Catering
1807 Second Street
Santa Fe, New Mexico 87501
tel: 505-989-7674
fax: 505-982-7350
email: adobocat@comcast.net

Ronnie Davis
Ronnie Davis Productions
Great Performances
287 Spring Street
New York, New York 10013
tel: 212-337-6076
fax: 212-727-2820
e-mail:
ronnie.davis@greatperformances.com

Simon Andrews
Swamp Fox
The Francis Marion Hotel
387 King Street
Charleston, South Carolina 29403
tel: 843-722-0600
fax: 843-853-2186
website: francismarioncharleston.com

Stanley Poll
William Poll Caterers
1051 Lexington Avenue
New York, New York 10023
tel: 212-288-0501
fax: 212-288-2844
e-mail: wpollny@aol.com

Sylvia Weinstock
Sylvia Weinstock's Cakes
273 Church Street
New York, New York 10013
tel: 212-925-6698
fax: 212-925-5021
website: www.sylviaweinstock.com
e-mail: sylvia@swcakes.com

William Henry, Executive Chef
Monika Henry, Food & Beverage
Manager
The Westin Resort Hilton Head
Island
Two Grasslawn Avenue
Hilton Head Island, South Carolina
29928
tel: 843-681-1048
fax: 843-681-1087
website:
www.westinresorthiltonhead.com

APPENDIX B

Public Service Perishable Food Distribution

Food networking is one way to acknowledge the hunger that many of our neighbors live with. Surplus perishable and prepared food is often difficult to distribute, and many people have reported that their offerings have been refused. Now federal and state "Good Samaritan" laws that permit the unlicensed redistribution of fresh and cooked food protect everyone who donates food in good faith. If you have any doubt, check with your state government on the Internet. Any of the groups listed below will assist you in the process of distributing food to those who need it.

There are food rescue organizations nationwide that handle the redistribution of unused, unserved, perishable, prepared cooked, uncooked, or ready-to-eat food. Any oversupply has to be handled quickly and cautiously. These local organizations not only adhere to local food safety and sanitation regulations, but are up to date in a network of needful recipients so that donated food is delivered in a timely and genuinely useful way.

The following organizations support an extensive community in a link that redistributes over two million pounds of perishable food each month. By all means, add to this list any additional programs you know of. Some of the groups may have changed by the time you need to reach one of them, but please don't be discouraged. A few phone calls starting with the Foodchain FCA Information Hotline (800-845-3008) will assist you in finding a neighborhood link. They are the national network for "Prepared and Perishable Food Programs," or PPFRP. You can also contact the USDA National Hunger Clearinghouse (800-GLEAN IT).

These are some excellent starting points for food redistribution and recovery:

City Harvest
575 Eighth Avenue
New York, New York 10018
tel: 917-351-8700
fax: 917-351-8720
website: www.cityharvest.org

Foodchain
912 Baltimore, Suite 300
Kansas City, Missouri 64105
tel: 800-845-3008

Second Harvest
116 South Michigan Avenue, Suite 4
Chicago, Illinois 60603
tel: 312-262-2303
website: www.secondharvest.org

USDA Gleaning and Food Recovery
Home Page
website: www.usda.gov/fcs/glean.htm

World Hunger Year
website: www.iglou.com/why/glean/

**FOODCHAIN MEMBERS
AND ASSOCIATE MEMBERS**

(Please note that for brevity no more than 3 groups are listed for each state. If you need one closer, contact the one nearest to you and they will direct you to a group that you can get to easily.)

ALABAMA

Magic City Harvest
1720 16 Avenue, South
Birmingham, Alabama 35205
tel: 205-933-5806

Selma Area Food Bank
P.O. Box 2513
497 Oak Street
Selma, Alabama 36702
tel: 205-872-4111

Twelve Baskets Program
Montgomery Area Food Bank, Inc.
521 Trade Center Street
Montgomery, Alabama 36108
tel: 205-263-3784
fax: 205-262-6854

ALASKA

Food Bank of Alaska
2121 Spar Avenue
Anchorage, Alaska 99501
tel: 907-272-3663
fax: 907-277-7368

Fairbanks Community Food Bank
517 Gaffney Road
Fairbanks, Alaska 99701
tel: 907-452-7761
fax: 907-456-2377

Southeast Alaska Food Bank
5597 Aisek Street
Juneau, Alaska 99801
tel: 907-780-4359
fax: 907-780-4098

ARIZONA

Association of Arizona Food Banks
234 North Central, suite 125
Phoenix, Arizona 85004
tel: 602-252-9088

Tucson's Table
23 West 27 Street
P.O. Box 26727
Tucson, Arizona 85726
tel: 520-622-0525
fax: 520-384-7924

Waste Not, Inc.
P.O. Box 25606
Phoenix, Arizona 85002
Tel: 602-941-1841

ARKANSAS

Ozark Food Bank
1901 Townwest Drive
Rogers, Arkansas 72756
tel: 501-631-8774

Potluck, Inc.
8400 Asher Avenue
Little Rock, Arkansas 72204
tel: 501-568-1147
fax: 501-568-1167

SW Arkansas Foodbank
P.O. Box 585
Arka Delphia, Arkansas 71923
tel: 501-246-8244

CALIFORNIA

Extra Helpings
L.A. Regional Foodbank
1734 East 41 Street
Los Angeles, California 90058
tel: 213-234-3030, ext. 131
fax: 213-234-0943

Foodrunners
2579 Washington Street
San Francisco, California 94115
tel: 415-929-1866
fax: 415-788-8924

Love's Gift Hunger Relief Program
P.O. Box 370900
San Diego, California 92137
tel: 619-581-3663

COLORADO

Community Food Share
5547 Central Avenue
Boulder, Colorado 80303
tel: 303-443-0623
fax: 303-449-7004

Denver's Table
Food Bank of the Rockies
10975 East 47th Avenue
Denver, Colorado 80239
tel: 303-371-9250
fax: 303-371-9259

The Prepared Food Program
The FDC of Larimer County
1301 Blue Spruce
Fort Collins, Colorado 80524
tel: 303-493-4477
fax: 303-493-5122

CONNECTICUT

Connecticut Food Bank
P.O. Box 8686
New Haven, Connecticut 06531
tel: 203-469-5000
fax: 203-469-4871

Foodshare of Greater Hartford
P.O. Box 2019
Hartford, Connecticut 06144-2019
tel: 203-688-6500
fax: 203-688-2776

Table To Table
Foodbank of Lower Fairfield County
538 Canal Street
Stamford, Connecticut 06902
tel: 203-323-3211
fax: 203-358-8306

DELAWARE

Food Bank of Delaware
14 Garfield Way
Newark, Delaware 19713
tel: 302-292-1305
fax: 302-292-1309

DISTRICT OF COLUMBIA

Capital Area Community Food
645 Taylor Street N.E.
Washington, D.C. 20017
tel: 202-526-5344
fax: 202-529-1767

D.C. Central Kitchen
425 Second Street N.W.
Washington, D.C. 20001
tel: 202-234-0707
fax: 202-986-1051

FLORIDA

Extra Helpings of Daily Bread
Daily Bread Food Bank
5850 N.W. 32nd Avenue
Miami, Florida 33142
tel: 305-634-5088
fax: 305-633-0036

First Coast Food Runners
Food Bank of Jacksonville
1502 Jessie Street
Jacksonville, Florida 32206
tel: 904-353-3663
fax: 904-358-4281

Second Helpings
Second Harvest Food Bank of
Central Florida
2515 Shader Road
Orlando, Florida 32804
tel: 407-292-8988
fax: 407-292-4758

GEORGIA

Atlanta's Table
Atlanta Community Food Bank
970 Jefferson Street N.W.
Atlanta, Georgia 30318
tel: 404-892-1250
fax: 404-892-4026

Second Servings
Second Harvest of Coastal Georgia
5 Carolan Street
Savannah, Georgia 31401
tel: 912-236-6750
fax: 912-238-1391

Unto Others
Middle Georgia Community
Food Bank
P.O. Box 5024
Macon, Georgia 31208
tel: 912-743-4580
fax: 912-741-8777

HAWAII

Hawaii Island Foodbank
140 Holomua Street
Hilo, Hawaii 96720
tel: 808-935-3050
fax: 808-935-3794

Hawaii Food Bank, Inc
2611 A Kilihau Street
Honolulu, Hawaii 96819
tel: 808-836-3600
fax: 808-836-2272

IDAHO

Idaho Food Bank
4375 South Apple
Boise, Idaho 83701
tel: 208-336-9643
fax: 208-336-9692

Cooooperative Extension System
University of Idaho
Moscow, Idaho 83844
tel: 208-885-6972

ILLINOIS

Prepared Foods Program
Greater Chicago Food Depository
4501 South Tripp Avenue
Chicago, Illinois 60632
tel: 312-247-4282
fax: 312-247-4232

Heart of Illinois Harvest
c/o Salvation Army
P.O. Box 9702
Peoria, Illinois 61612
tel: 309-679-1379
fax: 309-693-1413

Southern Illinois Food Warehouse
RR1, Box 121A
Opdyke, Illinois 62872
tel: 618-244-6146

INDIANA

Meal Share
Hoosier Hills Food Bank
615 North Fairview
Bloomington, Indiana 47404
tel: 812-334-8374
fax: 812-334-8377

Second Helping
27 Pasco Avenue
Evansville, Indiana 47708
tel: 812-425-4241
fax: 812-425-4225

Community Harvest Food Bank
P.O. Box 10967
Fort Wayne, Indiana 46855
tel: 219-447-3696
fax: 219-447-4859

IOWA

Food Bank of Iowa
30 Northeast 48th Place
Des Moines, Iowa 50313
tel: 515-244-6555
fax: 515-244-6556

HACAP Food Reservoir
1201 Continental Place NE
Cedar Rapids, Iowa 52402
tel: 319-393-7811
fax: 319-393-6263

Siouxland Food Bank
P.O. Box 985
Sioux City, Iowa 51102
tel: 800-792-3663

KANSAS

Flint Hills Breadbasket
905 Yuma
Manhattan, Kansas 66502
tel: 913-537-0730
fax: 913-537-1353

Kansas Foodbank Warehouse
806 East Boston
Wichita, Kansas 67211
tel: 316-265-4421
fax: 316-265-9747

Let's Help Food Bank
302 Van Buren
Topeka, Kansas 66033
tel: 913-232-4357
fax: 913-234-6208

KENTUCKY

Dare to Care
5803 Fem Valley Road
Louisville, Kentucky 40232
tel: 502-966-3821
fax: 502-966-3827

God's Pantry Food Bank
104 South Forbes Road
Lexington, Kentucky 40511
tel: 606-255-6592
fax: 606-254-6330

Kentucky Food Bank
105 Warehouse Court
Elizabethtown, Kentucky 42702
tel: 502-769-6997
fax: 502-769-9340

LOUISIANA

Foodbank of Central Louisiana
3223 Baldwin Avenue
Alexandria, Louisiana 71301
tel: 318-445-2773
fax: 318-484-2898

Greater Baton Rouge Food Bank
766 Chippewa Street
Baton Rouge, Louisiana 70821
tel: 504-359-9940
fax: 504-355-1445

Second Harvest of Greater New
Orleans
1201 Sams Avenue
New Orleans, Louisiana 70123
tel: 504-734-1322
fax: 504-733-8336

MAINE

Cooperative Extension Service
University of Maine
Orono, Maine 04469
tel: 207-581-3310

Good Shepherd Foodbank
415 Lisbon Street
Lewiston, Maine 04240
tel: 207-782-3554
fax: 207-782-9893

MARYLAND

Food Link
80 West Street
Annapolis, Maryland 21401
tel: 410-974-8599
fax: 410-974-8566

Hartford County Foodbank
P.O. Box 1005
Edgewood, Maryland 21040
tel: 410-679-8186
fax: 410-679-4306

Second Helping
The Maryland Food Bank, Inc.
241 N. Franklintown Road
Baltimore, Maryland 21223
fax: 410-947-4442
fax: 410-947-1853

MASSACHUSETTS

Cape Cod Food Bank
P.O. Box 236
Harwich, Massachusetts 02671
tel: 508-432-6519

Rachel's Table
633 Salisburg Street
Worcester, Massachusetts 01609
tel: 508-799-7699
fax: 508-798-0962

Second Helping
Greater Boston Food Bank
99 Atkinson Street
Boston, Massachusetts 02118
tel: 617-427-5200
fax: 617-427-0146

MICHIGAN

Food Gatherers
1731 Dhu Varren Road
Ann Arbor, MI 48105
tel: 313-761-2796
fax: 313-930-0550

Forgotten Harvest
21711 West 10 Mile Road #200
Southfield, MI 48075
tel: 810-350-3663
fax: 810-350-9928

Gleaners Community Food Bank
2131 Beaufait
Detroit, Michigan 48207
tel: 313-923-3535
fax: 313-924-6313

MINNESOTA

Second Harvest of Greater
Minneapolis
8405 10th Avenue North
Minneapolis, Minnesota 55427
tel: 612-593-9844
fax: 612-593-2712

Twelve Baskets
Second Harvest St. Paul
Food Bank
1140 Gervais Avenue
St. Paul, Minnesota 55109
tel: 612-484-5117
fax: 612-484-1064

Second Harvest North Central
Food Bank
118 10th Street SE
Grand Rapids, Minnesota 55744
tel: 218-326-4420
fax: 218-326-0254

MISSISSIPPI

The Gleaners, Inc.
P.O. Box 9883
Jackson, Mississippi 39286
tel: 601-981-4240

Twelve Baskets Food Bank
P.O. Box 1457
Biloxi, Mississippi 39533
tel: 601-388-6881

MISSOURI

Kansas City Harvest
Harvesters-The Corn. Fd. Network
1811 North Topping
Kansas City, Missouri 64120
tel: 816-231-3173
fax: 816-231-7044

Operation Food Search, Inc.
9657 Dielman Rock Island Drive
St. Louis, Missouri 63132
Contact: Mr. William E. Nordmann
tel: 314-569-0053
fax: 314-569-0381

Ozarks Share-A-Meal
Ozarks Food Harvest
615 North Glenstone
Springfield, Missouri 65802
tel: 417-865-3411
fax: 417-865-0504

NEBRASKA

Food Bank of Lincoln, Inc.
4800 North 57th Street
Lincoln, Nebraska 68507
tel: 402-466-8170
fax: 402-466-6124

The Nebraska Food Bank
723 North 18th Street
Omaha, Nebraska 68102
tel: 402-341-1915

NEVADA

Community Food Bank
of Clark County
3505 East Charleston
Las Vegas, Nevada 89104
tel: 702-459-3663
fax: 702-459-3663

Foodbank of Northern Nevada
994 Packer Way
Sparks, Nevada 89431
tel: 702-331-3663
fax: 702-331-3765

NEW HAMPSHIRE

Cooperative Extension Services
University of New Hampshire
Durham, New Hampshire 03824
tel: 603-862-2465

New Hampshire Food Bank
62 West Brook Street
Manchester, New Hampshire 03101
tel: 603-669-6821
fax: 603-669-0270

NEW JERSEY

Cooperative Extension Service
Rutgers University
Camden, New Jersey 08102
tel: 609-225-6169
Extra Helping
Community Food Bank of New Jersey
31 Evans Terminal Road
Hillside, New Jersey 07205
tel: 908-355-4991
fax: 908-355-0270

Greater Mercer Food Co-op
151 Mercer Street
Trenton, New Jersey 08611
tel: 609-396-1506
fax: 609-396-8363

NEW MEXICO

The Food Brigade of Santa Fe
121 Don Gaspar
Santa Fe, New Mexico 87501
tel: 505-986-8288
fax: 505-988-4645

Second Harvest Roadrunner
P.O. Box 12924
Albuquerque, New Mexico 87195
tel: 505-247-2052
fax: 505-242-6471

NEW YORK

City Harvest
575 Eighth Avenue
New York, New York 10018
tel: 917-351-8700
fax: 917-351-8720

Food Shuttle of Western New York, Inc.
250 St. Gregory Court
Williamsville, New York 14221
tel: 716-688-2527

Foodlink
P.O. Box 11290
Rochester, New York 14611
tel: 716-380-3380
fax: 716-328-9951

NORTH CAROLINA

Greensboro's Table
305 West Lee Street
Greensboro, North Carolina 27406
tel: 919-271-5975

Inter-Faith Food Shuttle
216 Lord Anson Drive
Raleigh, North Carolina 27610
tel: 919-250-0043
fax: 919-250-0416

Second Helpings of Winston Salem
3655 Reed Street
Winston Salem, North Carolina
27107
tel: 910-784-5770
fax: 910-784-7369

NORTH DAKOTA

Daily Bread
Great Plains Food Bank
P.O. Box 389
Fargo, North Dakota 58107
tel: 701-232-2624
fax: 701-232-3871

OHIO

Cleveland Food Bank
1557 East 27th Street
Cleveland, Ohio 44114
tel: 216-696-6007
fax: 216-696-6236

Queen City Servings
1250 Tennessee Avenue
Cincinnati, Ohio 45229
tel: 513-482-4533
fax: 513-482-4504

Second Servings
Mid-Ohio Food Bank
1625 West Mound Street
Columbus, Ohio 43223
tel: 614-274-7770
fax: 614-274-8063

OKLAHOMA

Second Helpings
Oklahoma City Food Bank
P.O. Box 26306
Oklahoma City, Oklahoma 73126
tel: 405-236-8349
fax: 405-236-5119

Table to Table
1150 North Iroquois Avenue
Tulsa, Oklahoma 74106
tel: 918-585-2800
fax: 918-585-2862

OREGON

Food Rescue Express
Food for Lane County
255 Madison Street
Eugene, Oregon 97402
tel: 503-343-2822
fax: 503-343-5019

Food Train/Food Depot
The Society of St. Vincent de Paul
3601 S.E. 27th
Portland, Oregon 97202
tel: 503-234-1114
fax: 503-233-5581

The Gleaning Network
211 North Front Street
Central Point, Oregon 97502
tel: 503-664-5244

Channels
331 Bridge Street
New Cumberland, Pennsylvania
17070
tel: 717-774-8220
fax: 717-774-3655

Greater Pittsburgh Community
Food Bank
3200 Walnut Street
McKeesport, Pennsylvania 15134
tel: 412-672-4949
fax: 412-672-4740

Philabundance
6950 Germantown Avenue
Philadelphia, Pennsylvania 19119
tel: 215-844-3663
fax: 215-844-4556

Rhode Island Community Food Bank
104 Hay Street
West Warwick, Rhode Island 02893
tel: 401-826-3072
fax: 401-826-2420

Loaves & Fishes
1900 Augusta Street
Greenville, South Carolina 29605
tel: 803-232-3595

Second Helpings, Inc.
P.O. Box 23621
Hilton Head Island, South Carolina
29925
tel: 803-842-7305

The Soup Kitchen
Charleston InterFaith Crisis Ministry
P.O. Box 20038
Charleston, South Carolina 29413
tel: 803-723-2726
fax: 803-577-6667

Black Hills Regional Food Bank
1844 Lombardy Drive
Rapid City, South Dakota 57701
tel: 605-348-2689
fax: 605-348-8440

Second Harvest of South Dakota
3511 North First Avenue
Sioux Falls, South Dakota 57104
tel: 605-335-0364
fax: 605-335-6617

Knoxville Harvest
Second Harvest
922 Delaware
Knoxville, Tennessee 37921
tel: 423-521-0000
fax: 423-521-0040

Nashville's Table, Inc.
1416 Lebanon Road
Nashville, Tennessee 37210
tel: 615-244-4564
fax: 615-244-6312

Round Up
Memphis Food Bank
239 South Dudley Street
Memphis, Tennessee 38104
tel: 901-527-0841
fax: 901-528-1172

TEXAS

Capital Area Food Bank of Texas
P.O. Box 18311
Austin, Texas 78760
tel: 512-448-2111
fax: 512-448-2524

The Dallas Hunger Link
North Texas Food Bank
4306 Shilling Way
Dallas, Texas 75237
tel: 214-330-1396
fax: 214-331-4104

End Hunger Network Food Loop
1770 St. James, Suite 204
Houston, Texas 70056
tel: 713-963-0099
fax: 713-963-0199

UTAH

Give S.OM.E.
Utah Food Bank
1025 South 700 West
Salt Lake City, Utah 84104
tel: 801-978-2452
fax: 801-978-9565

VERMONT

Cooperative Extension System
University of Vermont
Burlington, Vermont 05405
tel: 802-656-0669

Vermont Foodbank
P.O. Box 254
South Barre, Vermont 05670
tel: 802-476-3341
fax: 802-476-3326

VIRGINIA

Southwest Virginia Second Harvest
Food Bank
1111 Shenandoah Avenue, N.W.
P.O. Box 2868
Roanoke, Virginia 24001
tel: 703-342-3011
fax: 703-342-0056

Virginia's Table–Peninsula
Foodbank of the Virginia Peninsula
9912 Hosier Street
Newport News, Virginia 23601
tel: 804-596-7188
fax: 804-595-2507

Public Service Perishable Food
Distribution 269
Virginia's Table
Central Virginia Food Bank
4444 Sarellen Road
Richmond, Virginia 23231
tel: 804-226-1899
fax: 804-226-9034

WASHINGTON

Seattle's Table
Food Lifeline
15230 15th Avenue, N.E.
Seattle, Washington 98155
tel: 206-545-6567
fax: 206-545-6616

Spokane Food Bank
1234 East Front Avenue
Spokane, Washington 99202
tel: 509-534-6678
fax: 509-534-8252

Klickitat-Skamania Development
Council
P.O. Box 1580
White Salmon, Washington 98672
tel: 509-493-3954

WEST VIRGINIA

South West Virginia Evangelical
Association
P.O. Box 6
Coal Mountain, West Virginia 24823
tel: 304-583-2104

Cooperative Extension Service
West Virginia University
Morgantown, West Virginia 26506
tel: 304-293-2694

WISCONSIN

Second Harvest of Southern
Wisconsin
2802 Dairy Drive
Madison, Wisconsin 53704
tel: 608-223-9121
fax: 608-223-9840

Second Harvest Food Bank of
Wisconsin
1700 West Fond Du Lac Avenue
Milwaukee, Wisconsin 53205
tel: 414-931-7400
fax: 414-931-1996

WYOMING

Joshua's Distribution Center
714 CY Avenue
Casper, Wyoming 82601
tel: 307-265-0242

Wyoming Food Bank
P.O. Box 5553
Cheyenne, Wyoming 82003

CANADA

Second Harvest Food Support
Committee
444 Yonge Street
Toronto, Ontario M5B 2H4
Canada
tel: 416-408-2594
fax: 416-408-2598

GENERAL INDEX

liquor service, 285
staffing, 125–126
Liabilities, personal financial résumé, 89–90
Licenses, business setup, 92
Lighthouse Incorporated, 155
Lila Vine Consulting, 23
LilaVine (newsletter), 282–283
Lilavois, Eric
interview with, 23–25
newsletter of, 282–283
Limited liability corporation (LLC), business setup, 88
Linens, rental equipment, 137–138
Linwood's, Linwood Catering, and Due (Baltimore, Maryland), 52–54
Liquor laws
bartenders, 127
business setup, 92
licensing, 282
Local markets, 5
Location
of commissary, 10
of office, 10, 52–53
Location directory, 293–295
Lucas, Dione, 46
Lutèce (New York, New York), 23

Mae Mae Café (New York, New York), 60
Management. *See* Event management
Market Place Catereres (Seattle, Washington), 46
Maryland Higher Education Commission, 28
Maverick Southern Kitchens, 38–39
McDonnal, Joe
interview with, 46–49
recipes of, 49–51
McMullen, Jim
interview with, 41–43
recipes of, 44–45
Meer, Henry, 23

Menus, 151–155. *See also* Menu and recipe index
client interviews, 102–103, 151–154
cost estimates, 152–153
freshness, 152
number of, 154–155
organization of, 6
paperwork sample for, 111–115
printing of, 154, 155
resources for planning, 9–10
Microwave ovens, food safety and sanitation, 149
Mondavi Vineyards, 38
Morgans Mill, 38
Music and musicians
event management, 103
rental equipment, 140

National Restaurant Association, 144
Natural Gourmet Cookery School, 13–15
Neumark, Liz
interview with, 58–60
menu suggestions of, 60–61
recipes of, 62–63
New account credit form, paperwork sample for, 110
Notebook, importance of, 38–39
Note taking, catering, 4
Nutrition, computer software, 96

Occupational Safety and Health Administration (OSHA), 129
Office
business setup, 92–93
location of, 10
Office kit, 140
Office staff, staffing, 127–128
Off-premise catering
difficulties in, 18
event management, 103
requirements for, 1–2

S corporation, business setup, 87–88
Seafood Hazard Analysis Critical Control Point (HACCP), 144
Services, paperwork sample for, 109
Serving pieces, rental equipment, 137
Simplicity, 46–49
Site
  paperwork checklist for, 122
  selection of, 131–133
Small Business Administration (SBA), 7–8, 88–89, 90, 126
Smith, Allen, 65
Smoothies, 288–289
Software. *See* Computer software
Soho Cub Room (New York, New York), 23
Sole proprietorships
  business setup, 87
  example of, 64–65
Sommelier, 23–25
Spirit Education Trust, 23
Spirits. *See* Beverages
Staffing
  bakery, 127
  bartenders, 127
  buspersons, 128
  chef, 126–127
  dress codes, 129–130
  drivers, 128
  event management, 103, 104
  importance of, 125
  legal requirements, 125–126
  manager, 128
  office staff, 127–128
  personal hygiene, food safety and sanitation, 146–147
  production assistants, 127
  responsibilities, 130
  rules for, 130
  safety rules, 129
  sales people, 128
  scheduling, 129
  wait staff, 127
  working conditions, 129

Subcontractors, paperwork sample for, 109, 116, 120–122
Swamp Fox, The Francis Marian (Charleston, South Carolina), 71–73
Sylvia Weinstock's Cakes (New York, New York), 77–78
Szathmary, Louis, 9

Tea, 287–288
Temperature, food safety and sanitation, 144, 147–149
Tents, rental equipment, 138
Time management, importance of, 26–28
Timing. *See* Scheduling

Uniforms, rental equipment, 137–138
U.S. Department of Agriculture, food safety, 144–145
U.S. Department of Labor, staffing, 126
U.S. Government Printing Office, 146

Venues. *See* Site

Wait staff, staffing, 127
Washington Street Café (New York, New York), 68
Water, 288–289
Weinstock, Sylvia, interview with, 77–78
Wholistic nutrition, defined, 14
William Poll Caterers (New York, New York), 74–75
Wine. *See* Beverages
Wine sommelier, 23–25
Word of mouth, 6
Working conditions, staffing, 129
Wyman, Virginia, 48

Zoning, office location, 10

RECIPE AND MENU INDEX